CAMBRIDGE STUDIES IN LATIN AMERICAN
AND IBERIAN LITERATURE 2

The Spanish American regional novel

Carlos J. Alonso's new study provides a radical re-examination of the *novela de la tierra* or regional novel, which plays a central part in the development of Latin American fiction in the first half of the twentieth century. He identifies the regional novel as a specific literary manifestation of the persistent meditation on cultural autochthony that has characterized Latin American cultural production from its beginnings, and which in his view springs from Latin America's problematic relationship with modernity. He proposes a new view of the autochthonous as a discourse rather than a referent, but a discourse that is characterized by an internal crisis that manifests itself as a profound questioning of its own foundations.

Professor Alonso presents his argument through challenging readings of three works that are universally acknowledged as archetypes of the autochthonous modality: Rivera's *La vorágine*, Gallegos' *Doña Bárbara* and Güiraldes' *Don Segundo Sombra*.

In the same series:

Gustavo Pérez Firmat: *The Cuban Condition: Translation and identity in modern Cuban literature*

The Spanish American regional novel

Modernity and autochthony

CARLOS J. ALONSO

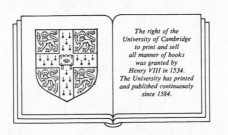

The right of the
University of Cambridge
to print and sell
all manner of books
was granted by
Henry VIII in 1534.
The University has printed
and published continuously
since 1584.

CAMBRIDGE UNIVERSITY PRESS

CAMBRIDGE
NEW YORK   PORT CHESTER
MELBOURNE   SYDNEY

Published by the Press Syndicate of the University of Cambridge
The Pitt Building, Trumpington Street, Cambridge CB2 1RP
40 West 20th Street, New York, NY 10011, USA
10 Stamford Road, Oakleigh, Melbourne 3166, Australia

First published 1990

Printed in Great Britain at
the University Press, Cambridge

British Library cataloguing in publication data
Alonso, Carlos J.
The Spanish American regional novel: modernity and autochthony.
1. Fiction in Spanish. Latin American writers, 1910–
Critical studies
I. Title
863

Library of Congress cataloguing in publication data
Alonso, Carlos J.
The Spanish American regional novel: modernity and autochthony/Carlos J. Alonso
p.   cm. – (Cambridge studies in Latin American and Iberian literature: 2)
Bibliography.
ISBN 0-521-37210-0
1. Spanish American fiction – 20th century – History and criticism.
2. Regionalism in literature.
I. Title.
II. Series.
PQ7082.N7A58   1989
863 – dc19   89-3124   CIP

ISBN 0 521 37210 0

To my parents, the enduring ground

Autochthon [Gr. *autochthōn*, sprung from the land itself; *autos*, self, and *chthon*, the earth, the ground.]
Webster's New Universal Unabridged Dictionary, p. 126

Even now, a century and a half later, no one can explain satisfactorily the "national" differences between Argentines and Uruguayans, Peruvians and Ecuadorians, Guatemalans and Mexicans.
Octavio Paz, *El laberinto de la soledad*, p. 110

And if a text always gives itself a certain representation of its own roots, those roots live only by that representation, by never touching the soil, so to speak. Which undoubtedly destroys their *radical essence*, but not the necessity of their racinating *function*.
Jacques Derrida, *Of Grammatology*, p. 101

Contents

	Acknowledgements	*page* viii
1	Introduction: the exoticism of the autochthonous	1
2	The *novela de la tierra*	38
3	*Don Segundo Sombra*	79
4	*Doña Bárbara*	109
5	*La vorágine*	136
6	Epilogue	163
	Notes	167
	Bibliography	193
	Index	209

Acknowledgements

I have a long-outstanding debt of friendship, intellectual stimulation and unstinting support with Marilyn Rugg, Roberto González Echevarría, Josué V. Harari, Sylvia Molloy, Enrique Pupo Walker and Paul Olson. The desire not to betray the generosity they have consistently displayed towards me was perhaps the most powerful incentive to accomplish this study.

My constant friends Servando Echeandía, Aníbal González Pérez and Jill Netchinsky have helped me with their differing examples of intellectual rigor to persevere in my own projects. They deserve to be restituted the many hours they have wasted listening patiently to my ideas and obsessions throughout the years.

And then there is Anne, who gives meaning to everything, and who has filled my life with such joy.

I

Introduction: the exoticism of the autochthonous

> Therein lies the gist of the American's terrible complex: the belief that his expression is not accomplished form, but rather a problem, something to be resolved. Fatigued and inhibited by such presumptuous complexes, he seeks in autochthony the luxury that escaped him; and cornered between this insignificance and the mirage of European accomplishments he examines his facts.
>
> José Lezama Lima[1]

In a remarkable piece called "The Argentine Writer and Tradition" – a title not unrelated to that of T. S. Eliot's powerful and enduring essay – Borges attempted to come to terms with the then contested issue of writing within a national literary tradition.[2] His observations on the subject seem to exhibit at times both the hindsight of someone who had not remained unmoved in the early part of his career by the appeal of autochthonous materials, and the uncanny desire to articulate a proleptic rejoinder to a number of his future critics. From the outset Borges characterizes the concern for an indigenous literature as a "pseudo-problem," and goes on to show the historical contingency of the expectation – the requirement in the eyes of some – that literature and nationality be somehow intertwined:

Besides, I do not know if it is necessary to say that the idea that a literature must be defined in terms of its national traits is a relatively new idea; also new and arbitrary is the idea that writers must seek themes from their own countries. Without going any further, I think Racine would not have even understood a person who denied him his right to the title of French poet because he cultivated Greek and Roman themes. I think Shakespeare would have been astonished if people had tried to limit him to English themes, and if they had told him that as an Englishman, he had no right to compose *Hamlet*, whose theme is Scandinavian, or *Macbeth*, whose theme is Scottish. The Argentine cult of local color is a recent European cult which the nationalists should reject as foreign.[3]

There is, Borges affirms, an insurmountable contradiction at the very core of the demand in certain Argentine circles for a literature reflective of autochthonous reality, a prescriptive stipulation that at the time appeared to have acquired almost dogmatic strength. To begin with, what the literary nationalists perceive as a necessary link between literature and national essence is a relatively recent conception, one that has no historical depth and, on account of that very fact, probably only transitory validity. Moreover, he avers, the postulation of such a relationship is a belated reflection of a similar European preoccupation, and therefore one that, for the sake of consistency with their avowed beliefs, should be eschewed by those who passionately argue for it. But Borges' devastating critique does not stop there:

Some days ago I found a curious confirmation of the fact that what is truly native can and often does dispense with local color; I found this confirmation in Gibbon's *Decline and Fall of the Roman Empire*. Gibbon observes that in the Arabian book *par excellence*, the Koran, there are no camels; I believe that if there were any doubt as to the authenticity of the Koran, this absence of camels would be sufficient to prove that it was an Arabian work. It was written by Mohammed, and Mohammed, as an Arab, had no reason to know that camels were especially Arabian; for him they were a part of reality, he had no reason to single them out; on the other hand the first thing a falsifier, a tourist, or an Arab nationalist would do is to have a surfeit of camels, caravans of camels in every page; but Mohammed, as an Arab, was not concerned; he knew he could be an Arab without camels.[4]

Borges' jocular and somewhat sarcastic tone is a reflection of the distrust mixed with contempt that he felt regarding the tawdry and melodramatic nationalism that he had seen flourish during the Perón regime.[5] But the light satiric slant of the comment cannot entirely mask the compelling nature of his more profound critique. For when it is considered outside of its immediate contextual circumstances, Borges' interpretation of Gibbon's observation opens the way to a radical examination of the attempt to *produce* a national literature: The whole enterprise – when viewed precisely as such – cannot be regarded as the direct and uncomplicated project that it would seem to be upon first consideration. If I interpret it correctly, Borges' entire critique is predicated on an almost literal, etymological interpretation of the concept of autochthony ("sprung from the earth itself") that allows him to identify cultural autochthony with an absence of cultural self-reflexiveness. Therefore, he would contend, simply by raising the issue of the autochthonous, the subject has already done irredeemable violence to the notion that it claims to uphold since it has brought to consciousness that which by definition can only exist in its absence. In other words, the very desire for an autochthonous expression becomes the guarantee that that desire will never be fulfilled, since the nature of the concept precludes the possibility of its ever becoming an object of desire. From this perspective Mohammed, who never entertained the thought of writing an indigenous text, must be judged nonetheless more successful on this score than the most ardent nationalist ever could be. Hence, the argument would seem to propose with unflinching logic, it is the *absence* of particular cultural traits identified as such in a text that could provide the strongest evidence of autochthonous production. This conclusion delineates the existence of a concomitant interpretive impasse inherent in the nationalists' stance: not finding what they are looking for in a text would constitute the confirmation that they had found the text they were looking for in the first place. In this fashion, those who would seek to affirm autochthonous values would be defeated from the outset by the peculiar nature of the concept they purport to sustain.

But the difficulties identified above have less to do with the concept of the autochthonous as such than with the nature of the project of cultural definition that invokes it. For this situation represents an extreme version of a predicament that could be described in the following manner: no one can posit as a problem the specificity of one's own culture and pretend to remain innocently and unreflexively within the horizon delimited by it. That is, through its preoccupation with autochthony the subject necessarily enters into a relationship of mediation with respect to its own culture, a circumstance that opens the way to counterfeit, exoticism or ideological expediency: "a falsifier, a tourist, or an Arab nationalist." In any event, the outcome of this inevitably centrifugal displacement is the formulation of a partial vision of cultural essence that willfully isolates certain elements – camels, for instance – and advances them as representative of the totality of cultural experience. This last comment should not be interpreted as pointing accusingly to the incompleteness of such a vision, that is, the way in which it purports to represent synecdochically the entire culture of which in reality it is merely a fragment. Its intention is rather to establish the inescapably *artificial* nature of that discourse that wishes to speak of the autochthonous, given that its rhetorical point of articulation and its perspective are necessarily extrinsic. This point would seem to be emphasized even by the tropological structure of Borges' argument: the success of his own critique of the obsession with autochthony depends on the existence of an assumption shared by him and his reader that camels are indeed "especially Arabian," obviously the perspective of an outsider to that specific cultural reality. Paradoxically enough, then, there would appear to be a common rhetorical ground underlying both the discourse of the ardent cultural nationalist and that of the gawking, exoticizing foreigner.

The issues that have been addressed above belong to subject/object philosophy, but the context of cultural exegesis in which they manifest themselves brings to mind the fundamental interpretive problematics of anthropology. It is indeed instructive to consider the enterprise of cultural definition that concerns us from the perspective of the paradigmatic anthropological situation. Lévi-Strauss has summarized the latter rigorously and sensitively in the following fashion:

In choosing a subject and an object radically distant from one another, anthropology runs a risk: that the knowledge obtained from the object does not attain its intrinsic properties but is limited to expressing the relative and always shifting position of the subject in relation to the object. It may very well be, indeed, that the so-called ethnological knowledge is condemned to remain as bizarre and inadequate as that which an exotic visitor would have of our own society. The Kwakiutl Indian whom Boas sometimes invited to New York to serve him as an informant was quite indifferent to the panorama of skyscrapers and of streets ploughed and furrowed by cars. He reserved all his intellectual curiosity for the dwarfs, giants and bearded ladies who were exhibited in Times Square at the time, for automats, and for the brass balls decorating staircase banisters . . . All these things challenged his own culture, and it was that culture alone which he was seeking to recognize in certain aspects of ours.[6]

In the works of Lévi-Strauss, one can see the attempt at a resolution of this impasse in the transition from *Tristes Tropiques* to *La Pensée sauvage*: from the tragic awareness of epistemological impossibility arrived at during his Brazilian expedition – his discovery of "true" primitives with whom, nonetheless, he could not communicate – to the confident advancing and wielding of a systematic theory for cultural analysis in the latter work. In the passage from one text to the other Lévi-Strauss manages, as Clifford Geertz has observed, to change the terms of the original situation – physical closeness and intellectual distance – into intellectual closeness and physical distance, no mere inversion since the transposition entails the anthropologist now being in a position to both comprehend and discourse about his subject.[7] Hence, the space defined by the displacement from one text to the other is brazenly occupied by a theoretical strategy that enables the anthropologist's knowledge to obtain, but which is simultaneously keenly aware of its mediating function.

The specific interpretive concerns voiced by Lévi-Strauss would not seem to inhere in the project of autochthonous cultural affirmation that occupies our attention here: The writer of an "autochthonous" text speaks from a position of physical and intellectual proximity to his own culture that should not entail the sort of difficulties that anthropology is forever encountering in its path. And yet, culling what has been established thus far, it could be suggested that what we have in the autochthonous discursive situation is an anthropology that cannot recognize itself as such, precisely on account of the overwhelming and dizzying familiarity between subject and object that is constitutive of it. The mediating analytical construct that is almost palpable in the relationship that anthropology establishes with its object is concealed in this case by the linguistic accessibility and physical proximity that characterize the encounter. But becoming an anthropologist to one's own culture cannot guarantee the transcendence of the vicissitudes of cultural hermeneutics, since in the end the latter is but an extreme instance of intersubjective interpretation, and therefore partakes of its unavoidable difficulties and vagaries. And yet, the particular characteristics of the autochthonous discursive situation conspire to foster the illusion that the cultural exegete has immediate and uncomplicated access to the phenomena of his own culture, when in fact the enterprise is grounded on the sort of interpretive construct revealed by Borges' critique.[8]

I would like to invoke the insights derived from our examination of these issues for the formulation of a proposition that will, in time, manifest its importance to this work. For one could advance as a corollary to the foregoing discussion that the project of writing an autochthonous literary text is as much a critical endeavor as a literary one, or more exactly, one where literature and criticism swiftly become inextricably entangled. As we have seen, "The Argentine Writer and Tradition" underscores the self-reflexiveness that accompanies the enterprise of producing an autochthonous literary text, a self-reflexiveness that constitutes the core of every critical act. Moreover, if we are attuned to the etymological roots of the word "criticism" in the Greek verb *krínein* (to separate), the inescapable cultural eccentricity of this project allows us to realize that the creation of an autochthonous text configures further the outline of a *critical* scene: that is, the attempt to produce a text of autochthony places the writer in an eccentric perspective with respect to his or her own cultural circumstance; in the resulting displacement, the author necessarily becomes also a critic in spite of the unproblematic assumption of immediacy on which his project is predicated. From its inception, then, self-reflection and distance are structurally built into the enterprise, endowing all such attempts with a dimension that is reminiscent of the paradigmatic situation of the critical act regardless of all attendant assumptions or protestations to the contrary.

Furthermore, the possibility of employing the adjective "critical" to describe the discourse of cultural specificity is delineated even more sharply when one considers the fact that affirmations of cultural identity customarily explain their emergence as constituting a response to a perceived crisis, a disruption caused by a situation or event that threatens a loss of cultural organicity or integrity. All discourse produced by a culture – and if interpreted broadly this category could encompass every manifestation of a given group – is to some degree confirmatory of that culture's identity, inasmuch as it is expressive of the set of beliefs or practices that impart a sense of closure to that cultural experience. But the kind of self-conscious affirmation of cultural essence under consideration here originates from an express desire to confirm those boundaries in the face of a situation that is experienced as a critical juncture. In an essay that explores the intimate connection between the concept of crisis and the activity of criticism, Paul de Man has proposed that one can speak of a crisis when "a 'separation' takes place, by self-reflection, between what . . . is in conformity with the original intent and what has irrevocably fallen away from this source."[9] De Man's point of departure is the resemblance that he claims exists between the language of crisis and the rhetoric of criticism, a similarity that arises because "even in its most naïve form, that of evaluation, the critical act is concerned with conformity to origin or specificity: when we say of art that it is good or bad, we are in fact judging a certain degree of conformity to an original intent called artistic."[10] Bringing to bear this statement on the issue at hand, one could propose that the text of cultural affirmation intends to call attention to the existence of a fissure, a concrete or threatened separation from that culture's essence that it construes as a crisis. But given the cultural eccentricity that has been established as constitutive of this discursive mode it could be argued that the autochthonous text purports to arise in response to a perceived fall from cultural grace, *when in fact it is itself constituted by the crisis that it designates.* In other words, the crisis, the separation that the autochthonous text pretends to elucidate has already been internalized by it as a condition for its own articulation. In this fashion, what is perceived to be fundamentally an ontological crisis of cultural proportions can only be rendered, it seems, through a discourse that is itself the rhetorical representation of that crisis. One could propose, then, that all formulations of cultural autochthony exist thoroughly in the mode of crisis, not only because they purport to arise in answer to a critical predicament, but also because they reenact that crisis in their own rhetorical structure. Hence, the tendency of crisis statements to exist "in the mode of error" as de Man has called it, is confirmed by these texts:[11] they would propose to engage in an affirmation of cultural organicity, but through a discourse that has abandoned that presumed connectedness as a condition for its very existence. The result appears to suggest that the text that seeks to affirm a culture's essence seems nonetheless condemned to be perpetually interdicted from participating in it.

The difficulties that have been identified above are expressive, I believe, of the complications and contradictions that issue when the entity that we refer to as a "culture" has recourse to the concept of *culture* itself to examine its own phenomena. For the wielding of the concept dictates by its very nature what statements can be made and what concerns arise when thinking about one's reality. A "culture" is conceived as a particularly meaningful arrangement, or conversely, as an arrangement that *means* in a particular way; it allows certain questions to be asked of that reality, and the answers that it elicits are couched in a vocabulary that refers to the categories implicit in the concept from the outset. Most importantly, the inquiry assumes the existence of an entity to be discerned called "culture," when in fact the latter can essentially be understood to be an effect of the questioning activity itself.

To begin with, the organicity and self-referentiality that are part and parcel of the concept impose on the lived experience of a group the requirement that it exhibit a comprehensive intelligibility and sense of purpose. In turn, this stipulation determines that certain tropological formations be employed to portray and evaluate "cultural" life. César Graña has succinctly described perhaps the two most compelling among these, referring to them respectively as the "anthropological fallacy" and the "anthropomorphic metaphor." The first of these, the anthropological fallacy,

is the notion that a culture, in order to be a "culture," must be a closed organism each one of whose manifestations is understandable as an expressive facet of the general entity. One has only to think of Spengler's *Decline of the West* to recall the spell of this idea, suggesting as it does that the history of peoples or periods is something akin to the dance in time of a single organism, making of each cultural event one of the dance's movements and gestures.[12]

The second, the "anthropomorphic metaphor," is a particular version of the anthropological fallacy. Its foundation can be construed as a biographical narrative that is nonetheless extended to encompass the culture as a whole. That is to say, through it the culture in question is perceived as constituting a collective subject whose development can be then narrated and interpreted in biographical terms. The resulting homology allows a culture to be endowed with the purposefulness and passion that are derived from considerations of personal intentionality. But according to Graña, there is a proclivity, once this analogy is established, to demand from a culture an unusual degree of intelligibility and consistency. In his words, the anthropomorphic metaphor

portrays societies as personages and historical *events* as biographical *acts* which stem from a body of motives. And curiously too . . . it regards the biographies of societies as more inexorably coherent than those of the biological individuals of daily life. In the latter we presume or permit ambivalence, doubt, caprice, self-contradiction, or just nonsense. But social anthropomorphism depends on an application of the theory of the personal soul to whole collectives in nothing but the most unqualified way. Either a culture is of a piece or it is nothing. Either it radiates a core of disposition or it is empty. And if we cannot sense the pulse of its *character* in every feature of its *life*, we think that either it hides itself from us or is engaged in betraying its own integrity. The outcome is a tendency to blend anthropomorphic and anthropological attitudes to portray whole cultures as finished "compositions," as pageants of choreographed values or panoplies of symmetrically arranged parts.[13]

These two major tropes of cultural figuration attest quite explicitly to what is perhaps the most significant attribute inherent in the concept of culture: its assumption that a culture is a static and perfectly synchronic order of meaning. But this characterization also encompasses the description of a community's displacement in time; for the temporality that a "culture" inhabits is not chronology but teleology, not simple succession but "significant season," to borrow Frank Kermode's felicitous formulation.[14] In other words, the depiction of a culture's movement in time is as closed and self-referential an order as the culture is understood to be when it is considered as a synchronic entity. In this fashion, the openendedness of historical experience is effectively suppressed, transformed into a teleological projection into the future of the culture's immanent deployment in time.

This realization leads to a reconsideration of a previous remark. Earlier I had observed that it is customary to see affirmations of cultural essence represent themselves as a response to a specific situation that is felt to engender a cultural crisis. And yet, by now one can begin to ascertain that there is an element of syllogistic circularity in this formulation, given that the notion of "cultural crisis" is intimately related to the conception of culture under scrutiny. For one must first conceive of a culture as a closed, internally homogeneous system, before it can be described as having lost or as being in danger of losing its immanent integrity and connectedness. Hence, one could submit that the "source" of the perceived cultural crisis lies not in the supposedly threatening historical situation that confronts the group under consideration, but rather in having internalized from the beginning a paradigm of culture that makes it impossible to account for historicity and chronological flux *except in the mode of crisis*; that is, historical eventuality must be experienced as a crisis because the epistemological figure that is employed to comprehend cultural life cannot encompass history except as the scene for an unremitting possibility of fallenness. Given the inescapable and Protean nature of temporal experience, the "culture" in question is thereby fated to be perceived by its interpreters as existing in a perennial critical state. The interpretive circle is finally completed with the appearance of the belief that historical misfortune will beset the community unabatedly as long as the schism, the ontological crisis at the heart of the culture, remains unresolved. In the end, then, the succession of discrete pronouncements of crisis becomes the culture's peculiar manner of marking time, of participating in history as it were, if only in the desperate, poignant manner allowed by this tortuous state of discursive affairs.

This transmutation of worldly historical experience into cultural crisis dictates in turn the rhetorical characteristics of the discourse produced by the cultural exegete. For as it was seen earlier, the peculiar structure of the crisis statement necessitates the designation of an original state or circumstance that has been abandoned, violated or otherwise compromised. This primordial situation is conceived of as a condition of perfect correspondence between the content and the forms deployed by a given culture, a situation that could be conceptualized as a sort of cultural ataraxia. More importantly, however, it is a *cultural* state that is interpreted as having generated itself in a *natural* fashion, that is, arising automatically from the midst of the collectivity and in perfect consonance with the surrounding environment. This seeming transcending of the nature/culture dichotomy through the figure of an autochthonous cultural order explains both its power and its irresistible appeal as a trope of cultural affirmation. But the avowedly spontaneous character of this mode of cultural generation cannot but put in check the very interpretive effort that propounds it as a reality: if such a generation were possible, it would have necessarily taken place, rendering superfluous the attempt at cultural exegesis that seeks to reaffirm its existence. Caught in this intrinsic contradiction, the only escape from it consists in arguing that the organic relationship that it posits and reaffirms has been somehow prevented from translating itself into a concrete cultural order. Therefore, the explanation of a culture's failure to incarnate a paradigm of cultural development that is deemed nonetheless coextensive with it must be sought in that culture's historical unfolding. This proposition engenders what could be referred to as the "diagnostic" dimension of the crisis statement: an investigation that quickly becomes a historical indictment – the unmasking of events, circumstances or characters whose individual "deviations" have participated in or continue the "great betrayal" that inaugurated the descent into cultural fallenness. But since the latter moment can potentially be made to recede endlessly in history, the diagnostic inquiry and its putative results also share in that ceaselessly recessive movement. In the end, the summation of all such indictments cannot help but coincide perfectly with the culture's own history. The outcome of this approach is a manifest desire to place history under erasure, since the latter is irrevocably envisaged as the theater for a post-lapsarian cultural condition. Historical consciousness is portrayed as a false consciousness, and if in the process of diagnosing the present predicament history is indeed reconstructed and examined, it is only in order to exorcise it more thoroughly.

And yet, if the forsaken autochthonous cultural order is to reintegrate itself, future history must be the instrument and stage for that epiphany as well. That is to say, the designation of a cultural crisis is also implicitly if not expressly accompanied by an enterprise of cultural redemption that projects itself temporally into the future. This aspect of the cultural crisis statement implies an antithetical perspective on history from the one just identified. The juxtaposition of the two mutually contradictory attitudes towards history surfaces unresolved in the fact that calls for an autochthonous culture usually alternate between nostalgia for a relinquished state of cultural plenitude that is associated with an unspecified moment in the past, and the affirmation of the present as a moment that announces proleptically the future cultural redemption. The result is that affirmations of cultural autochthony exhibit simultaneously two irreconcilable attributes: an essentialist, *ahistorical* conception of cultural identity, and an explicitly *historical* agenda for facilitating the imminent manifestation of that essence. In this fashion, the proponent of autochthonous cultural values manages to use the rhetoric of radical historical change, but in order to argue for the actualization of an immutable, ahistorical cultural essence that is identified with a zero-degree of cultural time. Thus, the discourse of the autochthonous cultural interpreter is suspended rhetorically between two moments that are in essence identical to each other, illustrating in the process the appropriateness of Hegel's remark concerning teleological schemes: "The outcome is the same as the beginning only because the beginning is an end."[15] From this point of view it could be argued that there is a fundamentally conservative dimension to the enterprise that is concealed by the radical, chiliastic tone that also characterizes it. In more essentialist terms, one could conceive the situation in the following way: the cultural crisis statement derives its militant force from measuring how far the culture has strayed from its "true" source; and yet, to make a case for the coextensive nature of the cultural order it envisions with the culture in question it must also be able to argue that the culture never *really* left there in the first place. Pronouncements of cultural crisis are constructed from such juxtaposed denunciations of difference and affirmations of immutable self-identity.

To a large degree both the sense of urgency and the exhortative tone of such crisis declarations derive from the latter contradictory supposition. Since the autochthonous cultural order is judged consubstantial with the community, its recoverability can always be portrayed as an imminent achievement, that is, as the effective realization of an immanent potentiality. Therefore, accession to it is conceived as a matter of collective volition, as a momentous project to be undertaken by the community in its entirety. In this sense, the cultural critic assumes the self-appointed role of officiant in a portentous ritual of collective redemption. In a discussion that attempts to establish a distinction between the differing mechanisms of ritual and game, Lévi-Strauss has contrasted the final heterogeneity that is created as a result of a contest with the unity that is the outcome of ritual. According to him, whereas competition establishes distinctions, ritual "conjoins, for it brings about a union (one might even say a communion in this context) or in any case an organic relation between two initially separate groups, one ideally merging with the person of the officiant and the other with the collectivity of the faithful . . . There is an asymmetry which is postulated in advance between profane and sacred, faithful and officiating, dead and living, initiated and uninitiated, etc., and the 'game' consists in making all the participants pass to the winning side."[16] The result of the textual ritual of cultural affirmation engaged in by the cultural interpreter in his role as officiant is a discursive performance that exhibits elements both prophetic and hortatory, and which possesses the combined rhetorical force of mantic vision and homily.

I believe it would not be difficult to sustain the proposition that in essence all of Latin America's cultural production since Independence can be understood as having been generated from within a discursive situation such as the one just examined. That is to say, the history of cultural discourse in Latin America can be accurately depicted as a succession of statements of cultural crisis that exhibit the contradictory attributes discussed above. Hence, when examined from the perspective afforded by the previous discussion one can begin to distinguish within this textual horizon the essential features of the two principal orientations identified earlier. The first of these is constituted by the diagnostic probing into Latin America's history in an attempt to inventory those elements that have avowedly hindered the manifestation of its intrinsic cultural essence. The diagnostic gesture delineated by this strategy can be perceived clearly in texts as diverse as Domingo F. Sarmiento's *Facundo*, *Nuestra América*, by Carlos Octavio Bunge, Alcides Arguedas' *Pueblo enfermo*, *Enfermedades sociales: los problemas contemporáneos* by Manuel Ugarte, *¿Existe América Latina?*, by Luis Alberto Sánchez and *Radiografía de la pampa*, by Ezequiel Martínez Estrada. The second tendency, the one that consists of a millenarian projection into the future, accounts for the epochal rhetoric that characterizes much of Latin American cultural discourse. In its most distilled form it has produced such works as "Alocución a la Poesía" by Andrés Bello, Francisco Bilbao's "Evangelio americano," *La raza cósmica* and *Indología* by José Vasconcelos, *El continente de siete colores* by Germán Arciniegas and Alfonso Reyes' *Ultima Tule*. Yet, as the discussion above suggests, the two projects are not antagonistic but complementary, and are therefore most often found concurrently in the same work; the simultaneous presence of both of these impulses can be detected in a large number of the texts that integrate this discursive tradition. A paradigmatic case of this internal dialectics is offered, for instance, by José Martí's influential essay "Nuestra América." In it, Martí identifies the persistent use of non-autochthonous epistemological constructs as the source of Latin America's cultural crisis, a disjunction that according to him is at the source of its political turmoil as well:

The good statesman in America is not the one who knows how Germany or France are governed, but rather he who knows the elements that comprise his country and how they can be guided to arrive, through methods and institutions born of the country itself, to that desired state where every man knows himself and acts accordingly, and where everybody enjoys the wealth that nature gave to all in the country they bless with their toil and defend with their lives. The government must be born of the country. The spirit of the government should be that of the country. The form of government must be adequate to the internal constitution of the country. A government should be nothing else but the equilibrium of the natural elements of the country.[17]

At the same time, however, the essay also purports to hail the advent of a new order that will redress the cultural schism denounced earlier by the author: "Standing tall, the new American men salute one another from their respective countries. Natural statesmen are born from the study of Nature. They read to adapt, not to copy. Economists study difficult matters at their source. Orators begin to be measured. Playwrights bring native characters to the stage. Academies discuss worthwhile themes . . . Prose, shimmering and taut, is pregnant with new ideas."[18] Martí's visionary harangue is a crescendo that reaches its maximum intensity with the hallucinatory rhapsody with which the essay closes: "The unanimous hymn can already be heard; the present generation carries with it, on the road made fertile by its sublime ancestors, the toiling masses of America; from the Bravo to the Strait of Magellan, riding the condor, the Great Semí has scattered, throughout the Romantic nations of the continent and the unfortunate islands of the ocean, the seeds of the new America!"[19] This final vision proclaims in no uncertain terms the momentous epiphany that will obtain through the recognition of and immersion in an indigenous cultural essence that until now has remained unheeded on account of the senseless misfortunes and heedless betrayals of history. In this way, Martí's essay can be seen to be generated by the dialectical interplay between the two essential and complementary modalities of diagnosis and revelation that have been discussed above.

If one takes into consideration that the demand for an autochthonous cultural expression has been the dominant concern in Latin American intellectual history, then it could be asserted that this rhetorical dialectics of crisis has both characterized and structured Latin American discursive space from the outset. Moreover, given the historical depth of the Latin American obsession with the actualization of an indigenous mode of cultural being, one could propose that cultural discourse in Latin America has always existed in a permanent state of crisis. The predictable outcome of this consistency has been that the crisis cannot be perceived as such anymore, allowing the various discourses generated by that crisis to become synonymous with cultural production. Indeed, the question of the autochthonous has acquired such intrinsic legitimacy and urgency that very few Latin American intellectuals and artists have not felt the necessity, and even the responsibility, to come to terms with it as a matter of course. All the more when one considers that the determination of the specificity of national or continental essence has been customarily wielded as an instrument for interpreting present economic and political instability and for advancing specific reforms for the future. By extension, the collective import and urgency associated with the question of the autochthonous have precluded the assumption of a critical perspective, a vantage point from which the search can begin to be conceived of as a cultural and ideological project instead. One could even propose that the very assumed naturalness of such an evidently cultural enterprise, the way in which it portrays itself as the natural breathing space for Latin American thought, has determined that it become itself a second-order postulation of the autochthonous. In this way the nature/culture dichotomy is transcended in a manner of speaking, through the undertaking of a resolutely cultural project as an unquestioned, "natural" activity.

The fact that the persistent identification of a cultural crisis should have become the essential modality of cultural discourse in Latin America has brought implicit with it significant consequences. In this rhetorical circumstance, the contention that the culture has abandoned its specificity becomes the heart of the culture's discursive production. One would almost be tempted to consider such a belief a constitutive aspect of cultural identity, since it appears to encompass an invariant trait of the culture's own discourse. In other words it could be argued that the essence of Latin American cultural production is the ever-renewed affirmation of having lost or abandoned such an essence. This oxymoronic proposition allows nonetheless some insight into the nature of the discursive enterprise that it describes. For it appears evident that what it summarizes is a succession of rhetorical performances that repeat an identical gesture, but which at the same time purport to advance a radically novel interpretation of the primordial cultural predicament. Hence, I would suggest that the preoccupation with cultural autochthony has operated as an enabling rhetorical formula that has generated cultural discourse in Latin America through its iterative use. That is: the identification of a cultural crisis has functioned as a rhetorical device, a discursive operator that has engendered the variegated collection of texts that constitutes Latin American cultural production.

This interpretation would seem to account for what could be referred to as the fundamental intransitivity of cultural discourse in Latin America, an aspect that is signalled distinctly by the most salient quality of that textual tradition: the conventional and repetitive nature of the discrete formulations that have arisen in response to the cultural crisis that they avowedly identify. Roberto González Echevarría has produced a concise catalogue of some of these: "the universal in the local, the mestizo continent, crossroads of the great cultures and races of the world, the Faustian presence of Indians and Africans,"[20] to which one would have to add the long-lived, multifaceted formula of "Civilization vs. Barbarism." The fact that the same concepts and answers recur time and again is indicative of the fact that the exploration of the autochthonous is not ultimately answerable to a specific contextual set of circumstances, but rather that it performs a generative role in the production of cultural discourse. Thus, the issue of cultural autochthony in Latin America can be interpreted as a rhetorical artifice that has furnished the space, the occasion and the possibility of the extended discursive performance that is Latin American cultural production. One could say – *mutatis mutandis* – that in the realm of intellectual discourse in Latin America the autochthonous has had a role similar to the one that, according to Emile Benveniste, "shifters" have in specific instances of language use. There are some "empty" structures, he proposes,

that are non-referential with respect to "reality," always available, and which become "full" as soon as a speaker avails himself of them in each instance of his discourse. Since they lack material reference they cannot be misused; since they do not assert anything, they are not subject to the condition of truth and escape all denial. Their role is to provide the instrument of a conversion that one could call the conversion of language into discourse. It is by identifying himself as a unique person pronouncing *I* that each speaker sets himself up in turn as the "subject." . . . [*I*] can be assumed by each speaker on the condition that he refers each time only to the instance of his own discourse. This sign is thus linked to the *exercise* of language and announces the speaker as speaker. It is this property that establishes the basis for individual discourse, in which each speaker takes over all the resources of the language for his own behalf.[21]

Thus, the preoccupation with an autochthonous cultural order has consistently served as a vehicle for the validation and generation of intellectual production in Latin America. Its effect has been to legitimize the production of cultural discourse through its performance as a rhetorical formula that could be readily appropriated by any potential "speaker." By invoking it, it becomes possible not only to write, but to write *as a Latin American*, no matter how compellingly the crisis statement decries the fact that this anchoring essence has been somehow compromised.

Nevertheless, one should not rush to conclude that history does not constitute a powerful component in the generation of cultural discourse in Latin America: the very opposite, in fact, is the case. For as it was established earlier, this perennial sense of cultural crisis is characterized by an inability to experience historical flux except in the mode of crisis; that is, historical situations or events are perceived as having precipitated a cultural crisis, when in fact such an interpretation of historical events was dictated from the beginning by the epistemological model of cultural life employed by the interpreter. And yet, the sequence of cultural crisis statements duplicates in its own succession the very movement of history, in so far as the sense of crisis that the texts avowedly respond to is perceived to issue from specific historical events. This explains also the blindness within the boundaries of this textual tradition regarding its repetitive, conventional nature, since every text claims to find its own validation in the critical moment in history that it purports to address. In this sense, Latin American cultural discourse finds its justification in a willful forgetfulness of history, a plunging into the immediacy of the present moment of crisis that is belied by the repetitive – and therefore historical – nature of that act.

According to de Man, the predicament defined by the last assertion constitutes the rhetorical structure of all statements of modernity. After identifying modernity as the desire to eradicate the past by affirming the preeminence of and the desire to participate in the present moment,[22] he proceeds to make problematic that very gesture in terms that recall the rhetorical circumstance I have been discussing: "Modernity and history relate to each other in a curiously contradictory way that goes beyond antithesis or opposition. If history is not to become sheer regression or paralysis, it depends on modernity for its duration and renewal; but modernity cannot assert itself without being at once swallowed up and reintegrated into a regressive historical process."[23] In my view, this resemblance between the structure of cultural discourse in Latin America and the rhetoric of modernity is indicative of the existence of an intimate and indissoluble relationship between the two; in fact, I shall argue below that Latin America's obsession with the determination of its cultural specificity is a phenomenon related to its peculiar and paradoxical experience of modernity. In the remainder of this chapter I shall explore the grounds for such an interpretation of Latin American cultural production. This will allow us to understand finally the necessary connection between the rhetorical appropriation of the concept of culture discussed above and the permanent experience of cultural crisis that has always been at the center of intellectual discourse in Latin America.

Modernity and autochthony

> Even now, at the dusk of modernity, we still cannot
> manage to be modern.   Octavio Paz[24]

In our earlier discussion of the discourse of cultural affirmation it was established that assertions of cultural specificity arise in response to an avowed cultural crisis, a crisis that is nonetheless internalized and performed rhetorically by the autochthonous work. I further suggested that given the relentless nature of Latin America's preoccupation with its cultural specificity, the history of Latin American cultural thought could be viewed as the naturalization of a state of crisis. If this is the case, though, one can presume that there is a genetic paradigm for that crisis that the history of repeated inquiries into the question of cultural specificity seems intent on reenacting. I will argue here that this primordial crisis, the separation repeatedly enacted by the ever-renewed attempts at articulating an autochthonous cultural definition for Latin America, was inaugurated by the chasm that opened between the rhetoric of modernity with which Latin American intellectuals and revolutionaries called Latin America into being, and the concrete historical and economic circumstances out of which the latter sprang. For if Octavio Paz is correct in proposing that the emancipation struggle in Latin America was a movement inspired by the French Revolution and the American Revolution, the two great political archetypes of the modern era, it is also true that material conditions of production in Latin America were at the time, and would progressively become yet more resistant to the demands of that rhetoric.[25]

Stating the situation in a diachronic dimension, the crisis that has characterized Latin American thought from the very beginning originated in the impossibility of reconciling the rhetoric that gave legitimacy and authority to the emancipation movement with the historical development that ensued from that moment. This primordial disjunction has translated itself into a succession of statements of cultural crisis that have arisen in response to the contingencies of history, since historical movement only managed to emphasize the chasm that produced the original crisis in the first place. The outcome has been, as I intend to show, the generation of a corpus of texts that attempt to formulate an autochthonous cultural definition, texts that, as I argued earlier, are themselves constituted by a parallel rhetorical crisis of their own; in other words, one could propose that the response to the crisis has only succeeded in replicating in its rhetorical structure the crisis that it was supposed to redress. Hence, each formulation of autochthony has had its discrete nature and has evolved out of a specific context, but each harks back to a genetic disjunction that can most accurately be described as a rhetorical predicament: how to reconcile the ideological appeal to modernity that legitimized the founding of Latin America with a historical reality that proved consistently intractable from the perspective of that rhetoric. Nevertheless, in order to understand fully the fascination with autochthony in the context delimited by Latin America's participation in modernity, it will become necessary to examine thoroughly the specific nature of Latin America's inscription in the modern.

In a study that constitutes one of the most rigorous considerations of the concept of the modern in any language, Octavio Paz has offered a most compelling picture of modernity in Spain and Latin America.[26] Central to his argument is what he diagnoses as the absence in Spain of a real Enlightenment that would have instituted the authority of Criticism, which for Paz is synonymous with modernity. This absence explains, in turn, the weak, epigonic nature of Spanish Romanticism, since Romanticism was essentially a critique of modernity from within itself. According to Paz, in a development that exemplifies modernity's inevitable criticism of its own foundations, Romanticism sought to dismantle the chimeras of critical reason: "Romanticism was a reaction against the Enlightenment, and was therefore determined by it; it was one of its contradictory products" (p. 81). Likewise, Paz asserts that "Romanticism was the reaction of bourgeois consciousness to and against itself – against its own critical production: the Enlightenment" (p. 84). Spain, then, could not engage in a critique of Criticism, since it had not had an Enlightenment to begin with:

The eighteenth century was a critical century but criticism was forbidden in Spain . . . In Spain the middle class and the intellectuals voiced no criticism of traditional institutions or, if they did, it was insufficient. How could they criticize a modern era which they had never had? (pp. 83–84)

Or, as Paz had proposed in an earlier passage: "In Spain this reaction against the modern age could not appear, because actually Spain did not have a modern age" (p. 82).

For Paz, Latin America's experience of modernity essentially paralleled that of Spain; on the other hand, he claims, Latin America's revolution for independence began a separation from Spanish tradition, a process that according to him culminated in the second half of the nineteenth century with the resolute embracing of Positivism by Latin American intellectuals. Aside from signifying an irretrievable break with Spanish intellectual preoccupations, the adoption of Positivist theories allowed for Latin America's participation in modernity through the critique of traditional institutions and beliefs in which Latin American *positivismo* engaged. In fact, Paz perceives in the historical development represented by *positivismo* a Latin American equivalent to European Enlightenment: "Positivism in Latin America . . . was a radical criticism of religion and of traditional ideology . . . This development was similar to the eighteenth-century Enlightenment; the intellectual classes of Latin America lived out a crisis to a certain extent analogous to that which had tormented Europeans a century earlier" (p. 87).

Paz's subsequent characterization and estimation of the late-nineteenth-century literary movement of *modernismo* is a direct consequence of the historical parallelism that he has thus established: If as he argued before Romanticism arose as a critique of the rational pretensions of the Enlightenment, there had to be then an equivalent moment in Latin America's experience of modernity, once an analogue for European Enlightenment was identified in

Latin American *positivismo*. This was, Paz asserts, the historical role of *modernismo*: "*Modernismo* was the answer to positivism, the criticism of sensibility – the heart and also the nerves – to empiricism and positivistic scientism. In this sense its historical function was similar to that of the Romantic reaction in the early days of the nineteenth century. *Modernismo* was our real Romanticism" (p. 88). In this way, the dialectic of modernity that determined the historical displacement from *positivismo* to *modernismo* in Latin America would be homologous to the one that resulted in the European Romantic reaction to Enlightenment beliefs and concerns.

While Paz has produced in his essay an insightful characterization of the essential traits of modernity, I would advance nonetheless that his account of modernity in Latin America is distorted by the powerful diachronic thrust that he identifies as the most salient feature attendant on modernity. In other words, Paz's own discourse on modernity in Latin America is – I would argue – itself marked by the dialectical, chronological drive at the heart of modernity that he so thoroughly exposed in his study. This contamination of the critical discourse by its subject matter ultimately prevents Paz from visualizing fully the distinctive nature of Latin America's insertion in modernity. As the previous synopsis shows, Paz would like to picture the existence of opposing tendencies and desires within modernity as a successive, dialectical process, exemplified by the transition that leads from the Enlightenment to Romanticism. He later superimposes this chronological scheme on Latin America's experience of modernity through the analogy that posits a similarity between the Enlightenment and Latin American *positivismo* and the subsequent critique of them represented by Romanticism and *modernismo* respectively. Nevertheless, Paz's faithfulness to the diachronic principle at the heart of the concept he wishes to elucidate determines his incapacity to conceptualize in a radical fashion the essence of modernity in Latin America.

I would contend that, for this reason, Paz's account of Latin America's experience of modernity fails to ascertain the essentially *rhetorical* nature of that experience and its implications. Or rather, it seems to be unable to profit from the insight gained by having established – albeit indirectly – that very fact. For in his discussion of Positivism's impact in Latin America, for instance, Paz had made the following remark: "Positivism in Latin America was not the ideology of a liberal bourgeoisie interested in industrial and social progress, as it was in Europe, but of an oligarchy of big landowners. It was a mystification, a self-deceit as well as a deceit" (87).[27] Paz, therefore, is aware of the circumstance that Latin America did not experience modernity as a historical reality; but lost in that denial is the all-important fact that this *was*, nonetheless, the essence of Latin America's historical experience of modernity. If the previous sentence seems alternately oxymoronic and pleonastic, it is merely because its structure is emblematic of the character of modernity in Latin America: it was an absence, a negation, but one that in turn generated a rhetorical predicament that has been the irreducible constitutive element of Latin America's relationship to modernity. Hence, I would propose that it is only when confronting the realization that Latin American modernity was a rhetorical phenomenon above all that we can begin to engage it in all its complexity. Furthermore, an understanding of the situation in rhetorical terms will place us in a position not only to advance a different formulation of the troublesome manifestation of modernity in Latin America, but also to understand more clearly the latter's obsessive concern with the determination of an autochthonous cultural expression.

The assertion that Latin America's experience of modernity was fundamentally *rhetorical* is meant to convey more than the fact that it was in essence a phenomenon or effect of discourse, that is to say, a discursive event that was not accompanied by the material trappings of modernity. This interpretation echoes the pejorative connotation that the adjective "rhetorical" has acquired in common parlance: that is to say, a discourse that is fundamentally devoid of referential ground. It is indeed the case that modernity in Latin America manifested itself superficially as an almost indiscriminate appropriation of discourses that were considered "modern," with the somewhat ingenuous intention of attaining modernity itself in the process of wielding them. Nevertheless, my principal objective in using the term rhetorical is not to underscore or reflect this circumstance, but rather to suggest that modernity was experienced by Latin American writers and intellectuals as a predicament that was rhetorical *in nature*. The fundamental features of this predicament could be summarized in the following fashion: Given that Latin America did not possess objective historical conditions to sustain the discourse of modernity, the adoption of the rhetoric of modernity had to be accompanied by a surreptitious gesture that sought to take leave from the constative exigencies of that rhetoric.[28] That is to say, while invoking the values, goals and ideology of modernity, Latin American writers also needed to define simultaneously a space outside that rhetoric, since the discourse of modernity unremittingly put in question the discursive authority of the Latin American writing subject. This contradictory rhetorical situation manifests itself textually in that the work adopts a rhetorical mode that it identifies with modernity, and simultaneously proceeds to argue in a way that suggests that that rhetorical mode is somehow not commensurate with the Latin American text.

Seen in this light, Latin America's relationship with modernity has incorporated from the outset a dimension that could be best described as critical, if one keeps in mind the displacement or separation that is part of the adjective's etymological charge. Hence, Latin American writers and intellectuals have consistently engaged modernity with a critical stance, but not of the sort that Paz identifies with European Romanticism or its Latin American "counterpart," *modernismo*. In Paz's scheme this critique is philosophical and existential, expressed through the Romantic insistence on Analogy as an epistemological principle that supersedes rationalism. In my view, though, this critical move reveals itself in the Latin American text as an internal rhetorical difference, a turning away from itself that originates in and is expressive of an incongruous discursive predicament. Since the resolute embracing of modern values and categories is also resolutely challenged by the rhetorical exigencies of the Latin American discursive situation, it becomes impossible to assert with any degree of assurance whether Latin American cultural discourse is modern or anti-modern; what must be understood, though, is that this undecidability is the essence of Latin America's experience of, and participation in modernity.[29] It might seem, on account of the necessary breadth of my argument, that I am disregarding the fact that the chasm between the rhetoric of modernity and Latin American circumstance has varied greatly from Buenos Aires to Venezuela to Bolivia. I am keenly aware of those differences; but my principal intention here is to point to the existence of that fissure itself, regardless of its specific features, and to delineate in general terms the complex maneuver of rhetorical enabling with which Latin American writers addressed the resulting crisis. Furthermore, the task that confronts us now is to understand the relationship that exists between this contradictory rhetorical inscription within the modern and the relentless, long-standing inquiry into the specific nature of Latin American cultural expression.

It is not difficult to visualize how this internal rhetorical displacement should have hypostatized itself into an exaggerated affirmation of another difference, one centered on the specificity and singularity of autochthonous cultural characteristics and values. Through a literal rendition and inversion of the traditional metaphor that conceives of discourse as a series of rhetorical *topoi* or *loci*, the problematics of rhetorical legitimation then surfaces thematized as a preoccupation with the *place* whence that discourse emerges.[30] The rhetorical difference intrinsic to the text is thereby projected, reified outside the realm of discourse; in turn, this externality enables it to become the object of a discursive cultural enterprise defined as the ceaseless exploration of that very difference; the outcome is Latin American cultural discourse, where Latin America becomes a historical and geographic space for which an irreducible difference is claimed in a persistent and repetitive fashion. This is the case even in those texts that appear to argue strenuously for the eradication of that essential difference through the total incorporation of Latin America into a modernity that is conceived as an intrinsically European phenomenon. In these works Latin America's historical and socio-economic idiosyncrasies are depicted as detrimental from the point of view of modernity; but the difference represented by those idiosyncrasies is also the thematic rendition of a displacement away from its chosen rhetorical mode that is an essential discursive maneuver for the text's coming into being. The result is that, when examined from this perspective, even those works that purport to diagnose the ills that postpone Latin America's participation in the modern can be shown to affirm, in their own discursive performance, the fundamental eccentricity of Latin America *vis-à-vis* modernity. Hence, the successive projects that would subsume Latin America under the mantle of modernity are simultaneously and paradoxically engaged in the affirmation of a radical cultural difference, a cultural claim to exception from the demands of modernity that is the expression of a discursive will-to-power; an attempt to stave off the rhetorical disenfranchisement with which modernity threatened the Latin American writer at every turn.[31]

The compelling enactment of this surreptitious rhetorical schism can be discerned, then, even in texts whose authors would seem to be unequivocally aligned with the ideology of modernity, or who would eschew any identification with autochthonous categories. Both of these qualities characterize, for instance, Sarmiento's *Facundo*, perhaps the most momentous pronouncement for modernity in nineteenth-century Latin America. Yet regardless of the author's explicit desire to incorporate Argentina (and by extension all of Latin America) into modernity, in this work Sarmiento's discursive authority is explicitly linked to the eccentricity, the irreducibility of Argentine reality to the requirements of modernity. This relationship is expressed through fragments such as the following, where Sarmiento relates his discursive performance, his interpretive authority, to the uniqueness of the Argentine situation: "South America in general, and Argentina in particular has been missing a Tocqueville, who . . . would penetrate to the heart of our public life, as in a vast field not yet surveyed or described by science, and could reveal to Europe, to France . . . this new mode of being that has no clearly defined or well-known antecedents."[32] It is precisely this recalcitrant nature of the Argentine situation that has baffled, according to Sarmiento, all European attempts to fathom it: "[France's] most cunning politicians have not managed to understand what their eyes have seen . . . When they see the rivers of molten lava that tumble, turn and collide noisily in this large nucleus of internal strife, those who pride themselves on being the sharpest have said: It is a secondary volcano, without name, one of the many that show up in America: it will soon extinguish itself; and have turned their gazes somewhere else, satisfied to have given such an easy and exact solution to social phenomena that they have only seen collectively and superficially" (p. 9). Elaborating on this very point, Sarmiento refers at various times to the Argentine "case" as a *secret* (p. 7), an *enigma* (p. 9), a *vortex* (p. 9) and a *mystery* (p. 10); he finally compares it to a Gordian knot that can only be untangled through a study such as the one he is about to undertake in his essay: "To untie that knot that the sword has been unable to cut one must study carefully the twists and turns of the threads that comprise it, searching in the national past, in the topography of the soil, in popular customs and traditions the points where they become entangled" (p. 9).[33] The rhetorical reliance on the eccentricity of the Argentine situation also surfaces in Sarmiento's paradoxical claim that the potential originality of Latin American literature lies in its use of the human and natural indigenous element that his argument also proposes should be eradicated, a recommendation that he follows to the letter by turning his work into a detailed depiction and exploration of that autochthonous component. Almost inevitably then, one begins to sense after a while a complicity between the author and the barbarism that he nonetheless claims is endemic to the country: "If you raise just a bit the lapel of the swallow-tailed coat with which the Argentine disguises himself, you will find a more or less civilized gaucho, but always a gaucho" (p. 162). Few readers of Sarmiento's text have failed to notice the consequences of this underlying continuity, which has elicited assertions such as Pedro Henríquez Ureña's well-known insight on *Facundo*'s author: "Sarmiento, as a civilizer in need of action and spurred by haste, chose for the future of his country the European and North American shortcut instead of the native path, still unfinished, slow, endless perhaps or leading to a dead end; *but no one felt more than he the untamed energy, the coarse originality of the barbarism that he endeavored to destroy*" (my emphasis).[34] Cultural discourse in Latin America has been consistently – one would be almost tempted to say systematically – produced in the midst of the disjunction that Sarmiento's work exemplifies so thoroughly. In turn, this rhetorical predicament has found its most persistent expression in the assertion of Latin America's irrepressible and irreducible cultural difference.

And yet, one can intuit readily the complications that arise when the discursive authority of a text is sustained through the effective disavowal or dismantling of its chosen rhetorical structure. It is this contradictory quality that makes Sarmiento's masterpiece, for instance, such a complex work; that endows it with a difficult nature that can never be adequately resolved. This incongruous circumstance further reveals itself in the fact that all the projects, solutions, reforms and manifestoes that have been advanced in order to make Latin America consonant with modernity have always exhibited a simplistic, doctrinaire and generally hyperbolic nature, betraying in their exaggerated gesturing the ambivalent wellspring that nurtures their explicit reformist designs. Considered in this light, one begins to understand the source of that "desperate incandescence" that according to Marshall Berman is characteristic of what he denominates "the modernism of underdevelopment":

The contrast of Baudelaire and Dostoevsky, and of Paris and Petersburg in the middle of the nineteenth century, should help us to see a larger polarity in the world history of modernism. At one pole we can see the modernism of advanced nations, building directly on the materials of economic and political modernization and drawing vision and energy from a modernized reality – Marx's factories and railways, Baudelaire's boulevards – even when it challenges that reality in radical ways. At an opposite pole we find a modernism that arises from backwardness and underdevelopment. This modernism first arose in Russia, most dramatically in St. Petersburg, in the nineteenth century; in our own era, with the spread of modernization – but generally, as in old Russia, a truncated and warped modernization – it has spread throughout the Third World. The modernism of underdevelopment is forced to build on fantasies and dreams of modernity, to nourish itself on an intimacy and to struggle with mirages and ghosts. In order to be true to the life from which it springs, it is forced to be shrill, uncouth and inchoate. It turns in on itself and tortures itself for its inability to singlehandedly make history – or else throws itself into extravagant attempts to take on itself the whole burden of history. It whips itself into frenzies of self-loathing, and preserves itself only through vast reserves of self-irony. But the bizarre reality from which this modernism grows, and the unbearable pressures under which it moves and lives – social and political pressures as well as spiritual ones – infuse it with a desperate incandescence that Western modernism, so much more at home in its world, can rarely hope to match.[35]

One could, of course, object to Berman's terminology; but I believe that his description of the phenomenon he alludes to is extremely compelling and essentially accurate. While his discussion of the "modernism of underdevelopment" curiously does not mention Latin America in the nineteenth century, most of the issues he raises in his consideration of modernism in Russia are apposite to the case. My argument would be, though, that the somewhat garish and extreme aspect of this particular modernism is the result of the rhetorical quandary in the midst of which it is forced to reside, rather than the expression of an existential conflict of cultural proportions, as Berman would seem to envision it. This circumstance can also be invoked to account, in turn, for the profoundly aesthetic character, the intensely gestural nature of Latin American modernity; in other words, the propensity to excess and superfluity that Berman has so aptly identified.

The phenomenon that I have been analyzing in its Latin American manifestation could be reformulated in less specific terms in order to thereby render it more universally applicable: the awareness of modernity provokes a crisis in the intellectual circles of communities that perceive the modern to be the province of another society. That at least one of the outcomes of this crisis is the affirmation of an intrinsic cultural essence is exemplified by the emergence of *Kultur* theories in Germany during the late eighteenth century and the early years of the nineteenth, a paradigmatic case that Alfred Mayer has summarized in the following fashion:

> *Kultur* theories can be explained to a considerable extent as an ideological expression of, or reaction to, Germany's political, social and economic backwardness in comparison with France and England. But the ideological reaction to this backwardness went in different and mutually hostile directions. For Kant and other representatives of eighteenth-century enlightenment in Germany, the enlightenment itself, the growth of rationalist and utilitarian philosophy, the flourishing of political and economic institutions, represented *Kultur*, and to emulate the achievements of *Kultur* was the task they set for Germany. *Kultur* thus had a universal, patently international flavor.
>
> The other ideological strand tended to regard *Kultur* as a complex of qualities, achievements, and behavior patterns which were local or national in origin and significance, unique, non-transferable, non-repetitive, and therefore irrelevant for the outsider. Herder's relativism did much to pave the way for this conception of *Kultur*. The stress on such unique culture patterns as against the political, scientific, or philosophical achievements of Western civilization can be regarded as an attempt to compensate for a deep-seated feeling of inferiority on the part of German intellectuals once they had come in contact with the advanced nations. Similarly . . . Russian cultural nationalism developed in the measure as Russian contacts with the West intensified. These *Kultur* theories, then, are a typical ideological expression – though by no means the only one – of the rise of backwards societies against the encroachments of the West on their traditional culture. *They consist in asserting the reality of something which is just about to be destroyed.*[36]

One can recognize in these two antagonistic postures towards modernity many of the characteristic qualities of cultural discourse in Latin America that have been discussed above. Nonetheless, I believe that the dichotomous nature of Mayer's scheme conceals the complexity of the dialectical interaction between the two essential attitudes. His static description allows him to transform and effectively reduce the confrontation with modernity to psychological dimensions. In his view, the formulation and upholding of an intrinsic cultural essence is a compensatory mechanism that betrays a "deep-seated feeling of inferiority"; a retrenchment into the self in order to prop up a cultural ego that knows it cannot possibly compete with, let alone vanquish, its competitor. This characterization implicitly advances the proposition that the first conception of *Kultur*, the one that seeks to embrace modernity wholeheartedly, is a more "mature," less "neurotic" reaction to the situation it confronts, inasmuch as it translates its concerns into concrete projects of social, political and economic reform to achieve the culture's incorporation into the realm of the modern. Such an interpretation obscures the fact that the attitude that this position represents – the enthusiastic immersion in modernity – is also a particular response to the crisis, and that it is therefore caught in a contradictory problematics of its own. This disjunction is ultimately reflected in Mayer's tendency to regard as mutually exclusive the two principal attitudes towards modernity that it identifies, blinded by the superficial discrepancies between them. By contrast, my argument proposes that when considered from a rhetorical perspective, the two postures are in fact related by virtue of the discursive predicament they have in common, their shared condition as crisis statements. For regardless of their dissimilarities, both of them share a rhetorical space that depends on cultural specificity and difference for its survival. In other words, the answers represented by the two attitudes may differ radically on the surface, but they both have an investment in the continued affirmation of an ineradicable cultural specificity, since their rhetorical authority is grounded on the persistence of the difference assumed by that specificity. This is why even works such as *Facundo*, that from all indications place themselves squarely on the side of modernity, signal in a number of ways the irreducibility of Latin America to the coordinates of the modern. But this is also why, by the same token, it would be misguided to interpret the passionate assertion of cultural difference as an attempt to withdraw from modernity, as Mayer suggests was explicitly the case in both nineteenth-century Germany and Russia. For even the most vehement proposals of cultural autochthony in Latin America seem to be motivated by the ulterior desire to make possible Latin America's participation in contemporaneous history, in the temporal flux that is the mainspring of the concept of modernity. When Martí, for instance, argues for the determination of a cultural essence specific to Latin America, he is envisioning that project as a preliminary stage to a comprehensive integration of the continent in modern world history. In the specific case of Latin America this incapacity to abjure or renege modernity altogether is further heightened by the circumstance that, as Paz averred, Latin America is itself a product of modernity; hence it cannot put the latter in question without simultaneously questioning the validity of its own legitimation.

In light of this discussion, the unremitting Latin American affirmation of an autochthonous cultural essence would have to be interpreted in a novel fashion. It should be construed as a strategy designed to fashion a rhetorical foundation, a position of rhetorical authority from within the difficult discursive situation described above. In the end, this ceaseless search for a cultural identity must be understood and addressed as an equally inexhaustible stratagem to empower rhetorically the Latin American writer in the face of modernity's threat to undermine the legitimacy of his discourse. That is to say, the assumption of Latin America's difference *has created* the rhetorical space and possibility for a Latin American discourse, a space that by definition can never be foreclosed by the demands and challenges of modernity, since that difference guarantees that Latin America is from the outset *hors jeu* with respect to modernity. This would account for the apparent naïveté that always seems to allow for yet one more formulation of autochthony, since each text must repeat anew the gesture that underwrites its discursive authority.[37] In this sense, the thematic repetitiveness within the textual tradition of cultural definition that was remarked on before could be considered another symptom of the blindness that necessarily accompanies this requisite maneuver of rhetorical foundation.

Given the discursive situation that I have outlined, there might seem to be an area of overlapping interests with a conception of cultural production that has evolved from a paradigm borrowed from the social sciences: dependency theory.[38] But regardless of the extensive influence that this scheme has exerted in some quarters and its commendable attempt to produce a comprehensive interpretation of Latin American cultural production, I would like to discourage such an association. In its cultural avatar, dependency theory concentrates on the distortions and incongruities that seemingly occur when a dominant discursive modality is transplanted to a context that is linked through a relationship of dependence to the metropolis that originated the hegemonic discourse; it concerns itself with the ensuing deformation that it considers to be the inevitable result of this discursive transplantation. To its credit, this view of cultural relationships undermines the organicist concept of cultural development as a series of specific stages that must be achieved if the "developing" culture is to mature as a cultural entity. It proposes in its stead a dynamic relationship determined by the dependence that structures cultural exchange between the metropolis and its periphery. I would argue, however, that in this scheme the discourse of "dependent" cultures is invariably viewed as evincing a catachretic quality with respect to the dominant cultural discourse; that is, the dependent subject is condemned to produce a "faulty" actualization of the dominant form, even if that deviation is subsequently interpreted by the critic as possessing critical or resistive significance *vis-à-vis* the hegemonic discourse. Hence, there is a permanent and irreducible Otherness associated with the dependent culture that amounts to a dangerous form of disguised exoticism. In general terms this cultural extrapolation of economic dependency theory construes dependent cultural pro-duction as essentially an echo of hegemonic cultural manifestations, however many difficulties or discrepancies it may identify in the re-creation of those forms in the context of a dependent situation. In the end, the theoretical scaffolding borrowed from the social sciences only serves to give renewed legitimacy to an old truism: that Latin American cultural production is a deficient or epigonic rendition of European cultural concerns.

In contradistinction to this view, I would argue as follows: Although it is impossible to deny the economic and cultural penetration of Latin America by European powers in the nineteenth century, it is my belief that the crisis produced by Latin America's insertion in the modern world historical order – which I have proposed to characterize as a rhetorical predicament – is "resolved" *creatively* by Latin American intellectuals in the continual affir-mation of a cultural specificity that is perceived to be, consciously or not, discontinuous with modernity. But I believe we would err in interpreting such a gesture as significant merely on account of its divergent stance *vis-à-vis* the discourse of modernity, a discourse associated with the metropolis; nor should the internal contra-dictions evinced by this discourse be taken as indicative of the stammering, flawed rhetoric of a subject immersed in a relationship of dependency. For as Paz, de Man, Calinescu and others have

established, even in its metropolitan European enclaves the discourse of modernity is inherently undermined by a persistent
questioning of its own desires and assumptions that endows it with
the unsettledness that is characteristic of it. Interpreting Latin
America's discourse of modernity strictly in terms of its European
manifestation deprives Latin America's experience of its specific
significance and its productive, creative character. Such an interpretation represents a reaffirmation of a subject/object model of
history, where Europe is understood to be the historical agent acting
on a dependent object whose prerogatives are limited to reacting to
what is done to it.[39] Instead, I would argue that Latin American
modernity must be understood as a cultural activity possessing
meaning unto itself; that is, as an ongoing process of cultural
production that engages in a symbolic appropriation of historical
and cultural experience.[40]

Moreover, I believe there is another compelling reason to refrain
from endowing Latin America's posture with respect to modernity
with any subversive power with respect to Western hegemonic
discourse: If we succumb to the temptation of identifying a revolutionary or demystifying value in the difference supposedly
entailed by Latin America, we run the risk of fetishizing that
difference, of becoming enamored of the critical opportunities that it
affords, thereby drawing attention away from the very concrete
situation of exploitation from which it arises. What I would like to
propose can be summarized in the following fashion: let us indeed
explore the ways in which, for example, Borges' *écriture* or Lezama's
gnostic formulations question or subvert the Western *épistème*, but
let us not make that critique contingent on their *being Latin American*.
For the price of engaging in such a critique can become an
investment in sustaining the condition of economic and political
subjection on which the affirmation of cultural difference is predicated, as well as the acceptance (however joyously embraced) of a
marginality that the hegemonic cultural discourse is always only too
willing to confirm in the first place.[41]

To summarize then, Latin America's preoccupation with the
affirmation of its cultural specificity has constituted the essence of its
experience of modernity. In this respect, the Latin American case is
analogous to that of other traditional communities faced with the
difficulties represented by their participation in an epoch of increasing industrialization. The earliest manifestation of these develop-

ments was the wave of successive nationalisms that characterized nineteenth-century political history; its most recent avatars are the widespread nationalist movements of the post-colonial period.[42] Every one of these nationalistic crusades has sought to legitimize its historical claims by representing itself as the political manifestation of a cultural essence that can no longer be suppressed. The process by which these national cultures are formulated is an imaginative act of creation that does not lack a certain arbitrariness as Ernest Gellner has contended: "The cultural shreds and patches used by nationalism are often arbitrary historical inventions. Any old shred and patch would have served as well ... Nationalism is not what it seems, and above all it is not what it seems to itself. The cultures it claims to defend and revive are often its own inventions, or are modified out of all recognition."[43] But regardless of its imaginative quality, nationalism invariably grounds the legitimacy of its existence and agenda on two very specific elements: a cultural essence whose origins are assumed to regress into a fathomless past, and the need to create political boundaries that are expressive of linguistic homogeneity. With respect to the first of these it can be said that, even if the emerging states regard themselves as very much the product of new historical developments, the spiritual essence of which they are a living political manifestation is nonetheless assumed to hark back to a remote point lost in the beginnings of cultural time. But the criterion of linguistic specificity is no less important than the first: language is the irreducible criterion of a nation's demand to exist as a separate political entity. As Kedourie has pithily said, "a group speaking the same language is known as a nation, and a nation ought to constitute a state. It is not merely that a group of people speaking a certain language may claim the right to preserve its language; rather, such a group, which is a nation, will cease to be one if it is not constituted into a state."[44] The enterprise of configuring a cultural essence from the study of the past manifestations of a group bounded by linguistic homogeneity is – as I shall examine in more detail in the next chapter – expressive of the relationship of mutual implication that obtained between the earliest instances of cultural nationalism and the birth of the discipline of philology at the beginning of the nineteenth century. It also accounts for why so many Latin American writers and intellectuals – among others Bello, Sarmiento, Reyes, Henríquez Ureña and

Picón Salas – have also been trained as philologists or have undertaken extensive philological work.[45]

With these observations in mind, one can begin to understand how Latin America's need to formulate a cultural specificity of its own became a totally incongruous endeavor. First, its demands conflicted insolubly with Latin America's founding cultural myth: its claim to being a quintessential outcome of modernity. For Latin America's assertion that it represented a radically new beginning foreclosed the possibility of engaging in the enterprise of "recovering" or "reconstructing" that purportedly ageless autochthonous essence that was the decisive accomplishment of other cultural nationalisms. If modernity represents a desire to obliterate the past, Latin America's thorough identification with modernity rendered problematic the formulation of cultural specificity and difference with which it proposed to answer the rhetorical challenges of modernity. But equally troublesome was the assumption of the existence of a linguistic specificity for Latin America; for even those linguistic traits or forms that could be construed initially as instances of idiomatic idiosyncrasy, autochthonous poetry or native legend could quickly be shown to be derived from Spanish sources, or to be mere anachronisms, examples of archaic pronunciation or usage that reflected sixteenth- or seventeenth-century Castilian norms. One is reminded here of Juan Marinello's observation regarding this very point: "If we struggled to introduce creole terms into the mother tongue, and if in our speech we made a serious attempt at innovation, we would arrive at words that were common currency centuries ago in Andalusia or Estremadura."[46] Juxtaposing these two essential difficulties, Latin America's predicament of cultural definition can be described in the following way: it seeks to affirm a difference that it cannot articulate in the terms prescribed by the paradigm of difference that it invokes. Prevented thus from anchoring its avowed cultural difference in the bedrock of the past or the uniqueness of its language, Latin America has engaged in the affirmation of its cultural specificity by making it the object of an epistemological *project*. Cultural identity became then a category whose referent was assumed to be transparent but which nonetheless had to be decoded; an affirmed reality that nevertheless had to be discovered – in short, a problem. Hence, far from providing the kind of reassurance and determination that a community could derive from its uninterrupted historical connection with a collective essence, Latin American cultural being has been experienced as a category that is subject to the vagaries and uncertainties of interpretation. Clifford Geertz has described the process of creating a collective cultural subject by proposing that it "tends to revolve around the question of the content, relative weight, and proper relationship of two rather towering abstractions: 'The Indigenous Way of Life' and 'The Spirit of the Age.' To stress the first of these is to look to local mores, established institutions, and the unities of common experience – to 'tradition,' 'culture,' 'national character,' or even 'race' – for the roots of a new identity. To stress the second is to look for the general outlines of the history of [the] time, and in particular to what one takes to be the overall direction and significance of history."[47] For Latin America the difficulties encountered in the articulation of a cultural essence have resulted in the collapsing together of these two tendencies, resulting in a conception of identity understood to be the putative final outcome of an ongoing historical project.

More decisive still, such a circumstance transforms the historical experience of a community into the final arbiter of the success or failure of collective conceptions of identity. In this instance only the lived historical existence of a culture can provide the authority to validate a collective myth, whereas in the case of a culture that can point to the past as a confirmation of its avowed identity, present historical circumstances can be either embraced or resisted because they are judged harmonious or incompatible with that presumed essence. But where Latin America is concerned, the difficulties and failures of its history have continually eroded the interpretive and tropological authority of the figurations that have been advanced to provide it with a mythology of cultural foundations. Hence, the belief that Latin America's economic and political problems arise from its failure to determine conclusively its "real" cultural essence, its historical "destiny," must be turned on its head: cultural identity is a perpetual preoccupation of Latin American intellectuals and writers *because* of the vicissitudes of Latin American history. That is to say, historical misfortune is not the outcome of Latin America's cultural errancy or self-ignorance, but the condition of its possibility. In this regard, Latin America's situation can be illuminated by comparing it to that of the United States. Born of modernity as well, the United States shared from the beginning the linguistic and historical difficulties attendant on the formulation of a cultural essence that have been identified in the case of Latin America. But in contrast to the latter, the ascendance of the United States to a position of historical hegemony has managed to invest with authority the myths of cultural identity that were generated by that country's intelligentsia.[48]

But this comparison also leads us to suspect that if the determination of cultural specificity has played such a generative role in the production and sustenance of cultural discourse in Latin America, it is because it has nevertheless allowed the causal understanding of real, concrete and difficult historical problems as a function of a presumed cultural crisis. Interpreted in this ideological vein, the Latin American quest for cultural identity can itself be regarded then as a cultural myth of foundations; but a myth that narrates the story of an essential cultural schism, capable nonetheless of endowing the affairs of the collectivity with the requisite meaning and purpose. In the end, through this myth of permanent cultural crisis Latin American intellectuals have paradoxically found an effective narrative of cultural identity. Only, of course, that the cultural meaning that it advances is that cultural meaning must be rigorously sought and just as rigorously never found. This incongruous myth of cultural definition, in which interpretive desire and its thwarted teleology coexist, has left its imprint in the Latin American discursive tradition that it has engendered: texts of vehement rhetoric and passionate verve that ultimately redound in the repeated affirmation of a collection of stereotypical, conventional formulations.

And yet, regardless of the argument that I have advanced, or the broad critique of the concept of identity that has marked the last fifteen years of Latin American critical debate, I have no illusions that the topic of cultural essence will soon lose its sway.[49] First, one must take into consideration that the entire academic and institutional framework that supports and legitimizes Latin American discourse is centered on the project of securing an answer to this cultural question. But more importantly, it must be realized that my undertaking of the dismantling of the concept of identity does not escape the fact that I am nonetheless borrowing its authority to provide the foundation for my own discursive performance. The question that imposes itself is the following: will there ever be a Latin American discourse that is no longer centered on either the question of identity or its dismantling – the pieties of cultural essence or the ever-renewed attempts to demystify them? Or better yet: will such a discourse be able – or wish, for that matter – to call itself Latin American?

The chapters that follow will examine in detail the *novela de la tierra*, a group of texts that represent the intersection of literary discourse and the difficult project of cultural definition that I have analyzed. In general terms, the discussion will address the specific ways in which literature inserted itself in the comprehensive enterprise of determining Latin America's cultural specificity. First, I will attempt to situate the historical context from which the project of literary autochthony emerged. Subsequently the specific characteristics of a literary discourse that claims to be reflective of essential cultural categories and values will be addressed. My overarching aim will be to consider the specific textual enterprise represented by the *novela de la tierra* in light of the contradictory nature of cultural discourse in Latin America that has been established above.

2

The *novela de la tierra*

> He also thought he recognized trees and crop fields
> that he could not have named, because his actual
> knowledge of the countryside was quite inferior to
> his nostalgic and literary knowledge of it.
>
> Jorge Luis Borges[1]

Judging from current attitudes prevalent among most literary critics, the expression *novela de la tierra* would seem to be more than simply an attempt to reflect the thematics of the texts that are conventionally grouped under that rubric; for the term could be interpreted metaphorically as well to describe the position these works are deemed to occupy in the edifice of contemporary Latin American letters: they are considered to be the coarse, unfinished foundation of the structure, whose principal function is to give support to the building erected on them. This is, I believe, an accurate description of the manner in which most modern critics have confronted and analyzed these works, endeavoring to identify in them everything that present-day Latin American literature has transcended, has left behind on its way to achieving its current preeminence.

Hence, it is not surprising to find that contemporary critical discourse on the *novela de la tierra* almost invariably exudes an air of complacency *vis-à-vis* its subject matter. Such a comfortable posture clearly informs the following assertion by Mario Benedetti: "[Regionalist literature] has already exhausted itself in almost all Latin American countries, and one can say today that it is a thing of the past, an experience that only has a place (a well-earned place, nonetheless) in the manuals and histories of literature."[2] With equal authority but considerably less kindness, Mario Vargas Llosa has labeled these texts "primitive" and has argued that with them "the novel became a census, a matter of geographical data, a description of customs and usages, an ethnological document, a regional fair, a

38

sample case of folklore."[3] In both of these utterances the underlying assumption is that, as a whole, the works included under the rubric *novela de la tierra* have been thoroughly domesticated by now, and that they are irredeemably out of step with contemporary critical and literary preoccupations. Even when these works have been re-examined with the express intent of rectifying the neglect to which they have been subjected, the novels have not fared much better. In most instances, the desire to call for renewed attention to them is accompanied by a reading that only manages to reactivate – surreptitiously if not overtly – the most entrenched critical common-places about the *novela de la tierra*. In the least harmful variation of this revisionary turn, the reader is simply reminded by the critic that these are indeed significant works whose shortcomings are attribut-able to the literary and sociological contexts whence they arose.

Equally perplexing is the facile fashion in which the term *novela de la tierra* is bandied around in critical circles, where the label is commonly used as a catch-all, useful for making sweeping pro-nouncements in the realm of literary history. Take, for instance, the following passage in Emir Rodríguez Monegal's influential mono-graph *El boom de la novela latinoamericana*: "The decade of the 1940s, with the successive appearance of the novels already men-tioned, deals one blow after another to the *novela de la tierra* . . . until it transforms completely the literary panorama."[4] Such a discursive practice presupposes that an established consensus exists on the literary characteristics that the rubric *novela de la tierra* designates, when even the most superficial consultation of the critical and historiographic literature will establish the unwarranted character of such an assumption. And yet, the widespread flippant use of such a thoroughly imprecise category as *novela de la tierra* is itself a secondary manifestation of the unproblematic, homogeneous char-acter generally ascribed to the novels themselves. A related indi-cation of the concept's indeterminate nature is the plethora of terms that it has subsequently engendered. That the label stands on very imprecise theoretical foundations is demonstrated by the existence of a number of other related and equally vague denominations such as *novela criolla*, *novela rural*, *novela costumbrista*, *novela telúrica* and *novela regional*.[5] Even more specific categories have been produced in an attempt to further subdivide the field, such as *novela campesina*, *novela de la selva*, *novela gauchesca* and several others. Nevertheless, the taxonomical proliferation has not resulted in a more precise knowledge of the works involved, but rather in a purely thematic fragmentation (by geographical milieu, character, etc.) that has engendered – not surprisingly – a purely thematic criticism.

In all, the fluidity and imprecision of the category of *novela de la tierra* is symptomatic of the fact that its principal use by literary historians during the last fifty years has not been the designation of a specific field of study; its main function has consisted in serving in a heuristic capacity for the composition of the larger narrative of literary history. As a result, the critical valorization of the *novela de la tierra* has not been grounded in an examination of its intrinsic qualities, but has been determined rather as a function of preceding or subsequent literary developments. This last assertion becomes evident when the precipitous fall in critical fortunes of the *novela de la tierra* is remarked upon. If one invokes Northrop Frye's ingenious analogy of the history of literary taste as a voluble stock market, it could easily be claimed that few issues in the Latin American Literary Exchange have lost as many points in as little time;[6] one could advance as exemplary in this respect Arturo Torres Rioseco's outright prescriptive enthusiasm for the *novela de la tierra* in the 1930s, and the frankly condescending tone of Carlos Fuentes' thoughts on that novelistic promotion thirty years later.[7] Nonetheless, a closer examination reveals that both readings, although apparently irreconcilable are dictated by an identical underlying configuration of historical emplotment, and that the evident differences between the two are simply a mirage, a result of the chronological distance that separates them. Whereas Torres' privileging of the *novela de la tierra* stems from his sympathy for a novelistic production that constituted in his view the beginning of an authentic Latin American literary tradition, Fuentes is intent on showing how the deficiencies inherent in this founding act were overcome during the subsequent novelistic development they initiated. Hence, the nature of both critical enterprises is predicated on the postulation of the *novela de la tierra* as an origin – a place from which the future will unfold in Torres Rioseco's scheme, and an original point of reference against which to highlight and valorize the achievements of "la nueva novela hispanoamericana" in Fuentes' case.

As Edward Said has remarked in his powerful meditation on beginnings, all points of departure have two aspects that animate one another, and which constitute but two sides of the same coin: "One leads to the project being realized: this is the transitive aspect of the beginning – that is, beginning with (or for) an anticipated end, or at least expected continuity. The other aspect retains for the beginning its identity as *radical* starting point: the intransitive and conceptual aspect, that which has no object but its own constant clarification."[8] The first of these, according to Said, "foresees a continuity that flows from it. It is suited for work, for polemic, for discovery."[9] Fuentes' positing of the *novela de la tierra* as an origin corresponds to an underscoring of the first of these aspects, that is, the desire to provide a point of departure for a series that would culminate with the novel of the "Boom" that is his principal concern. Torres Rioseco is engaged, on the other hand, in an enterprise that emphasizes the second aspect, the description of what Said calls "a point that is stripped of every use but its categorization in the mind as beginning".[10] He wishes to present the *novela de la tierra* as the inception of a truly autochthonous literature, thereby emphasizing what there is at the point of origin that is unique and intransitive in itself.

For Fuentes, the *novela de la tierra* is a point of departure both rhetorically and conceptually. His monograph literally begins with a consideration of these novels; they are also designated as a beginning of sorts for novelistic development in Latin America. Here, the *novela de la tierra* becomes the repository of all the literature produced in Latin America during the preceding four centuries, from the chronicles of the Conquest through Sarmiento: "Until very recently the literary Solís, Grijalvas and Cabrals continued discovering with astonishment and fear a Latin American world that was above all an implacable presence of jungles and mountains on an inhuman scale."[11] Once all these diverse tendencies and currents are rhetorically subsumed by Fuentes into a single novelistic Text that is posited as an origin, the articulation of a Tradition becomes a possibility; the task in the remainder of his study will consist in narrating the story of its unfolding and eventual consummation in a development that amounts to an erasure of that origin and a new beginning: "*la nueva novela hispanoamericana.*"

Conversely, Torres' designation of the *novela de la tierra* as a beginning is more concerned with the exploration of the immanent qualities of the point of origin *qua* origin. For this reason his writings on the texts in question have a certain concreteness and wealth of detail that determines the usefulness that they will subsequently have for our study. But Torres cannot seem to escape the danger inherent in the enterprise he is engaged in: what Said refers to as the "tautological circuit of beginnings about to begin."[12] His description of the *novela de la tierra* as a point of origin is persistently undermined by the successive consideration of a number of works, each of which is purportedly more autochthonous than the last. Thus, the true beginning is forever being simultaneously posited and postponed, both hailed and predicted at once. This dialectics can be seen at work in the rhetorical organization of his treatise on the *novela de la tierra* as well. At the very end of his first critical consideration of the autochthonous novel, entitled *La novela en la América Hispana*, Torres can only promise that "in the second part literary americanism [will be] defined *in a more concrete fashion*"[13] (my emphasis). In this way, the avowed identification of an origin becomes in reality a series of provisional beginnings that are successively abandoned *en route* to a presumed final encounter with the most radical beginning of all. In the end, in Torres' writings the *novela de la tierra* is paradoxically its own postponement, merely an anticipation of what its unrealized and yet ungraspable culmination will be. This accounts for the tentative and preliminary tone of Torres' study on the *novela de la tierra*, since the dynamics of his own discourse ultimately prevents a direct critical confrontation with the works themselves. By the same token, Torres' desire to portray the *novela de la tierra* as an origin imposes on him the necessity of detaching it from the continuum of literary history. This explains the inordinate attention given to *modernismo* in Torres' work, since it is only against the backdrop provided by the latter that one can supposedly perceive the originality and uniqueness of the *novela de la tierra*. Therefore, Torres' fascination with beginnings determines that his discourse on the *novela de la tierra* be necessarily of a differential nature. But in order to define it, he must also articulate a parallel discourse on what it is not, that is, *modernismo*. Hence, Torres is fated to write two books while putatively discussing the *novela de la tierra*: one on the latter and another on *modernismo*: "Editorial necessities compel me to divide this work into two parts. The first one studies those writers that come closer to a genuinely American thematics; for this reason I have decided to call them the *novelistas de la tierra*. The second, devoted to the authors that show a more European orientation ... will be entitled *novelistas de la ciudad*."[14] The result of this internal dialectics is that *modernismo* reappears obsessively and obtrusively in Torres' discourse on the *novela de la tierra*, to the point that his writings sometimes seem less a study of the latter than an ardent and vigorous campaign against the former.

Hence, in spite of the evident differences in their valorization of the *novela de la tierra*, the two critical approximations that have been examined coincide in their metaphoric designation of it as a point of origin for further literary development. As recent theoretical meditations on the rhetoric of historical discourse have established, it is in the nature of all historical writing to fall captive to some configuration of emplotment;[15] but one can probably assert that the manner in which the *novela de la tierra* has been consistently characterized as a beginning in the realm of literary history has determined to a large extent that a certain exegetical optics be employed by critics when dealing with texts that are included in that category. One could propose then, that our received idea of the *novela de la tierra* is in many ways the result of a conceit of literary history that has dictated in turn the position of neglect that it now occupies.

It might seem from this overview of the critical literature on the *novela de la tierra* that perhaps my principal concern should be the determination of a set of generic criteria to define the category, as a means of redressing the lack of rigor and concentration that has characterized it. Furthermore, it would appear that arriving at some definition of generic specificity would be essential to this study, since it would furnish the criterion for inclusion that a necessarily limited interpretive enterprise such as mine must invoke. Nevertheless, I would like to argue from the beginning that undertaking to impose generic coherence on the *novela de la tierra* is a temptation that must be questioned and ultimately resisted. The justification for this stance is not necessarily related to the relentless critique to which the concept of genre has recently been subjected from a number of quarters.[16] My reasons for eschewing this approach arise from a desire to change the *nature* of the critical pressure that is brought to bear on the texts that are denominated *novelas de la tierra*. For whatever improvement in preciseness one could expect to derive from a more rigorous determination of generic specificity has to be weighed against the similarity that would link such an effort to traditional critical approximations to the *novela de la tierra*. For the attempt to construct a generic model that would encompass these texts would enter into the same relationship that criticism has traditionally entertained with them: that is, it would have to regard them as discrete positivities, as coherent actualizations (however faithful) of the specified generic paradigm. And as it will be shown, this critical approach has consistently resulted in a commentary that has only managed in essence to repeat the texts themselves through its unwitting appropriation of a critical discourse already present in the novels from the outset. This situation obtains because the enterprise of producing a literary text that is expressive of essential cultural values can only be understood and conceived – as the previous chapter has established – within a perspective that is necessarily critical in nature.

Hence, this study will not endeavor to arrive at a more precise definition of generic configuration for the *novela de la tierra* that will in turn canonize a collection of literary works. Instead, my purpose will be twofold: first, to document the discursive nature of "the autochthonous" by establishing the rhetorical nature of a literary discourse identified with the category of autochthony. Secondly, and just as important, I shall also explore in subsequent chapters the difficulties and contradictions that issue from the attempt by the texts in question to articulate such a discourse. My interpretive project takes as its point of departure the conviction that perhaps the most effective way to revitalize these works for a contemporary audience may be through such a paradoxical and contradictory reading, one that establishes how the text begins to differ radically from the presuppositions that avowedly sustain it.

My examination of the *novela de la tierra* begins with a consideration of the historical conjuncture that determined its emergence and viability as an instrument of cultural affirmation in Latin America.

The origins of the *novela de la tierra*

I too panamericanized with vague fervor and very
little faith in the country of diamonds and tropical
glee.   Rubén Darío[17]

On account of the historical depth of the preoccupation with the autochthonous in Latin America, it would appear somewhat futile to undertake the determination of the precise origins of the *novela de la tierra*. To begin with, one can readily find throughout the nineteenth century several manifestations of the desire to engender an autochthonous literature, from Andrés Bello through Domingo Sarmiento to José Martí. Indeed the entire period presents many instances that attest to the belief that linguistic and literary specificity were regarded as correlatives of the political and cultural otherness that Latin America had recently achieved as an outcome of the battle for independence. In this regard one can cite the ever-expanding collections of *cubanismos, argentinismos* or *venezolanismos*, the periodic reformist projects to adjust Spanish orthography to Latin American phonetics (Bello and Sarmiento are well-known examples of this endeavor) and the founding of Academias Nacionales de la Lengua throughout the continent.[18] Moreover, although there are essential differences that separate the *cuadro de costumbres* and the *novela de la tierra*, Enrique Pupo-Walker has rightly proposed that "it is evident that in Latin America the *cuadro de costumbres* exhibits a desire for cultural affirmation and critical responsibility that distinguishes it from the simple *roman des moeurs*. Frequently, the loose structure of these compositions manifests a dialectical tension that brings it closer to the essay, and which announces the intellectual orientation of the creole narrative of the twentieth century."[19] It could also be remarked in this regard that notwithstanding the commonplace critical notion that affirms the cosmopolitan thrust of *modernismo*, the concern for an indigenous literary expression arose as one of the persistent preoccupations of its practitioners. In sum one would have to agree with Pedro Henríquez Ureña when he says that "the literary history of our last hundred years could be described as the history of the ebb and flow of aspirations and theories in search of an expression that is most perfectly ours."[20] Hence, the "origins" of the *novela de la tierra* have a diachronic dimension that cannot be apprehended strictly as a concrete point in time. And yet, the explosive intensity and continent-wide character of the cultural preoccupation with autochthony that marks the first thirty years of this century in Latin America is in itself a phenomenon whose historical coordinates cannot be overlooked. Furthermore, the distinctive response to the question of the autochthonous articulated by the *novela de la tierra* can and must be examined with a view to establishing its specific nature, even while acknowledging that the enterprise of which it is an instance has very extended historical roots.

Traditionally, the literary movement that concerns us has been regarded as one of several manifestations of the more comprehensive cultural phenomenon that one critic has denominated "the redis-covery of America."[21] According to this interpretation, the vigorous meditation on cultural essence that characterized the first thirty years of this century in Latin America was a reflection of the Neo-Kantianism or Neo-Spiritualism that in Europe had come to be associated with the vitalism of Bergson, the contingency of Boutroux, the Nietzschean emphasis on the Will, and the aesthetic influence of Croce. And yet, the altogether haphazard and slow diffusion of these ideas throughout Latin America during this period cannot account for the unanimity and depth of the nativist explosion in the entire continent.[22] The other conventional explanation for the surfacing of a literature of autochthony in this period is that it represents a nostalgia for an agrarian past in the face of an encroaching industrialization that threatened the hegemony of the landed aristocracy. This interpretation is undermined by the dissi-milar economic development of individual countries in Latin America, by the widely differing class alliances that can be attri-buted to the authors involved and by the obvious overtures to modernization present in some of these works (Gallegos' *Doña Bárbara* immediately comes to mind in this regard). I would like to argue that although the influence exerted by these intellectual trends should not be undervalued, a cultural development of such magnitude and extension must be understood as having its source in the primordial rhetorical predicament that was discussed in our previous chapter; that is, in the troubled inscription of Latin America in the context of the modern.

A careful consideration of cultural discourse in Latin America reveals that the end of the nineteenth century coincided with a decided change in Latin America's problematic relationship with modernity. It was a variation that can be more accurately described as a difference in orientation rather than as a radical trans-formation; a modification that had been in preparation for decades, but which finally surfaced fully and with an irrepressible force at the very close of the century. If 1898 is a date that customarily serves to mark the ascent of the United States to the rank of international power, it is no less true that the moment signaled a significant shift in the ceaseless meditation about modernity that had characterized Latin American cultural discourse. One could assert, in fact, that perhaps the most important outcome of the Spanish-American War, from a Latin American perspective, was that the United States became the new icon of modernity, the new focus of Latin America's contradictory connection with the modern, swiftly assuming a role that until that moment had been reserved for England, France and, to a lesser degree, Germany. This shift only managed to exacerbate the troubled nature of that relationship because of the consummate identification with modernity that had characterized the coming into being of *both* the United States and Latin America; that is, in the figure of the United States Latin American intellectuals could well discern a strikingly familiar rhetorical posturing towards modernity that had indeed been fulfilled by historical eventuality. This potential specularity, which is arduously repressed by the claims of cultural difference that will be examined below, sometimes surfaces distinctly even in the midst of the most fervent anti-United States pronouncements. Such is the case of the following surprising remark by Manuel Ugarte, perhaps the most vibrant voice against the United States in the Latin American intellectual circles of the times: "We have the example of what Latin America should be in what was and is Anglo-Saxon America."[23] The same can be asserted regarding these harsh, self-critical words by José Vasconcelos: "Let us admit that it was unfortunate that we did not act with the unity shown by the Northerners; the amazing race, the one that we are tired of insulting only because it has defeated us in every contest in the historical struggle. It is triumphant because it manages to unite its pragmatism with the clear vision of a great destiny. It keeps in mind the intuition of a well-defined historical mission, while we get lost in a labyrinth of verbal chimeras."[24] Latin America's relationship to modernity is from that moment on mediated by the United States, and one can identify the traces of that mediation in the Latin American cultural discourse of the time.[25]

Following this line of thought, I would like to propose that the historico-cultural crisis that provides the immediate background from which the project of the *novela de la tierra* arose resulted from a profound anxiety experienced by Latin American intellectuals in their consideration of the United States; a crisis that originated during the last years of the nineteenth century and continued unabated well into the next. One finds particularly during the first decade of the twentieth century a seemingly inexhaustible collection of works in which the United States is an obsessive concern. Some attempt to discern the nature of American intentions in Latin America, others address directly the essence of American culture and society, and still others go as far as perceiving the lines of an imminent confrontation between Latin America and the United States as already drawn.[26] Traditionally, this consuming concern with the northern neighbor has been regarded as an understandable reaction to the repeated interventions and abuses by the United States in Latin America throughout the nineteenth century, and especially to the heightened frequency with which they occurred in the aftermath of the Spanish-American War. In light of that historical development one can understand, for example, why Martí's cautionary comments concerning the United States should have acquired the reputation of clairvoyance that they enjoy to this day.

Still, it is customary to interpret these texts as delineating two identifiably different positions and attitudes towards the United States. The first is an aggressive denunciation of the arrogant, imperialistic behavior of the northern country that is invariably accompanied by a call to unity of all Latin American nations against the common enemy. This perspective is summarized by the efforts of the Argentine Manuel Ugarte, who in countless books, articles, conferences and lecture tours railed against the menace that he saw advancing against the southern hemisphere.[27] The second position merely argues that the United States represents a radically distinct cultural reality from that of Latin America and proceeds to delineate the specificity of that difference. This second perspective has become synonymous with what is undoubtedly the most famous of the works of this period, the essay *Ariel* (1900), by the Uruguayan writer José Enrique Rodó. And yet, although the subject that preoccupies both schools of thought is the same, the United States, critics have tended to dissociate the concerns of one from those of the other. The following commentary is typical in that regard: "The link between the *arielistas* and the 'anti-Yankee' trend in the Spanish American essay is very tenuous. Had Rodó never lived, I think it certain that essayists like Manuel Ugarte or Rufino Blanco Fombona would have produced their sharp criticisms of the Colossus of the North. The expansionist policies of the United States, her political intervention, and her economic penetration of Latin America elicited in these writers a kind of reaction quite different from Rodó's analysis of cultural contrasts between the Latin world and North America."[28] For this critic the historical coexistence of the two tendencies does not amount, in fact, to much more than a coincidence.[29] At the most general level, then, the perceived difference between the two attitudes could be formulated in the following fashion: intellectuals such as Ugarte appear concerned with how to address the United States as a concrete historical and political menace, whereas Rodó's interests seem to lie essentially in the examination of the United States as a specific cultural and spiritual entity. This presumed difference is lent credibility by the fact that even in the most superficial, stylistic plane, the writings of Ugarte and Rodó appear quite dissimilar: it would be very difficult, for instance, to relate the stridency and urgent unevenness of the former's prose with Rodó's mellifluous, sumptuous style.

I believe, nevertheless, that these two essential viewpoints can be reconciled when one remarks on the fact that their solutions to the crises that they each designate are in essence the same. This resemblance begins to surface when it is realized that Ugarte's answer to the imperialist designs of Latin America's northern neighbor is not the deployment of a concrete political or economic strategy of resistance, but rather the affirmation of a cultural unanimity among the Latin American nations that must be tapped in order to confront the United States.[30] Similarly, Rodó's essay is predicated on the belief that Latin American countries share a cultural essence and project that is incompatible with the conception of culture represented by the United States. Hence, both authors coincide in their affirmation of a continent-wide cultural specificity for Latin America as an answer to the contingency to which their texts are a response. What was, indeed, this perceived crisis that elicited in both of these writers the affirmation of a continental cultural essence for Latin America as a response? I shall propose that perhaps the solution to this question can be gleaned precisely from the specific characteristics evinced by the response.

As was mentioned previously, it is commonly assumed that the concern shown at the time by Latin American intellectuals regarding the United States was the result of the latter's accession to a position of clear hegemony in the American hemisphere in the aftermath of the Spanish-American War. But what has not been remarked on up till now is that that accession was prepared and sustained by the resolute advancing by the imperial nation of a powerful myth, a vision regarding the future trajectory of the hemisphere as a totality – a concept that was christened with the rubric of "Pan-Americanism" and which was resoundingly heralded throughout the Americas by the United States. Pan-Americanism, the belief in a geographic, economic and historical order that would encompass both North and South America, became the historico-political myth through which the United States conceived of its relations with Latin America in the last ten years of the nineteenth century and beyond. The genesis of this formula can be traced to the year 1889, when then Secretary of State James G. Blaine coined the term "Pan-American Conference," and convoked the first of a series of such meetings of representatives of American nations, a conclave that was held in Washington, D.C. in the fall of that year.[31] As part of a concerted campaign to publicize and muster support for the concept, official delegations from the United States were sent at various times to most countries in Latin America.[32]

To some extent, Pan-Americanism attempted a revival of the Anti-European rhetoric of the Monroe Doctrine that understood the New World strictly as the scenario for the development of the nations in it. But in this particular instance the emphasis was rather on the formulation of a project for the achievement of a hemispheric order that would only encompass the Americas. From a review of the future agenda that was presented to the participants of the first conference in 1889, one can establish the comprehensive thrust of the proposal: adoption of a common currency, provisions for cultural exchange, a uniform system of weights and measures, a continent-wide set of customs regulations, the creation of a Pan-American Bank, the construction of an intercontinental railway and a number of other similar undertakings. This summary should also leave no doubt that the emergence of the Pan-American ideal must be understood as a decidedly ideological stratagem on the part of the United States meant to facilitate its hegemony over the continent. Nevertheless, what should be underscored is the sense of cultural crisis that the doctrine elicited in Latin American intellectual circles and the figural strategy through which they attempted to transcend the perceived threat.

Perhaps the most symptomatic manifestation of the crisis represented by the United States' initiative was the ensuing continent-wide controversy surrounding the legitimacy of the very concept of Pan-Americanism as an instrument for envisioning the future of Latin American nations.[33] The enthusiastic espousal and fostering of the Pan-American proposal by the United States did not find a strong echo among countries that perceived the Spanish-American War as an abusive conflict deliberately provoked by the United States, and which had witnessed with increasing alarm a series of successive interventions by the northern power in Latin America. As early as 1897 one encounters a biting indictment of the Pan-American doctrine in a book entitled *Le Pan-Américanisme et l'équilibre américain* by Fourcy Chatelain, a Haitian diplomat and lawyer. Comparing the Pan-American idea to the Bismarckian notion of the *Zollverein*, Chatelain advances the following interpretation of its inception:

Using once again an old and once popular theme, [Anglo-Saxon politicians] have denounced the former masters of the Americas: old Europe, now incapable of aspiring to political hegemony, will be depicted as the hereditary enemy of the New World's economic development. In these circumstances, the *brothers* of the North, those tried and true collaborators of South American independence, have offered their services and their sympathy, and while pointing to European perfidy, always ready to strike, have invited the *brothers* of the South to strengthen even more their ties with the United States.

Such is the diplomatic comedy imagined by Mr. Blaine, and on the basis of which he sent out invitations for the two meetings of October 4 and 16, 1889, so sadly famous in the political and economic history of our *fin de siècle*.[34]

The sarcasm evident in Chatelain's prose turns into disbelief at the preposterous nature of the doctrine in the following fragment from Manuel Ugarte's *Las nuevas tendencias literarias*. Speaking about the prospect for the cultural union envisioned by Pan-Americanism he proclaims:

A vertigo of domination and hegemony leads them [the United States] to fantasize that there is only one America. The astonishment with which they discover that Spanish American literature exists is proof of their limited judgment and of the self-centeredness that ails them. Excited by their victories, they seem not to know that half the continent was civilized by Spain, whose spirit . . . perpetuates in nineteen republics the traditions of the Latin soul. It is clear that in the New World there have to be two irreconcilable literatures, just as there are two different ethnic and political groups. To imagine artistic or territorial fusions is to desire the impossible, because certain facts escape the will of men.[35]

These vigorous protestations notwithstanding, the myth of Pan-Americanism had to be neutralized with a parallel creation, another cultural trope that would articulate a particular mytho/poetic reality exclusively for Latin America. This necessity was the well-spring for the affirmation of a continental cultural order that would encompass all Latin American nations, a belief that circulated under various labels such as *pan-latinismo*, *pan-iberismo*, *pan-hispanismo* or *hispanoamericanismo*. The following formulation of the concept is characteristic: "Although fragmented into twenty republics, it is plain to see that notwithstanding that dispersal – which is explained by territorial extension and other circumstances – we constitute from Mexico to the Patagonia a large *whole* solidly bonded by indestructible ethnic, historical and social affinities. We are a vast organism whose parts, except for a few insignificant differences, are thoroughly linked by physical and spiritual factors that have a similar origin."[36] Ugarte himself described the notion in this fashion: "From the border of Mexico to the Austral seas, in the nineteen republics that occupy twenty million square kilometers and comprise a population of fifty million inhabitants, there is . . . a univocal and homogeneous intellectual movement. It is not a mosaic of local efforts, but rather a single mind, a single soul, a single literature that is surprising on account of its unity and spiritual uniformity."[37] The desideratum represented by *pan-latinismo* was, of course, not entirely new in Latin American circles; there had been some feeble and largely unsuccessful attempts to form some sort of union among Latin American nations during the nineteenth century.[38] But the force and unanimity with which the ideal dominated Latin American intellectual concerns during the first thirty years of the twentieth century attest to its nature as a continent-wide cultural myth, as a collective response to a threat and a challenge issuing from an outside source. Speaking to a Spanish audience, Manuel Ugarte defined the problem thus:

Of the two tendencies that vie for the New World, only one is consonant with the broad vision that we must have regarding the future. *Panamer-icanismo*, which would lead us to distance our countries ethnically, economically and spiritually from Europe in order to enter into an artificial union with a country whose origins and background are different from ours, does not correspond in any way with the Romantic ideal and the unbending character of our race. On the other hand, *hispanoamericanismo*, the direct and enthusiastic turn to our spiritual tradition . . . is the popular movement that represents not only the vital instinct of our nations, but also the logical development of a policy respectful of all national rights, and especially of national moral integrity, without which the material integrity of nations cannot be maintained.[39]

The desire to postulate the existence of a cultural order and a historical project specific to Latin America resulted in an enterprise that produced books of major importance such as *Ariel* (1900); Manuel Ugarte's *Las nuevas tendencias literarias* (1908), *El porvenir de la América Latina* (1910) and *El destino de un continente* (1923); *La evolución política y social de Hispanoamérica* (1911) by Rufino Blanco Fombona; and Francisco García Calderón's *Les Démocraties latines de l'Amérique* (1912) and *La creación de un continente* (1912). In fact, it is perhaps only when one highlights the backdrop constituted by the debate on Pan-Americanism that one can understand fully the genesis and character of Rodó's ideas in *Ariel*. Most critics customarily explain the composition of Rodó's essay as a defense against a disdainful United States, as a decided affirmation of the immanent value of Latin American culture. But an attentive reading of the work reveals that there are no tangible textual grounds for such an interpretation of Rodó's purpose in writing his essay. On the other hand, when the author's argument is seen in the context provided by the United States' sponsorship of and proselytizing for Pan-Americanism, the hidden agenda of *Ariel* becomes clearly discernible: it constitutes a statement of absolute and irreducible cultural *difference* rather than an apology for Latin American culture. Rodó's implicit response to the union envisioned by the doctrine propounded by the United States is to aver that the two cultures that it proposes to conjoin are irreconcilable from their very core.

The formulation of a Pan-Hispanic cultural order soon had the opportunity to appropriate for its purposes a historical circumstance that provided an ideal context for its deployment: the 100th anniversary of the beginning of the Independence movement in Latin America, in 1910. There can be little doubt that the commemoration of the *Centenario*, as it was called, became the most significant cultural event in the decade between 1910 and 1920 in Latin America; the elaborate celebrations of the event that took place in all countries and at various times during the decade throughout Latin America attest to that fact.[40] Seen in the context of the desire to affirm a spiritual essence shared by all Latin American nations, it was perhaps inevitable that the *Centenario* would be interpreted in terms of the possibilities it afforded for that affirmation. In a masterful stroke of historical imagination, Latin American authors and intellectuals willed to perceive in 1910 a repetition of the circumstances and possibilities that in their view had characterized the corresponding moment one hundred years previously, in 1810. In other words, the preoccupation with a unity of continental proportions that had surfaced in the first decade of the twentieth century now seemed to hark back to the historical moment that could be characterized as the very origin of Latin America; an avowed pre-lapsarian instance of continental and cultural unity that preceded the fall into a history of fragmentation and fratricidal dissension known only too well; a moment and a possibility that had returned – so to speak – in the apotheosis of its celebration.[41] The following fragment from Francisco García Calderón's *La creación de un continente* is exemplary in this respect:

In the variegated collection of confused nations we discern an ancient harmony. There is a continent, a confederation without treaties, a moral league without coercion, an inevitable assembly commanded by both territory and race. Impotent men may work against unification . . . but a formidable pressure that arises from the grave leads our anarchical race towards unanimity. In the sorrowful dusk of the Liberators only the future union consoled their dying eyes. The great dead Fathers live once again in us and impose on us the vision of a unified continent regardless of the provisional divisions between us.[42]

The same idea of historical recuperation reappears in many widely-read works of the time, such as the ensuing one, where the past is represented as demanding its ultimate fulfillment from the present:

A collective ideal shook America from Mexico to Buenos Aires when the struggle for Liberation began; a single breath made trumpets sound in the thousand victories and the thousand defeats of the fight; a single heart heard bells ring on the day when territorial domination ended. One Motherland had just been born. For the supreme ideal of an American geographic demarcations are but a whim.

As a Motherland, Spanish America is One . . . There are no borders between us; the great project of our forefathers has not been accomplished yet. It is our duty to make it cohere: Let us unite![43]

The fascination exerted by this historical event accounts for the publication during this period of an untold number of studies devoted specifically to the protagonists, campaigns and other events related to the struggle for Latin American independence. Paradigmatic in this respect is the attention to the figure of Simón Bolívar displayed by Rufino Blanco Fombona in his *Bolívar pintado por sí mismo*, his critical editions of *Discursos y proclamas de Bolívar* and *Cartas de Bolívar*, and his founding of the Editorial América in Madrid.[44] One of the special series of this publishing enterprise was the Biblioteca Ayacucho, which consisted almost exclusively of memoirs and biographies of participants in the revolt against Spain and its immediate aftermath.[45] The celebration of this historical moment – a moment that was reconstructed and fashioned as much as it was celebrated in 1910 – also posited the return of the genetic possibilities that the event afforded when understood as the very beginning of cultural time. This explains the millennial and liminary rhetoric that is typical of the period, and which informs the following passage:

I remember once again the great days of the *Centenario*, and my hopes revive. I think that there is a mysterious meaning and a saving grace in the rituals of commemorations . . . We believe that time has secret forces, that time accomplishes deeds by itself; we believe that the eternal can turn the passing moment into sacred time, making it last; we believe that a moment marked thus by eternity – such as was the case with the *Centenario* – is a divine spell . . . Celebrations of that sort demand, with the centuries as witnesses, the most solemn of pledges.[46]

This rhetoric found expression, for instance, in formulas such as *mundonovismo*, a concept defined and circulated in a number of works by the Chilean critic Francisco Contreras.[47] It is also present in the many utopian texts of the period, such as *La raza cósmica* and *Indología* by the Mexican writer José Vasconcelos. Furthermore, it was not lost on Latin American intellectuals that at the precise time when Latin America was celebrating this feast of new beginnings, Europe appeared to be signaling its historical exhaustion in the apocalyptic "War to end all Wars."[48]

From the literary perspective that concerns us here, the possibility of a reenactment of an absolute origin of cultural history entailed the actualization of a moment when literature could effectively provide a founding myth for the collectivity; a new beginning where the emerging national or continental soul could find a synthesis of its essence and a prophetic vision of its future in the transcendent vehicle of a literary creation. Herein, I believe, lies the impetus for the enterprise of composing "autochthonous" literary texts that characterizes in broad terms literary production in Latin America during the first thirty years of the twentieth century. Yet, the problematic nature of that project in Latin America soon made itself evident: the postulation of a zero-degree of cultural time on which the entire enterprise was predicated simul-taneously had the effect of abolishing the history from which such an effort should putatively derive its legitimacy and strength; that master creation, that *Ur-text* could not be compiled and assembled from a presumably ageless reservoir of traditional myths or com-positions. Therefore, if this autochthonous Text were to be it would have to be constructed, produced, *made* (remembering the etymo-logy of the word "poetry" in the Greek *poiein*), rather than be recovered or reconstituted from literary fragments looming out of an immemorial past. But how could such a Text be produced, except through the internalization of a discourse that explained and defined the criteria for establishing its status as an autochthonous creation in the first place? In other words, the composition of that literary Text had to be effected within the boundaries of another discourse that could legitimize the text's claim to being an *indigenous* literary work; a disciplinary discourse whose postulates would have to be simultaneously incorporated in the text to certify the latter's pretensions to constitute an autochthonous literary creation. In the remainder of this chapter the specific characteristics of this discur-sive modality will be explored.

The discursive roots of the *novela de la tierra*

The concept of culture that has nurtured Latin America's obsession with an autochthonous cultural expression and thought is a synthe-sis of a number of beliefs that had their first formulation during the last years of the eighteenth century and the first decades of the nineteenth. This was the moment when, according to Michel Foucault, a radical break in Western epistemology occurred that transformed to the core all previous configurations of knowledge and representation. In the most general of terms, this new *épistème* can be envisaged as an abandonment of the "horizontal," grid-like epistemological models that were characteristic of Classical thought, and the adoption of paradigms of understanding traversed by a fundamental historicity, a vertical dimension that imparts a depth of field to knowledge and to the objects that it creates: "European culture is inventing for itself a depth in which what matters is no longer identities, distinctive characters, permanent tables with all their possible paths and routes, but great hidden forces developed on the basis of their primitive and inaccessible nucleus, origin, causality, history. From now on things will be represented only from the depths of this density, withdrawn into itself . . . inescapably grouped by the vigour that is hidden down below, in those depths."[49] This is why the knowledge of modernity will use for its articulation metaphors that are reflective of the depth through which it conceives its objects and in which the latter appear to be thoroughly immersed. Some of these, such as "source," "origin" and "seed," are genetic in nature and define that original nucleus from which all subsequent development sprang; others allude to the process that unfolded itself from that origin, the inner necessity that displayed itself in the object's temporal or historical existence. All of them are represented in the numerous versions of organic form that were deployed by the various discourses and disciplines that made their appearance throughout the nineteenth century.[50] The transformations that occurred specifically in the conception of language at this time are of particular interest, since they will allow for an understanding of the preeminent role played by the latter in the construction of an autochthonous cultural essence.

One of the outcomes of this epistemological shift was that language folded in on itself, acquiring in the process a certain concreteness capable of being apprehended and formulated as a set of internal laws. Moreover, language came to be considered as an entity possessing a fundamental historicity, a development in time that was unique to itself. The linguistic studies of Bopp, Schlegel, Grimm and von Humboldt engage in an intrinsic analysis of language as an object unto itself, with a history and rules of its own, rather than as a template for representation, as was the case in the Classical Age.[51] With the loss of the idea of language as a representational screen, discourse came to be understood more and more as an instrument for the expression of a subjectivity.[52] This realization impinged as well on the characterization of that historicity that was judged inseparable from language; the outcome was the interest that suddenly developed in the idea of the collectivity as a linguistic entity:

Language is no longer linked to civilizations by the level of learning to which they have attained . . . but by the mind of the peoples who have given rise to it, animate it, and are recognizable in it. Just as the living organism manifests, by its inner coherence, the functions that keep it alive, so language, in the whole architecture of its grammar, makes visible the fundamental will that keeps a whole people alive and gives it the power to speak a language belonging solely to itself. This means that the conditions of historicity of language are changed at once: its mutations no longer come from above (from the learned elite . . .), but take their being obscurely from below . . . In any language, the speaker, who never ceases to speak in a murmur that is not heard although it provides all the vividness of the language, is the people. Grimm thought that he overheard such a murmur when he listened to the *altdeutsche Meistergesang*, and Raynouard when he transcribed the *Poésies originales des troubadours*.[53]

This concern with the expressive capabilities of language was complemented by perhaps the most important change that occurred in the understanding of language in the nineteenth century: its thoroughly novel conceptualization as a totality of discrete phonetic elements. Language ceased to be considered a concatenation of visible signs and became a sonic entity, a totality that could be studied independently from the letters that might be employed to transcribe it:

Whereas for general grammar, language arose when the noise produced by the mouth or the lips had become a *letter*, it is accepted from now on that language exists when noises have been articulated and divided into a series of distinct *sounds*. The whole being of language is now one of sound. This explains the new interest, shown by Raynouard and the brothers Grimm, in non-written literature, in folk tales and spoken dialects. Language is sought in its most authentic state: in the spoken word – the word that is dried up and frozen into immobility by writing. A whole mystique is being born: that of the verb, of the pure poetic flash that disappears without a trace, leaving nothing behind but a vibration suspended in the air for one brief moment.[54]

In a development consistent with this description, the historicity of language was formulated anew as the summation of all the changes that had occurred throughout time in its pronunciation, the uttered sounds that in their peculiar combinations defined a linguistic system as a specific and unique entity. When juxtaposed to the expressive capabilities described above, one begins to understand how spoken language was attributed with a collective ontological significance that had a profoundly historical dimension as well. In this fashion, spoken language became the repository of immemorial collective desires, the aural record of collective projects and hopes.[55]

    In the end, speech was just one of the domains in which that collective volition expressed itself; traditions, legends, myths, popular art forms, and common law were other realms where this will had its manifestation. Herder, for instance, characterized folk poems as "archives of a nationality," "imprints of the soul of a nation," and as "the living voice of the nationalities."[56] In essence, all cultural and political practices and institutions were assumed to be generated organically from a spiritual kernel that deployed itself in time following the dictates of an internal necessity. This development marked all the creations of the community in question, imparting to them a specificity and exclusivity that made it impossible and even undesirable to make cross-cultural comparisons. Expressions such as "national soul," "spirit of the people" and "popular genius" were used to refer to this spiritual monad that unveiled itself throughout the history of a group in an almost impersonal fashion, not unlike a plant, perhaps without ever rising to the consciousness of the individuals that formed the collectivity. Consequently, what one would refer to as the creative act was conceptualized and described as anonymous, unreflecting and collective, as Renan vehemently argues in this passage from *L'Avenir de la science*:

The most sublime works are those that humanity has accomplished collectively, so that no proper name can be appended to them. The most beautiful things are anonymous . . . Why do you think you believe that you have ennobled such and such a national epic because you have discovered the name of the insignificant individual who consigned it to paper? Why should I care about the meaningless syllables of his name? That name itself is a lie; it is not he, but the nation, humanity working at a certain moment in time and space, which is the true author.[57]

The many botanical and biological metaphors that were used throughout the century to characterize cultural life and its evolution attest to the organicity that physical and spiritual processes were assumed to have in common; but it is also expressive of the relationship that was presumed to exist between a culture and the physical environment in which it obtained. The spirit of a people manifested itself also in the ways it manipulated and transformed its surroundings; but the conditions of possibility for that manifestation were determined to an important degree by the physical environment where it resided. As a result, the spiritual dimension of a culture reflected and was shaped by the daily contact of the collectivity with the various elements that constituted its environment. Herder, for instance, understood this relationship in a most direct and immediate way:

Since man is no independent substance, but is connected with all the elements of nature; living by inspiration of the air, and deriving nutriment from the most opposite productions of the Earth, in his meat and drink; consuming fire, while he absorbs light, and contaminates the air he breathes; awake or asleep, in motion or at rest, contributing to the change of the universe; shall he not be changed by it? It is far too little, to compare him to the absorbing sponge, the sparkling tinder: he is a multitudinous harmony, a living self, on whom the harmony of all the powers that surround him operates.[58]

For Herder, the environment was an amalgam of climactic and geographic elements that operate "rather on the mass than on the individual," an agent that "does not force, but incline; it gives the imperceptible disposition, which strikes us indeed in the general view of the life and manners of indigenous nations, but is very difficult to be delineated distinctly."[59] And yet, it is also evident that the environment, through its organic interaction with the spiritual monad of a people, molds every aspect of that culture's existence:

The Arab of the desert belongs to it, as much as his noble horse, and his patient, indefatigable camel . . . With this his simple clothing, his maxims of life, his manners, and his character, are in unison; and after the lapse of thousands of years, his tent still preserves the wisdom of his forefathers. A lover of liberty, he despises wealth and pleasure, is fleet in the course, a dextrous manager of his horse, of whom he is as careful as of himself, and equally dextrous in handling the javelin. His figure is lean and muscular; his complexion brown; his bones strong . . . He is bold and enterprising, faithful to his word, hospitable and magnanimous, and, connected with his fellows by the desert, he makes one common cause with all. From the dangers of his mode of life he has imbibed wariness and shy mistrust; from his solitary abode, the feelings of revenge, friendship, enthusiasm and pride.[60]

Culture and history, then, are to some extent inflected by geography since the latter invariably leaves its characteristic imprint on the spiritual structure of a people that lives within its boundaries. But this organic relationship opened the way for a correlative spiritualization of the environment, that is, a conception of the physical milieu as a telluric Agent secretly informing all human creations. Geography thus became a Force, a powerful and mysterious spiritual presence that modified the deployment in time of a people's "national soul." The recurrent metaphor that described a culture's development as essentially similar to that of a plant perceived this "nourishment" that a human collective spirit was deemed to derive from its sustained contact with the earth.[61]

One can see clearly that this conception of cultural essence brought implicit with it and was generated from within a comprehensive hermeneutical enterprise. By its very nature, the spiritual monad that was privative to each culture could not be apprehended directly but rather had to be decoded, reconstructed through the study of that culture's diverse tangible manifestations – particularly those of the culture's past, since they were considered to be more spontaneous and less contaminated by the collectivity's contact with other communities. This reconstruction became the project that defined the discourse of philology, a discipline whose birth can be traced back to the epistemological disjunction described earlier by Foucault. From its beginnings in the early nineteenth century philology underwent a series of internal transformations: from an "intuitive" stage in the Romantic period to Renan's confident and empowering definition of it as a "science exacte des choses de l'esprit," to the restricted stylistics associated with the more recent names of Vossler and Spitzer.[62] But throughout this intrinsic development the essential objective of philology remained unaltered: to arrive at a determination of the organic spiritual dimension that manifested itself in a culture's creations.

An understanding of the foundations of philological discourse allows us to appreciate the specific manifestations of the desire to produce an autochthonous literary text that dominated Latin American literature during the early part of this century.[63] One begins to realize that the enterprise of textualizing what is construed as a collective spiritual essence is a project that acquires its full intelligibility within the conceptual horizon delimited by the discipline of philology. Indeed, the realization of a deficiency that must be redressed through the engendering of an autochthonous literature is only possible inside the epistemological boundaries circumscribed by philological discourse. One could suggest, then, that the Latin American "autochthonous" *oeuvre* would like to fashion itself after the ideal text envisioned by philological interpretive practice: a work that evinces a transparent, unmediated relationship between Latin American cultural being and writing.

Some of the features of the literature produced in Latin America during the period under scrutiny express this connection quite directly. To begin with there was an obvious predilection for employing those forms that philology had designated as inherently "popular," that is spontaneously and anonymously produced by the collectivity: the *romance*, the ballad, the epic poem, the legend, etc. Indeed, a number of the poets of the period showed their understanding of the possibilities offered by this poetic conception, sometimes effecting as a result radical transformations in their poetic practice and personae. Among them is Rubén Darío, who wrote his "Canto a la Argentina" in celebration of that country's anniversary of its independence; his "Canto épico a las glorias de Chile" and the "Oda a Mitre" are further examples of writing in this modality. Leopoldo Lugones wrote his *Odas seculares* to coincide with the celebration of the *Centenario*, and the titles of some of his other collections are equally revealing: *Romancero*, *Poemas solariegos* and *Romances de Río Seco*. He also offered a cycle of public lectures that were subsequently gathered in the volume *El payador*, a meditation on the nineteenth-century Argentine equivalent of the anonymous medieval *juglar*. José Santos Chocano published the ambitious work *Alma América* and began the composition of his unfinished opus *La epopeya del Libertador*, an epic poem on Bolívar that was to have six cantos, but of which only the fourth ("Ayacucho y los Andes") was produced. Finally, although Manuel González Prada had written his *Baladas peruanas* much earlier, they found a hospitable context when they were posthumously published shortly after his death in 1918. In most of these authors the intensely lyrical persona of their previous writing now took on an impersonal, narrative tone – projecting in this fashion the depersonalized anonymous subject that philology demanded of all truly collective creations, a conception that is echoed by Manuel Ugarte in remarks that remind one of Renan's views on the matter:

One man condenses a moment of the collectivity. Through one human pore flows the sap of the whole. A single brain expresses a collective gesture. The thinker and the artist are nothing but a product of the communal ferment, just as a flower grows out of the earth's vitality . . . The greatest of geniuses will only manage to condense or idealize the thrust of a community or an epoch. If it is true that a people and a time must be grateful to the individual who gave them a voice, he in turn must be cognizant of the elements that sustain him and allow him to be the arm, the brain and the heart of an entire race.[64]

This relationship can also be identified in works such as Lugones' *El payador* where, as was suggested earlier, there is an attempt to superimpose on Latin American literary history genetic schemes regarding the formation of a national literary tradition that are derived from philological formulations. Such is the thrust of the following passage from Lugones' introduction to his treatise, where he expounds on this connection in no uncertain terms:

I have chosen as the title of this work the name of those wandering minstrels that used to traverse our countryside reciting *romances* and *endechas*, because they were the most important characters in the founding of our race. Just as happened in all other Greco-Roman groups, here also that moment coincided with the creation of a work of art. Poetry laid the differential foundation of the Motherland by creating a new language for the expression of the new spiritual entity constituted by the soul of a race as it came into being.[65]

Similarly, the autochthonous Latin American landscape became a privileged literary category, since it was through its constant contact with it that the spiritual essence of the continent's people was shaped. Herein find their justification the myriad works produced during this period that aspired to capture the specific geography of a region or country in a cycle of poems, such as José Eustasio Rivera's depiction of the jungle in *Tierra de promisión*, Cornelio Hispano's *Elegías caucanas* and the Argentine Miguel Camino's *Chacayaleras*, an attempt at a poetic representation of his native region of Neuquén that invokes the *chacay*, a shrub indigenous to the area. But perhaps the most succinct rendition of this conceit is the justly famous essay "Visión de Anáhuac" by Alfonso Reyes, the source for the following passage:

Regardless of the historical doctrine one may profess . . . we are in unison with the race of yesteryear not only through our blood, but more importantly through the effort to dominate the coarse and unyielding nature that surrounds us; such an effort is the foundation of history. We also share with them the profound emotional unanimity that arises from the daily encounter with a similar natural object. The confrontation between human sensibility and a common world carves and engenders a common soul.[66]

The works and authors mentioned thus far constitute only a representative sample; it would be impossible to summarize the total extent and the multifarious forms that this literary endeavor assumed throughout Latin America. What is of particular concern to this study is the reflection on the novel as a genre of this desire to create an autochthonous text, a dynamics that produced the large collection of texts that have come to be collectively known as the *novela de la tierra*. It is worth noting in this regard that at the same time that the novel as a literary form was undergoing its avowed crisis at the beginning of this century, in Latin America the genre was recruited to provide precisely the sort of totalizing, organic vision that most critics of the period were alleging it could no longer pretend to achieve. This, I would venture to say, is the principal reason why the *novela de la tierra* seems to possess a persistently anachronic character, even when confronted with some other novels produced in Latin America at the time. And yet, as it will be argued later, there are aspects of these novels that belie the transparency and homogeneity dictated by this presumption regarding the nature of their signifying function – elements that make them in fact very modern texts even in spite of themselves.

By now it should not be difficult to discern that the discourse of the autochthonous in the *novela de la tierra* represents a condensation of the paradigm of cultural construal and interpretation just studied. Hence, one could argue that the discipline of philology provides the essential concepts and relationships that legitimize and control the writing of these novels.[67] This explains why, at the most superficial level, the *novela de la tierra* appears to be an indiscriminate and uncomplicated collection of philological commonplaces: speech as a privileged instance of language; geography as a sempiternal telluric presence; the detailed depiction of a human activity that has arisen in perfect consonance with the environment. One could even partially attribute to this apparently unexamined, derivative relationship between the *novela de la tierra* and the most commonplace notions of philology the contemporary disregard for these novels as ingenuous and immature. It is indeed hard to repress a smile when confronted by the many passages such as the following one from *La vorágine*, where there is a calculated attempt to transcribe speech phonetically:

Boss, it's betta if we go back. My woman was left alone and my cattl's gone wild. I got four heifers about to give birth, and I betya they've burst by now. Forget those bonz, they're jinxed. It's bad to meddle with dead'uns.

That's why the litany says: "Here I bury ya, here I covah ya; the devil takes me if I uncovah ya."

[Camará, simpre es mejorcito que nos volvamos. Mi mama se quedó sola y mi ganao se mañosea. Tengo cuatro cachonas de primer parto, y de seguro que ya tan parías. Déjese de güesos, que son guiñosos. Es malo meterse en cosas de dijuntos. Por eso dice la letanía: "aquí te entierro y aquí te tapo; el diablo me yeve si un día te saco."] (pp. 233–34)

Likewise, one can recall moments such as the one quoted below from *Doña Bárbara*, which endeavor to describe in painstaking detail aspects of a human activity that binds man to his geographic milieu in a relationship of reciprocity, in this instance the rounding-up of cattle for branding:

The cries of the horsemen rang out. Old steers started running around everywhere, trying to break through the ring created by the horses; here and there wild bulls gathered, eager to launch; but the stampedes became irresistible at times; avalanches of tame cattle would overwhelm the wild beasts who were trying to break out, converting their rage into fear. Some small troops were already beginning to assemble where the calves had been herded; but others resisted, and the cowboys, in a tight ring around the animals, had to push from all sides, whirling their mounts around, bringing them to their haunches by stopping them at full gallop with forceful jerks of the bridle.[68]

And yet, I would like to argue that although the essential postulates of philological discourse seem to account for the fundamental characteristics of these texts, that relationship is not as uncomplicated as it would seem at first glance; for the seemingly subordinate relationship between the *novela de la tierra* and philology conceals, nonetheless, a thorough inversion of philological interpretive operations. The philologist's overriding purpose was the revelation of the ultimate spiritual structure that was posited as the underlying bedrock or foundation for the text under scrutiny. As a result of this hermeneutic stance, the concrete textuality of the work was considered nothing but a more or less transparent screen or veil, with the text's final truth to be arrived at by the critic only beyond it.[69] But whereas philology endeavored to collate and interpret texts in order to arrive at a collective ontological definition, the writers of the *novela de la tierra* take as their point of departure this supposed essence and *then* proceed to write the texts that will ostensibly embody it. Therefore, in the *novela de la tierra* there is a reversal of the hermeneutic trajectory that philology proposed; that is, these novels envision the process of their coming into being as a displacement from spiritual essence to text. On account of this tropological reversal of interpretive paths, one can detect in the *novelas de la tierra* a heightened awareness of their own textuality, of their own productivity, that defies all traditional readings of them. This knowledge manifests itself in the text as a self-critical gesture that seeks to guarantee, to authorize the organicity and necessity of the relationship between text and essence which philology simply posited as a given. Hence, the *novela de la tierra* purports to write a literary text that incorporates the autochthonous essence, but it also writes alongside it a parallel critical discourse that comments on the legitimacy and validity of the formulation of autochthony that it advances. This situation implies that the autochthonous writer is both author and commentator of his own work, a predicament that belies the customary claims of transparency advanced with almost ritual consistency by the authors of these texts and their critics. In other words, the *novela de la tierra* is simultaneously an attempt to create a genuinely autochthonous work, and an unwitting denaturalization of the concept of an indigenous text by exposing its intrinsically discursive nature, its effective repeatability as a modality of discourse.[70]

But if one can conclude that a self-critical gesture is an essential component of the autochthonous text, then one could describe the latter as constituted by a crisis, a fundamental "separation" that could throw into question its very essence. I am referring to the displacement away from their literary specificity that can be identified in these works as they assume the critical stance determined by their paradoxical rhetorical nature. The result is the presence in them of a critical discourse whose articulation represents an abandonment of, or deviation from, their presumed condition as "literary" texts. In this way, it could be affirmed that both literature and criticism coexist as simultaneous yet divergent intentionalities at the core of the text of the *novela de la tierra*. The adjective "literary" is not invoked here in any essentialist acceptation, but rather to denominate the specific set of ruling assumptions that are supposed to organize all aspects of the text's signifying practice as a "literary" text. Hence, it refers specifically to the ideology of signification that governs and generates the work's presentation of itself. By the same token, "criticism" alludes to the discourse that encompasses the crisis, the text's movement away from its stated practice of signifi-

cation. Therefore, "literature" and "criticism" serve only as metaphors to describe the coexistence in the work of diverging conceptions of its signifying labor. This state of affairs manifests itself as a
disjunction that arises between the explicitly literary presuppositions and affirmations made by the text, and the demands determined by the critical turn that is constitutive of the work's discourse
as well. All documents of literary autochthony exhibit to some
degree and in one level or another the traces of the difficult and
conflictive rhetorical predicament that engendered them.

And yet, the simultaneous presence of contradictory impulses in
the same text signals an internal difference, one that is not incidental
but rather an essential constituent of the autochthonous literary
text. It could be argued then, that the autochthonous work is both
determined and structured from the outset by a difference within
itself that renders necessarily problematic any formulation of that
text's specificity in unambiguous terms. Indeed, if one acknowledges Barbara Johnson's definition of a deconstructive reading as
one "which analyzes the *specificity* of a text's critical difference from
itself,"[71] one must assume that the autochthonous literary text is
ceaselessly engaged in the activity of dismantling itself, of naming its
own difference; of "criticizing" itself, by engaging in a "separation"
from itself. One would almost be tempted to say that the essence of
such a text is constituted by that difference, if it were not precisely
the impossibility of establishing the text's identity that is implied by
such a disjunction.

Moreover this self-critical gesture, this internal difference proves
particularly difficult to establish and explore since, as it has been
determined, it offers itself as a discourse that defines and vouches for
the text's own identity. The difference that is of concern here is
elucidated by the presence of an-other discourse in the text, a
discourse that is critical in nature and therefore divergent in
intention and stance from the one that sustains the literary assumptions that rule the text. But this discourse effectively masks the
difference that it embodies by relentlessly speaking the text's
supposed identity; for its principal intention is to guarantee, to
vouch precisely for the legitimacy of those characteristics and
relationships that are nevertheless *also* deemed to be the very essence
of the autochthonous work. In this fashion, the *novela de la tierra*
paradoxically marks the critical departure from its own essence
through the presence of a discourse that continuously affirms that

same essence. In other words, the autochthonous work is engaged in the ceaseless underwriting of that which is also assumed to be a given, an activity that can be characterized as both tautological and potentially interminable. Perhaps more significantly, it is an undertaking that must be described as supplementary to the work, since it endeavors to establish something that is already taken for granted by the text. Thus, it could be argued that in the *novela de la tierra* this discourse of critical difference takes the form of a naming of the text's essence and that, as an outcome, that essence is somehow also curiously projected as a supplement to itself. But by its very nature, then, this internal critical gesture is not easily identified, since the text manages to speak of itself at the moment of greatest difference from itself.[72]

This critical intention surfaces in these works, for instance, as specific moments when the text lapses into a commentary that tries to elucidate explicitly the relationships that presumably undergird the world it is depicting. One can clearly detect this intention in the following fragment from Gallegos' *Doña Bárbara*:

The return from work brought the patio in front of the cabins to life. As darkness came on, the cowboys came back in noisy groups, began to banter, and ended by singing their thoughts in ballad form, since for everything that must be said the man of the Plain already has a ballad which says it, and says it better than speech. For life in the Plain is simple and devoid of novelty, and the spirit of the people is prone to the use of picturesque and imaginative forms.

And between mouthfuls a discussion of the events of the day's work, barbs and boasts, a friendly joke and the quick, sharp retort, a story rising from the picturesque life of the cowboy and guide, the man of hard toil always with a ballad on the tip of his tongue.

And while the watchers by the corrals took turns going around . . . in the cabins, another more boisterous watch was taking place: the guitar and the *maracas*, the *corrido* and the *décima*. The birth of poetry.[73]

In passages such as this one, the text can be seen to engage in what could be referred to as an explication of its own discursive assumptions. In them, the work articulates explicitly and comments on those relationships that also allow it to conceive the cultural world it recreates as an organic whole in the first place. The critical, expatiating purpose of this particular fragment can be distinguished, for instance, in the causal structure of the first paragraph; but it is also evinced by the manifest explanatory intention of the entire passage. Through it, the text "explicates" the spontaneous birth of popular poetry (speech) from the interaction between man's activity and his geographic milieu. This is, of course, an organic relationship that is presumed by the autochthonous text to be an immanent aspect of its own discourse. And yet, the organic nature of the link that the fragment affirms is entirely compromised by the fragment's very presence in the text, since in order to comment critically on its own procedures the text must have abandoned that organicity in the first place. Hence, in its performance the passage points to the problematic rhetorical nature of "the autochthonous," that is, its status as a mode of discourse that undermines through its articulation the legitimacy of that which it affirms.

Sometimes this commentary assumes a more inconspicuous form that nonetheless cannot entirely conceal its interpretive, critical objective. In this particular instance, from *La vorágine*, it acquires an essentially definitory one; there is a sudden break in the narrative that allows for the insertion of a detailed commentary on a specific element of the autochthonous universe:

Tambochas! This meant suspending work, abandoning shelter, throwing barriers of fire across the trail, and seeking refuge elsewhere. It was [*Tratábase de*] an invasion of carnivorous ants, born who knows where, that migrate to die as winter comes, sweeping the hills for leagues and leagues with a noise that resembles a distant forest fire. Wingless wasps with red heads and yellow-green bodies, they overwhelm on account of their venomous bite and their swarming multitudes. Every cave, every crevice, every hole – tree, bush, nest, hive – endures the overpowering flow of that heavy and fetid wave that devours young birds, rodents, reptiles and puts to flight whole villages of men and beasts.[74]

At other times this intention manifests itself in extra-textual pro-nouncements by the author regarding his works, as in the following fragment from a letter that Güiraldes once wrote to a young writer: "There is an Indian, a Persian and an Arab literature, and as many literatures as there are languages and regions. In them, the truly autochthonous ones, there is no clash with the country's elements. Both the landscape and the climate find their way into the very soul of literature and they are neither foreign to it nor outside of it."[75] Such an overt declaration of philological first principles by an author finds its consummate expression in the voyage that customa-rily precedes the writing of these novels; a voyage where the author's roaming through the landscape begins to acquire all the trappings of the philologist's research on language and milieu. Other textual features, such as the glossaries that are appended to the majority of these works, and the singling out of particular words or expressions in the text through the use of quotation marks or italics, constitute further signs of the existence of this critical dimension in the *novela de la tierra*.

The rhetorical situation just examined has had important implications for the relationship that literary critics have customarily established with these texts. Perhaps the most significant observation to be made in this regard is that the works' critical dimension has consistently anticipated, channeled and, it could also be claimed, neutralized the traditional critical commentary on the novels. This circumstance obtains because literary critics have for the most part simply reenacted the critical trajectory already encompassed by the works in question, demonstrating in the process the continuity that exists between their discourse and the one articulated by the novels on their own. But since the works' critical dimension consists – as was determined earlier – of an affirmation of their essence, most commentary on the texts has usually taken the form of a restating of the works' enabling principles and assumptions. The specific rhetorical nature of the autochthonous discourse makes entirely problematic the establishment of boundaries between the text and the criticism on it, thereby allowing for the unwitting and unencumbered collapse of one discourse into the other. For this reason, critical work on these texts frequently appears to be a mere paraphrase if not an outright repetition of the novels themselves. Such slippage results from an extreme actualization in the *novela de la tierra* of a dynamics that is immanent to criticism in general, one that Jonathan Culler has summarized as follows:

The distinction between criticism and literature opposes a framing discourse to what it frames, or divides an external metalanguage from the work it describes . . . Curiously, the authority of critics' metalinguistic position depends to a considerable extent on metalinguistic discourse within the work: they feel securely outside and in control when they can bring out of the work passages of apparently authoritative commentary that expounds the views they are defending . . . This is a paradoxical situation: they are outside when their discourse prolongs and develops a discourse authorized by the text, a pocket of externality folded in, whose external authority derives from its place inside. But if the best examples of metalinguistic discourse appear within the work, then their authority, which depends on a relation of externality, is highly questionable: they can always be read as part of the work rather than as a description of it.[76]

Criticism on the *novela de la tierra* has customarily derived the authority of its commentary from its appropriation of a sustained critical discourse already present in the works themselves, a discourse that seeks to legitimize their ruling presuppositions. This results in the critics' heightened sense of mastery of the text, as well as in a renewed conviction of their being unambiguously outside the work they are interpreting. But true to the dialectics described by Culler, it would seem that the more their externality and authority are confirmed, the more their discourse is limited to repeating the text, to remaining inside it, as it were. At this point, criticism becomes mere description, an activity that would find its consummation in the word-for-word repetition of the text itself; but such an activity compromises both the assumed specificity and function of critical discourse since, as Tzvetan Todorov has proposed in the context of a related discussion, "in a certain sense, every work constitutes its own best description."[77]

Hence, traditional criticism on these texts has engaged in the task of essentially confirming what the novels proposed from the outset, that is, the successful achievement of a textual hypostatization of "the autochthonous." Ultimately, this critical continuity has resulted in the confirmation of the status of the autochthonous as referent rather than as discourse; through the focusing of the critical gaze on issues of incorporation, representation and appropriation of the autochthonous, the discursive dimension of the latter has never been adequately explored. In fact, the very rubric of *novela de la tierra* could be taken as emblematic of this critical stance, since the term could refer indistinctly to a text produced spontaneously by the autochthonous understood as a transcendent agent, or to one in which the indigenous unveiled itself without need for mediation.

Another aspect of the critical literature that confirms this connection is that in it "the autochthonous" appears to possess a curiously ambiguous nature even within this representational framework, since it is simultaneously interpreted as embodying both an ontological substance and a concrete referential "reality." This latter realization allows one, in turn, to understand some of the specific characteristics shown by the conventional critical discourse on the novels. For instance, many critics will praise the mimetic, almost documentary intention of the authors involved, their success in capturing in their works a reality identified as autochthonous. Examples in this vein are the countless critical works devoted to the praise of a given author's faithful representation of autochthony, as well as the number of "corrective" works that seek to detail the inaccuracies or insufficiencies of that same author's vision. Conversely, the same critics that extol the mimetic fidelity of the novels will, sometimes in the same piece, praise also their intensely symbolic dimension, their accession to some mythic or archetypal realm of identity or ethnicity. Needless to say, such a commingling of mimetic and symbolic criteria entails all sorts of difficulties that are never addressed directly in the critical canon. And yet, the most superficial examination would establish that this confusion was already present in the novels themselves; in the final analysis its survival in the critical literature merely confirms once again the manner in which critics have traditionally borrowed from the novels the categories for their critical practice.

Nonetheless, in order to establish the rhetorical figure that organizes and sustains the discourse of the autochthonous in the *novela de la tierra*, I propose to avail myself of the very circumstance that critics have customarily performed as ideal readers of these texts. As has been argued above, there is a continuity between the critical dimension that is constitutive of these works and the critical corpus on them; hence, one could read the criticism on the *novela de la tierra* as constituting a condensed repetition of that commentary that the texts make on their own signifying practice. My strategy then, will be to distill from the critical discourse on the novels the rhetorical figure that underlies and organizes the discourse of the autochthonous. Consequently, the critical literature on the *novela de la tierra* will be consulted less for the interpretive insights it might afford on a particular text than for its economic exposition of the discursive assumptions intrinsic to the texts it is supposedly elucidating. From this perspective, it would be difficult to ignore Torres Rioseco's liminary role in the history of critical speculation on the *novela de la tierra*. His writings on these novels show many of the inconsistencies and contradictory aspects already noted. But besides being responsible for placing in circulation the term *novela de la tierra*, his *oeuvre* is the only comprehensive examination of that novelistic production. Furthermore, Torres' lack of methodological rigor should not obscure the fact that his selection of specific works effectively identified legitimate ways of encoding the autochthonous in a novelistic text. This becomes apparent in passages such as the following, where he warns of the dangers of becoming *too* autochthonous: "There are some works that are excessively American, excessively indigenous, that overuse local color, native customs and the drama of primitive ways, that oftentimes become caricatures of novels."[78] More than strictly a demand for stylistic decorum, one could interpret Torres' comment as advancing implicitly that a certain rhetorical economy is required to incorporate successfully the genuinely American in a literary text. It is precisely this organizing configuration that I would like to establish and explore in the remainder of this chapter.

The principal criterion implicated in Torres' encomiastic account of the *novela de la tierra* (as well as in his correlative condemnation of *modernismo*) is that a relation of unison must exist between a particular literary style and the environment whence it came. This last term, in its Spanish rendition as *ambiente*, is a category that recurs obsessively in Torres' discourse on the *novela de la tierra*. Time and again, the concept of *ambiente* is invoked by Torres Rioseco in order to explain the difference represented by Latin America. But an attentive reading shows that throughout Torres' study the word *ambiente* evinces what could be referred to as a controlled polysemy, an oscillation between three well-defined semantic poles. The first of these endows the concept with a linguistic dimension, as the ensuing passage makes clear:

The regional literary work takes advantage of the idiomatic elements of everyday speech. Traditional writers (such as Larreta), for whom only archaic language has value, can only be understood when we remember that they have lived for many years in Spain. In them there is a purely superficial interest in language, and one could say that they are in limbo, disconnected from their environment [*ambiente*]. It is not my intent to defend literary anarchy, but to propose that literary style should evince a close relationship with its environment [*ambiente*].[79]

The extended context for this quotation is a discussion of the relationship between literary production and spoken language in Latin America. The word *ambiente* in this particular instance is meant to stand for a number of forces that have determined certain traits peculiar to oral expression in Latin America. Spoken language is presumed to encompass within it the weight of all the history and cultural traditions of the land. For Torres, the incorporation of spoken language in their works is perhaps the single most important contribution of the new novelists to the development of an autochthonous style. Indeed, it would be an understatement to say that oral language forms the very core of the *novela de la tierra*: the discourse of the autochthonous identifies in spoken language a certain ontological charge, to be measured precisely by its dialectal idiosyncrasies, as well as by its very sonic nature. For this reason one can feel throughout these works an element of fruition in the transcription of certain linguistic usages and modalities associated with a specific idiomatic reality. In fact, the urge to record the spoken voice is so overwhelming that at times dialogic situations seem contrived or lengthened beyond narrative exigencies in order to indulge in this consistent fascination with oral expression. This uncompromising "fidelity" to the spoken word has often resulted in accusations of artistic immaturity and class condescendence from some critical quarters. And yet, it is singularly important to underscore that the spoken word is at the very center of the literary discourse of the autochthonous and, as such, must be accounted for in any attempt to understand fully the phenomenon of the *novela de la tierra*.

But if Torres' concept of *ambiente* can be seen to refer to a cultural environment as inflected by linguistic peculiarity, it can also be found operating as a notation of geographical locus: "Upon discovering the autochthonous motif, our writers have had to study the environment [*ambiente*]. It is thus that one now encounters artistic descriptions of previously unknown regions: the delta of the Orinoco, the shores of the Amazonas, the jungles of Colombia, the Venezuelan plain, the mountain ranges of Peru, the Chilean salt fields and the pampas of Argentina."[80] Etymologically, the word "geography" could be considered a synonym for the expression *novela de la tierra*; one could argue that to write the ground, to textualize it, would serve adequately to describe the implicit intention of the novels under consideration. In general terms, geography performs in these texts as the scene where the action takes place. The term "scene" is employed in all its theatrical fullness, not only on account of the powerful topographic component of the *novela de la tierra*, but also because of the large amount of textual energy spent on the demarcation and description of the geographical expanse of the novels. Much has been written about the setting for these texts, to the point that perhaps the most commonplace assertion (and complaint) is that in them, nature, far from being just the background for the action, is essentially the protagonist of the story. Indeed, one of the ruling assumptions of the *novela de la tierra* is the postulation of a significant relationship between geography and literature in the context of a wider search for an autochthonous literary expression.

Moreover, the word *ambiente* reappears in Torres' study with yet another meaning: In an attempt to explain the scarcity of indigenous novels in Chile, Torres Rioseco advances the following conjecture:

The Chilean countryside is poor and backwards when compared with the large cattle farms and agricultural establishments of Argentina . . . This accounts for Argentine writers such as Sarmiento, Lynch, Güiraldes, Reyles and so many others, true experts of the rural environment [*ambiente*] . . . On the other hand the Chilean peasant, trapped between mountains and limited to small plots of land, was always at the mercy of the landowners' will and therefore never became his own master. His imagination did not develop, and the monosyllable became his favorite utterance.[81]

In this passage the viability of the *novela de la tierra* is related to a circumstance that is economic in nature. The implicit notion expressed by the fragment is that the meaning of *ambiente* encompasses also a semantic component defined by a *métier*, an organized and internally coherent human activity. This seemingly intriguing assertion becomes less so when it is remarked on that, for instance, the three novels that will be closely analyzed in this study in fact present us with a wealth of detail about three distinctive human activities – cattle-ranching (*Doña Bárbara*), cattle driving (*Don Segundo Sombra*) and the extraction of latex from wild rubber trees (*La vorágine*). Any reader of these works will also remember the proliferation of involved, protracted passages that describe the activity in question as a rigorous human endeavor, as a specific set of operations and codified practices. To accomplish this the novels use a specialized, almost technical lexicon that enhances further the distinct impression of disciplinary closure. The result is the postulation of a horizon of human activity that possesses the same density and import as the linguistic and geographic contexts that were commented on above.

For reasons of economy the term "autochthonous" has been

employed until now to subsume a number of concepts such as soul, identity, being, authenticity, etc., that are charged with ontological value and that recur throughout the *novela de la tierra* and its criticism. I would like to suggest that hereafter "the autochthonous" should be understood to be a discursive mode based on a rhetorical figure encompassing three elements: spoken language, geographical location and a given human activity, that is, the three registers among which the concept of *ambiente* effects a sort of counterpoint in Torres Rioseco's critical discourse on the *novela de la tierra*. But the fluidity that allowed the same word to encompass three distinct semantic fields in Torres' discourse should be remarked on, since it underscores the artificial and fractious nature of our tripartite discussion of them. On the contrary, the authority and effectiveness of the figure that organizes these categories derives from the fact that any one of them can be subsumed under the remaining two. The three categories are thoroughly intertwined in a complex synecdochical fashion; the land is the scene where the human activity takes place, but it is also the milieu from which the peculiarities of spoken language are supposed to have emerged. Language, in turn, is not only tied to the geography, but is also the lexicon, the argot that is itself an integral component of the human activity described. In the *novela de la tierra* then, "the autochthonous" is a discursive mode generated by a complex rhetorical figure that organizes a synecdochical interaction between the three specific semantic fields mentioned. The synecdochical relationships that the figure establishes between the three categories are meant to project rhetorically the organicity that binds together and relates to one another and to the environment every one of a culture's manifestations. The relative importance of each element in the figure can vary from text to text; but a given configuration of it underwrites and sustains the discourse of the autochthonous in each work. There are passages, such as the following from *Doña Bárbara*, that clearly manifest the condensed nature of this configuration:

And so it seemed to Luzardo. There was the sad and brutish tobacco planter on the little strip of land he worked, and the light-hearted, swaggering herdsman in the midst of the wide prairie, struggling with nature, . . . plucking the *bandurria*, strumming the guitar at night after the rude toils were over.

Luzardo saw that in his contest with life the man of the Plain was both indomitable and fatalistic, lazy yet indefatigable; in strife he was impulsive yet calculating; undisciplined yet loyally obedient to his superiors . . . humble on foot, proud on horseback – all these qualities at once, without clashing, such as are the virtues and faults in a newborn soul.

Something of this shines through the ballads in which the singer of the Plain combines the boastful jolliness of the Andalusian, the smiling fatalism of the submissive Negro, and the rebellious melancholy of the Indian – all the peculiar features of the souls that have contributed to make his own. And what was not clear in the ballads, or what Luzardo had forgotten, he learned from the tales he heard from his peons while he shared with them both their hard work and raucous leisure.[82]

An analysis would show that this fragment is constructed through a series of metonymical displacements enabled by the discursive figure described above: land, language and work are conceived as intersecting domains, if not as outright consubstantial with one another. This is what allows for the unhindered, almost imperceptible flux from one category to the others that the passage enacts as well: Work not only has a vocabulary of its own; it is also the subject matter and the occasion for a linguistic/poetic performance that arises from it. The land provides the space where human activity deploys itself, and work is also determined by the rhythms dictated by the geographic milieu. But the land is likewise transformed by the constant and integrated activity of man. The linguistic reality depicted is bounded by geographic limits, and its presence and force can also be felt in the men's language. Yet language also names and demarcates the land, making possible the transformation of topography into a toponymical space that serves as the familiar scene for man's activity.

Moreover, the three categories are capable of encompassing a large number of distinct manifestations, a fact that endows the figure that contains them with an almost inexhaustible generative capacity. Oral language, for instance, can be incorporated in a number of different ways, such as the retelling of legends and tales or the performance of popular poetry and song; it also accounts for certain textual features, such as the phonetic writing that is so prevalent in them, the glossaries that are almost a fixture as addenda to these texts, and the typographical highlighting of certain words by boldfacing, italicizing or enclosing them inside quotation marks. Similarly, the land can subsume all the multifarious elements of non-urban geography, and it sustains both the detailed descriptions of topographic features and the marked emphasis on spatial organization and orientation in the novels. By the same token, the intricate accounts of a given *métier* and the use of a specialized vocabulary to effect this description are some of the textual attributes that arise from the third category, one that can include the many facets and operations of the human activity depicted.

This re-conceptualization of the autochthonous as a rhetorical modality suggests that the project of writing an autochthonous literary text can be examined as a productivity, that is, as an activity that engenders a particular discursive performance. The outcome of this performance is "the autochthonous," a discursive construct that is sustained by the rhetorical figure described above, and not by the avowedly worldly, referential status of the essence to which it alludes. But as I have argued above, this productivity is also projected in the text in the guise of a discourse that endeavors to underscore and validate the relationships that are defined by the rhetorical figure that generates the discourse of the autochthonous. This is why all these works incorporate, at one level or another of the text, a commentary on their own procedures that could be called critical, given its nature and intention.

In the next chapters three of these novels will be examined closely in an effort to establish how this internal critical gesture finds its deployment in the texts, thereby granting them a more complex nature than that which they (and most critics) would explicitly claim for themselves. The discussion will focus on three novels that a number of critics have designated as paradigmatic instances of the *novela de la tierra*: *Don Segundo Sombra* by Ricardo Güiraldes, Rómulo Gallegos' *Doña Bárbara* and *La vorágine*, by José Eustasio Rivera.[83] My selection of these particular novelistic works is based on the existence of this "consensus" among critics regarding their exemplarity, a fact that acquires significance given the continuity that I have shown to exist between the *novela de la tierra* and its criticism. In the ensuing chapters I will attempt to establish the rhetorical density of the discourse of the autochthonous as it manifests itself in them, and will tease out specific textual practices that dismantle or otherwise render problematic the authority of that discursive mode.

3

Don Segundo Sombra

Every finished work always leaves a surplus, be it
large or small . . .
Ricardo Güiraldes on *Don Segundo Sombra*[1]

The accolades received by *Don Segundo Sombra* immediately after its
publication astounded all concerned – particularly Güiraldes
himself, already resigned to the general indifference with which the
public had greeted his earlier works. Concurrently, the popular
acclaim was given its benediction by the dominant literary figure of
the time, the poet Leopoldo Lugones, in an encomiastic appraisal
that proposed Güiraldes' novel as an exemplary instance of
autochthonous literature.[2] Güiraldes, a dying man at the time,
seemed finally destined to achieve, in the waning months of his life,
the unanimous approval that had persistently eluded him. And yet,
the very Sunday after Lugones published his review – and in the
same *Suplemento Literario* of the newspaper *La Nación* – the Franco-
Argentine man of letters Paul Groussac made a trenchant observation that encapsulated his misgivings regarding *Don Segundo Sombra*.
While reading the novel one had the impression – Groussac claimed
– that "[Güiraldes] had left his dinner jacket on top of his gaucho
pants [ha olvidado el smoking encima del chiripá]."[3] Güiraldes died
a few months later, bewildered both by the immense editorial
success of his masterpiece as well as by the unkind statements –
exemplified by Groussac's remark – that the novel continued to
elicit from other quarters.

Although couched in somewhat different terms, the two general
perspectives delineated by the previous anecdote have been restated
time and again during the intervening sixty-odd years since the
publication of *Don Segundo Sombra*; the chasm between Güiraldes the
gifted writer and Güiraldes the privileged landowner has never been
adequately bridged. Critical opinions on Güiraldes have usually

79

revolved around these two axes: praise for his achievements in the literary expression of a national essence on the one hand, and accusations of elitism and ideological imposture on the other – the dinner jacket or the *chiripá*.

The view exemplified by Groussac's needling remark acquires renewed force when it is noted that Güiraldes seems at times to have engaged in the sort of role-playing that recalls the pastoral games of some European monarchs. There are photographs that show Güiraldes dressed in full gaucho attire while enjoying a sojourn on his *estancia* – photographs which may seem preposterously solemn and self-important in our eyes, but which allow by contrast a measure of the investment that the Argentine of the time had collectively in the gaucho. The most famous of these shows the author handing a *mate* to don Segundo Ramírez, the man around whom Güiraldes ostensibly developed his portrayal of the novel's protagonist, both of them consciously striking a pose for the camera. Pictures of this sort form a marked contrast with others that capture Güiraldes the cosmopolite, the man who – it is claimed – introduced the tango to Paris in his youth, posing aristocratically while sitting in an elegant wicker chair, for example, or lounging on the deck of an ocean liner with his wife and friends.[4]

This putting on and off of costumes would seem to evince a certain naïveté on Güiraldes' part in the best of cases, and a deceitful intention in the worst. Nevertheless, whether pathetic or duplicitous, Güiraldes' play-acting has been construed ultimately as pointing to the unwitting admission of an irreconcilable difference, an inescapable otherness made all the more tragic or irksome by the recourse to costume and mask. It is precisely this otherness that is stressed by critics intent on debunking Güiraldes' literary vision of the autochthonous. To them, Güiraldes' avowed contact with, and subsequent representation of, the indigenous is a doomed project, a failed attempt at communion contaminated by the author's class extraction and lineage. This interpretive stance is succinctly summarized by the title of one such critical appraisal: "*Don Segundo Sombra* and the gaucho as seen by the boss's son."[5] One can perceive quite clearly that what is being impugned is Güiraldes' avowedly skewed presentation of the autochthonous element in his novel, given that his social background necessarily imposed a perspective that had to redound in falsification and deceit. It is no surprise, then, that most sociological interpretations of *Don Segundo Sombra* are

marked by an undercurrent of scorn towards Güiraldes that sometimes manifests itself in perplexing ways. In his book on *Don Segundo
Sombra*, for example, Aristóbulo Echegaray performs a textbook
projection in his reading of the final scene of the novel when the
critic ascribes to the character of don Segundo his own spite for the
novel's author: "There is a profound contempt in Don Segundo's
attitude. He shakes his godson's hand in silence. He cannot shout at
him 'You're such a . . . ' He rides off without turning his head, thus
showing him his back, the face of scorn . . . He flees from Fabio
Cáceres, but in fact it is Güiraldes who loses him."[6] Aside from not
explaining the correct way of riding away on a horse without
showing one's back, the critic fails to make explicit how such a
problematic and dangerously uncontrolled ending could find a
place in a broader ideologically-grounded reading of the novel.

On the other side of the polemic the commentary focuses on
Güiraldes the writer, and more precisely the Argentine writer who
successfully encompassed the essence of nationality in his novel.
From this critical perspective, for example, Güiraldes' ownership of
an *estancia* was nothing but an exceptional opportunity to participate
in, not just observe, the world of the gaucho. This intimate
knowledge would later become the instrument for the aesthetic
hypostatization of the autochthonous in the writing of *Don Segundo
Sombra*. According to this critical perspective, Güiraldes underwent
a biographical preparation of sorts in order to gain access to the
most intricate details of gaucho life. But, it is similarly proposed, he
also went through a parallel process of artistic *askesis* that made
possible the masterful literary portrayal of this universe. This is why
it is customary for these commentators to read Güiraldes' *oeuvre*
previous to *Don Segundo Sombra* as a function of the latter, not because
these earlier works present great affinities with it, but because critics
have tended to see in them an unsuccessful groping with literary
structure and content that would be eventually resolved in the
writing of Güiraldes' masterpiece. Hence, the author's literary
career is routinely described as a protracted aesthetic and existential
apprenticeship that had its culmination in the composition of *Don
Segundo Sombra*, as the ensuing quotation makes explicit: "It could be
said that Ricardo Güiraldes' trajectory consists of a series of failures
that the final goal justifies and redeems. One of Güiraldes' major
accomplishments is to have persevered beyond solitude and beyond
the lack of direction and will that sometimes afflicted him."[7] The

earlier texts chronicle, therefore, a sort of personal and aesthetic itinerary that marks the author's passage from inauthenticity and insecurity to a moment of literary fulfillment and self-knowledge through the writing of a text of collective transcendence.

The two critical perspectives that have been detailed above have dominated from the very outset the history of criticism on the novel:[8] Whereas one faction will praise the author's success in the transposition of the gaucho's world into the text down to its most intricate details, the other will assert that it would be impossible for Güiraldes, a member of the social elite, to effect such a textual transformation without introjecting his class perspective and interests; if someone claims that the writer aimed at an archetypal representation of the collective spirit by presenting the gaucho as a quasimythical figure, someone else will rejoin that he did so out of nostalgia for a past where a certain social order that subjugated and condemned the gaucho to marginality prevailed unquestioned and unperturbed. Indeed, given the irreducible differences that are inherent in the interpretive stances that they represent, there would appear to be very little hope of ever conciliating these two essential outlooks on Güiraldes' novel.

And yet, I would like to argue that these seemingly irreconcilable critical positions ultimately find a common ground in the similarity of the relationship that they entertain with Güiraldes' text. For both the literary and the ideological judgments on *Don Segundo Sombra* are based on critical narratives about Güiraldes that are specular reflections of the text's narrative itself. The following passage, for instance, epitomizes the first of these critical perspectives. It clearly summarizes Güiraldes' childhood and adolescence on his family's ranch as an experience of apprenticeship that purportedly culminates in the composition of *Don Segundo Sombra*:

In these new horizons that somehow have been known all along, the boy will acquire an intimate knowledge of things. First, the house . . . Then, beyond the tiled patio he will arrive at the peons' kitchen; he will go near the thatched huts, the corral and the mangers. And beyond, the horses and cattle that make the ground tremble; farther still, the peons, cowboys and horse tamers – demigods of dangerous chores whom he will learn to love and admire and whom he will transpose, many years later, to the printed page. From them and among them he will acquire their knowledge, and will immerse himself both in the difficult techniques and operations that they employ in their day-to-day toils, as well as in the peculiar spirit of the gaucho that comes up in the latter's sayings, conversations and campfire tales.[9]

The critical literature on *Don Segundo Sombra* presents many examples of descriptions that are in essence – if not in actual wording – identical to the one just cited. And yet, any reader of Güiraldes' text will recognize in this fragment a restatement of those elements of *Don Segundo Sombra* that define it as an instance of the *Bildungsroman*: the author's education as an adolescent described by the fragment can be readily identified as a close parallel to the apprenticeship undergone by the boy Fabio Cáceres in Güiraldes' text.[10] Just as the young protagonist of the novel slowly acquires as the narrative progresses a knowledge of all aspects of the gaucho's world, a similar pedagogical process is projected onto the bio-graphical account of Güiraldes' development as an author. Sig-nificantly enough, both pedagogical narratives end in an act of writing that endows the entire narration with meaning in a retro-spective fashion: the adolescent that was Güiraldes will write in time the book that will define him as a significant author and will therefore redeem him from the vagaries of his previous literary attempts, whereas in *Don Segundo Sombra* the adult narrator writes an autobiographical account that illuminates his real identity and his newly-found status as a landowner.

A similar conclusion can be established when we examine closely the second critical outlook, the ideological approximation to Güiral-des' text. According to this view Güiraldes, a member of the landowning elite, produced in *Don Segundo Sombra* a mystified version of the world of the gaucho that in turn was a response to the specific challenges that Argentine history of the period presented to that social class.[11] Hence, Güiraldes' class extraction inevitably condemns his literary depiction of the gaucho to falsification, given that his view of that world had to be distorted by the concerns and interest peculiar to his class:

Don Segundo Sombra evidences its creator's familiarity with the finer points of horsebreaking, with those essential trivialities of life on the trail, with the nuances of the language of the men of the pampas. And yet Güiraldes was among them but not of them, and could not be simply because of the circumstances of his birth. Consequently, even before he sat down in 1920 to transform that gaucho experience into art, that experience had inevitably come to signify to him something other than what it represented to those who lived it, something more than the picturesque images it summoned forth for the contemporary urban dweller. Rather, it had become the vision of an ideal world, one which would not be seen again and which perhaps never really existed in the first place.[12]

Consequently, when considered from this perspective, the task of the critic would consist in confronting *Don Segundo Sombra* as an ideological construct that would have to be subjected to a radical demystification. Nevertheless, one cannot fail to notice that this critical narrative which seeks to explain the necessity of a demystifying confrontation with Güiraldes' text constitutes in essence a summary of the basic plot of *Don Segundo Sombra*. Indeed, if one substitutes the name of the protagonist of the novel for that of Güiraldes in the phrase where it appears, the latter would appropriately serve as a condensed formulation of the text's argument: "And yet *Fabio* was among them but not of them, and could not be simply because of the circumstances of his birth." In the context of *Don Segundo Sombra*, the sentence would allude to the adolescent's banishment from the world of the gaucho upon being informed of his identity as heir of a wealthy landowner. Similarly, both Güiraldes in this critical narrative, and the protagonist in the novel attempt to translate their experiences in that world into a text that has nevertheless lost all contact with the ideal realm that it nostalgically evokes. As the reader will remember, in *Don Segundo Sombra* the writing of the text is identified in the final pages of the novel as a post-lapsarian undertaking, as a consciously doomed attempt to bridge the distance that now separates the protagonist from a world of which he was once part. This situation is analogous to the one proposed by the critical passage just cited, where Güiraldes is described as necessarily engaged in an act of mystification on account of the specific circumstances of his birth. The difference is, of course, that in the second instance the critic's discourse is purportedly necessary to dismantle, to demystify Güiraldes' idealized vision of the gaucho. And yet, one could argue convincingly that a demystifying reading of *Don Segundo Sombra* is already incorporated in the novel itself, since the writing of the text by its protagonist takes as its point of departure the knowledge that the ideological reading pretends to establish – that is, that being a landowner makes it impossible to participate in the privileged world of the gaucho. This is why in *Don Segundo Sombra* the writing of the text is depicted as following a moment of separation and exile from the state of communion that had once characterized the protagonist's relationship with the domain of the gaucho. In the end, one has to wonder about the mystified status of a critical discourse that bases its claim to interpret on the will to demystify, when the text it confronts can be shown to be involved in the process of its own demystification.[13]

It appears, then, that the two principal critical perspectives on *Don Segundo Sombra* are articulated as narratives that only manage to repeat fundamental aspects of the novel's argument. This observation paves the way for the correlative assertion that perhaps this situation obtains because the text of Güiraldes' work had already internalized the essential elements of a critical discourse on itself. From this perspective it could be proposed that the two critical factions have in essence appropriated this intrinsic commentary that the novel articulates on its own; the sign of this appropriation would be the manner in which criticism on *Don Segundo Sombra* has unwittingly engaged in a systematic repetition of the text that it has pretended to elucidate. This being the case, I would like to argue that maybe there is something to be gained by reading the criticism on *Don Segundo Sombra* in a direct, close manner; since the text incorporates already a critical discourse on itself, perhaps the best possibility of confronting the novel from a critical standpoint may be afforded by reading its criticism in a most literal fashion. I propose, therefore, to engage the critical polemics on *Don Segundo Sombra* as representing a particularly pointed instance of a dynamics succinctly described by Jonathan Culler:

Texts thematize, with varying degrees of explicitness, interpretive operations and their consequences and thus represent in advance the dramas that will give life to the tradition of their interpretation. Critical disputes about a text can frequently be identified as a displaced reenactment of conflicts dramatized in the text, so that while the text assays the consequences and implications of the various forces it contains, critical readings transform this difference within into a difference between mutually exclusive positions.[14]

Hence, it is conceivable that those aspects of the novel that have been isolated by the criticism on it may yield some insights into the way in which this self-critical dimension manifests itself in the text.

Upon close examination one can detect that regardless of their divergences, both critical perspectives coincide in their recognition of Güiraldes' possession of a precise and thorough knowledge of the gaucho and his world. Recalling one of the previously quoted passages, "*Don Segundo Sombra* evidences its creator's familiarity with the finer points of horsebreaking, with those essential trivialities of life on the trail, with the nuances of the language of the men of the pampas. And yet Güiraldes was among them but not of them, and could not be simply because of the circumstances of his birth." Turning to the other fragment, one finds an analogous proposition: "From them and among them he will acquire their knowledge, and will immerse himself both in the difficult techniques and operations that they employ in their day-to-day toils, as well as in the peculiar spirit of the gaucho that comes up in the latter's sayings, conversations and campfire tales." In both instances Güiraldes is depicted as having acquired this knowledge in a practical fashion, through direct participation in the "work and days" of the gaucho that he would later portray in his novel. It would seem, then, that for the two traditional factions of Güiraldean criticism the gaucho, faithfully represented textually or not, possesses referential specificity; the dispute would then center on whether or not Güiraldes could have been the subject responsible for its textual representation, given the social stratum whence he came; in any event, if Güiraldes was faithful in his depiction of this world, or if he falsified or mystified it by reason of class interest, the presumption concerning the referentiality of the gaucho still remains. In fact, the vehemence of the condemnation or praise shown by the two sides can be understood as a function of their shared assumption regarding the possibility of an unlimited mimesis in the representation of Güiraldes' subject. One begins to understand, then, the appearance of a number of critical efforts that, for instance, enthusiastically attempted to trace on a map or physically recreate the character's geographical displacement; or on the other hand, those which pretended to rectify Güiraldes' narrative by taking exception to some of the author's descriptions of the minutest details of gaucho life – the correct way to mount a horse, for example.[15]

But the assumption that Güiraldes' creation *can* be held up against a "real" gaucho immediately gives rise to innumerable problems, since it can be argued that the figure of the gaucho has always performed as a cultural construct throughout Argentine history. As Emir Rodríguez Monegal has suggested "before 1916 (the publication date of Lugones' *El payador*), the gaucho was not the symbol of Argentine nationality; on the contrary, he was the symbol of the barbarism that the new and proud nation attempted not only to eradicate but to obliterate through willful forgetfulness."[16] In fact, even before 1916 there are discernible changes in the conception of the gaucho as a cultural object. Thus, for example, the gaucho of Ascasubi has little to do with the outlaw Juan Moreira, and the latter much less in common with Hernández's creation, Martín Fierro. In a significant shift that was less a reversal than a reactivation of certain characteristics already inherent in the cultural construct of the gaucho, by Güiraldes' time the latter had evolved to constitute a repository of desirable national values. (It is precisely the symbolic potential of the gaucho as a figure of autochthony that allows the metaphoric structure of Sarmiento's argument in *Facundo* [the gaucho stands for indigenous barbarism], but also the ambivalence shown by Sarmiento throughout his work in its depiction of the gaucho. For Sarmiento the gaucho is the embodiment of a "bad" autochthony, but autochthony nonetheless.) In any event, the persistent status of the gaucho as a cultural symbol compromises any attempt to demystify or celebrate Güiraldes' creation through a comparison with a presumably referential conception of the gaucho, since such a contrast would necessarily take place within a shared dimension of cultural symbolic production.[17]

But if the referential specificity of the gaucho can be rendered problematic, how then can one interpret the contention shared by the two critical passages cited above, to the effect that the writing of *Don Segundo Sombra* is the result of a detailed and exact knowledge of the world of the gaucho painstakingly acquired by Güiraldes? At this point one could venture an answer by invoking the mimetic relationship that was shown earlier to obtain between the novel and its criticism: If the critical discourse on the novel takes the form of a narrative that mirrors the narrative that unfolds in the text, it might be because the text it addresses is about that very process of unfolding. Hence, I would argue that the insistence on perceiving the composition of Güiraldes' novel as the outcome of the acquisition of a certain knowledge is reflective of the importance that the very concepts of acquisition and knowledge have in the text of *Don Segundo Sombra* itself. In the remainder of this chapter I will attempt to explore the opportunities afforded by this interpretive line of questioning. My inquiry begins, however, not with *Don Segundo Sombra*, but with an earlier text by Güiraldes where the problematic just described surfaces in the context of another deliberation on the specific nature of the autochthonous.

The economy of national identity

In 1924, in the middle of a decade of intense cultural debate about national essence, the avant-garde Buenos Aires review *Martín Fierro* conducted a written survey of opinions on the specificity of the Argentine character. Those polled were asked to consider the issue by responding to the following two questions: 1. Do you believe in the existence of an Argentine sensibility, an Argentine mentality? 2. If you believe in just such a sensiblity and mentality, what are its attributes? Güiraldes, admitting that his answers were drawn somewhat hastily and almost in jest, provided *Martín Fierro* with the following reply:

First question

Yes, there is an Argentine sensibility and an Argentine mentality. If that were not the case, we would have no reason for being except as fallow land, ready to be sold by the lot [*vendible en lotes*].

We may be [*estamos*] in a moment of compromise [*transacción*] and amorphism. But since elementary school I know by heart that *estar* is not the same as *ser*.

Second question
A short balance sheet

Credits	*Debits*
Capacity to assimilate	Imitation, copy-catting
Hospitality	Self-destruction out of/self-denial
Individualism	Excessive self-reliance
Disinterest, generosity	Profligacy, squandering
Critical sense	Malevolence, slander
Faith in onself	Self-conceit
Audacity	Aggressiveness
Pride in one's virtues	Concern for appearances
Congeniality	Volubility
Respect for bravery	Senseless daring
Love of friendship	Lack of trust
etc.	etc.

Advice: keep to your left.

This rudimentary classification is arbitrary precisely because it attempts to classify. Within human conventionality we should render unto Caesar the things that are Caesar's and to God the things that are God's: from the Argentine emotional and mental qualities we should render unto Man the things that are Man's and the Argentine being unto himself.[18]

A mixture of platitudes and stereotypical personal attributes, the substance of Güiraldes' response was probably not unique nor is it especially enlightening. There is, however, something striking about this reply, a certain contradictory aspect of it that manages to provide a point of departure for the examination of the discourse of the autochthonous in *Don Segundo Sombra*.

One cannot help noticing the manner in which Güiraldes' answer is reinforced by – indeed built on – a rhetorical use of economic terms and metaphors. Significant in this respect is the somewhat peculiar use of the word *transacción*, with its double meaning of compromise and transaction. Moreover, Güiraldes claims there must be an Argentine character because if that were not the case, "we would have no reason for being except as fallow land, ready to be sold by the lot," an effective economic simile to describe the hypothetical disaster of ontological non-specificity. The same applies to the dictum "render unto Caesar the things that are Caesar's and to God the things that are God's" that organizes rhetorically the fourth paragraph, an expression that was originally used in the New Testament to address specifically the issue of taxation by Roman authority.

Of paramount importance, though, is the recourse to the balance-sheet format as a means of organizing the presentation of the supposed idiosyncrasies of the Argentine being. The column headings of *Credits* and *Debits* are meant to convey directly – again through an economic metaphor – the laudable and regrettable qualities respectively of the national character. This persistent use of economic metaphors by Güiraldes could be considered simply an extended rhetorical device – perhaps even a bit over-extended – were it not because, as we shall soon recognize, economics has an ambiguous presence in the text of Güiraldes' response.

For a careful examination shows that although economics provides the tropological backbone for the piece, there is conversely an implicit condemnation of economic considerations and operations throughout the text. The economic term *transacción* is coupled with *amorphism* in order to describe a present but transitory moment of national disorientation that is not a genuine reflection of the underlying ontological bedrock that sustains it: "We may be [*estamos*] in a moment of compromise [*transacción*] and amorphism. But since elementary school I know by heart that *estar* is not the same as *ser*." This idea is reinforced by Güiraldes' purposeful discrimination between *ser* and *estar*: the present moment – a moment of *transacción* – falls in the province of *estar*, and consequently should have no bearing in a discussion of the essential qualities of the national character. The same ambivalence can be seen at work in the decidedly affirmative response offered by Güiraldes to the first question: "Yes, there is an Argentine sensibility and an Argentine mentality. If that were not the case, we would have no reason for being except as fallow land, ready to be sold by the lot." In this case the activities of partitioning and selling are associated metaphorically with a preposterous state of existential non-specificity, through the presentation of those economic operations as the fragmentation that would accompany an ontological fall.

A similar contradiction informs Güiraldes' second answer, the *pequeño balance* of national characteristics. Upon examining closely the two columns of attributes, one can establish that in most cases the items that appear next to one another constitute the obverse and reverse of the same coin (so to say): power of assimilation vs. imitation, audacity vs. aggressiveness, critical acumen vs. pettiness. The idea implied by the balance-sheet format would be, of course, that the real Argentine character would have to be located in the middle between the two extremes or, in keeping with the rhetorical figure employed by the author, by adding together the opposing entries in each line item. And yet, precisely in the context of the metaphor used by Güiraldes, this would be the moment of perfect balance of credits and debits, the juncture at which economics would become a superfluous activity, signified by the now meaningless vertical line running the length of the empty page. It would seem that in the realm of true Being there is no justification for the existence of economic thought, an implication nonetheless violated by the form of Güiraldes' very attempt at a definition of the authentic Argentine being.

Economics, Güiraldes' answer to the survey appears to be signaling, is an arithmetic of the contingent, an account of fallenness from being. Still, one can only be perplexed by the fact that Güiraldes' attempt to describe the essence of the national character is couched in figures derived from economics, thereby subverting the message that his answer would like to convey; for economics functions in Güiraldes' response both as a rejected concept *and* as the trope that controls the rhetorical structure of the piece. Hence, it would seem from the above example that a successful formulation of the autochthonous would have to be accompanied by a repudiation of economic considerations, only to have them reassert themselves in a most insidious way. The betrayal of the conceptual dimension of Güiraldes' answer by its very own rhetorical organization is a most telling intimation of the way in which a metaphoric structure organized around the concept of economy will inscribe itself surreptitiously in *Don Segundo Sombra*, Güiraldes' most influential text.

Working knowledge

The world of the gaucho depicted by *Don Segundo Sombra* is a seamless, homogeneous universe of privileged ontology. Yet, as it was proposed in an earlier chapter, one should understand this organicity as an effect of discourse, that is, as a particular set of metonymic relations organized as a rhetorical figure. In my consideration of *Don Segundo Sombra* I would like to turn first to the examination of the homogeneous universe represented in the novel in terms of the rhetorical structure of the autochthonous. This discussion will allow us to see in some detail the specific manner in which "the autochthonous" is articulated in Güiraldes' text. Nonetheless, the discrete description of each category in relation to the remaining two must be understood for what it is: an exercise demanded by expository expedience. In reality the three are intertwined so as to create what could be called a textual nature, a set of already-given relations that are supposed to precede even writing itself. In fact, the strength of the discursive figure of the autochthonous stems precisely from this synecdochical fusion between its constitutive elements. My purpose here is to establish the essential features, the assumed relationships of the universe described by *Don Segundo Sombra*, before proceeding to explore another dimension of the text whose existence challenges those very presumptions of organicity.

It has been affirmed countless times that in *Don Segundo Sombra* Argentine geography rises to the status of character. It is understandable that the space where the action takes place should have been deemed that important, given the number of allusions to and descriptions of it produced by the narrative. In *Don Segundo Sombra*, the main geographic element is, of course, the Argentine pampas. The characterization that emerges from the novel is in its most general scope, that of a limitless, ever-new geographical expanse. This quality is pictured as a direct correlative to the ethos of freedom that is the avowed creed of the gaucho. Don Segundo is the archetype of this kind of man, one who does not settle anywhere simply because there is nothing to make one place stand out against another. This tacit axiom is encapsulated in a number of observations that the narrator makes: "To gallop is to abolish distance; for the gaucho arriving is but a pretext for leaving."[19] And: "They had the soul of the herder, which means having the horizon for a soul" (p. 373). The important fact is, however, that this characteristic of the land is seen to determine the nature and rhythm of the activity that the men pursue. This is why the principal ongoing action of the novel is described at various times by the protagonist as simply marching aimlessly. All beings appear to be invaded by the cadence that the land seems to dictate: "On the pampa impressions are swift, spasmodic, and they vanish without a trace in the enormous present . . . The trail was the same as the one before . . . Animals and men were possessed by one fixed idea: motion, motion, motion (p. 380). In this homogeneous horizon of human activity and geography, everything seems to have its place and purpose, even vicissitude. This explains why potentially disturbing occurrences are not perceived as setbacks, but as an integral part of experience. The observations that are made about destiny have no tragic taint; they are presented with an air of stoic resignation. This interpenetration of human action and geography belies the hasty commonplace assertion that the *novela de la tierra* in general seeks to portray the agonistic struggle between human beings and nature in Latin America. Appearances to the contrary, the possibility of genuine strife involving nature and man is eliminated in most of these novels by the characterization of the land as a sort of symbiotic stage for man's activity.

In a similar fashion, the particular linguistic register of the gaucho's world is made to echo the geographic milieu. This is accomplished through the use of figures that refer to fauna, flora, and topographic elements that are associated with the *pampas*. Examples of this are myriad: "Under the hearth's hood was a big soup kettle surrounded by little maté gourds, like chicks around the mother ostrich [*rodeada como un ñandú por sus charabones*]" (p. 363); "His face was full of coarse veins, like the belly of a just-skinned sheep" (p. 408); or: "Tatters of gray clouds scurried across without direction, like wild mustangs fleeing before a prairie fire" (p. 481). This is most evident in the boy's description of don

Segundo after their first encounter, in which the latter's physique is minutely described through a consistent use of attributes belonging to a horse.

Human activity in turn can be seen to inform the linguistic order through the use of a specialized vocabulary that encompasses all the facets of cattle ranching. The following example is characteristic in the density of allusions to specific operations, techniques and practices:

The oldest of the ranch hands helped us by roping the colts that we then threw in order to bridle and bit them while they were still down. Then we hitched them to the post with a few turns of the halter, and later saddled them. I for one kept my eyes on them, watching for signs of trouble to come. Would this one slip his cinch? Would that one throw me? Meantime, while I saddled, I had to be on guard against kicks, rushes, tramplings and rearings.   (p. 470)

Many pages have been devoted to the classification and clarification of this highly specialized lexicon, a critical enterprise that many other *novelas de la tierra* preempt by appending a glossary to their texts.[20] Through the presence of this specialized vocabulary we become aware of a *métier* in all its intricacies, essentially because it is projected as possessing a linguistic integrity that represents it as a closed order of human activity.

Such is the web of totalizing relationships that define the homogeneous world depicted in *Don Segundo Sombra*. Given the characteristics just discussed, it might seem that to speak about the presence of economics in such an ontologically charged novel could be taken as a foolhardy, if not an outright reductive enterprise. And yet, I believe there would be little disagreement with the observation that *Don Segundo Sombra* is above all a description of men performing a series of chores that are subsumed under the larger economic activity of cattle ranching: the gathering and driving of herds to pasture and market, branding, the taming of horses, etc. This is why the common complaint about the novel that very little actually *happens* in it is simultaneously understandable and inaccurate: the dearth of events in a large-scale conception of plot is more than compensated by the constant activity of the characters as they go about their daily business. The intricate and careful descriptions of these activities become at times so weighted with a profusion of detail that they almost acquire a clinical tone. Witness, for example, the following involved and precise account of the butchering of a cow:

Goyo was swift and clever; my own busy uselessness made him laugh. I had barely slit the skin at one foot when his knife tip, traveling all the way across the paunch, was almost in my face. His long strokes drew the hide from the flesh and once the breach had been made he inserted his fist in it, quickly skinning the beast. Circling the joints with his knife, he broke the four legs at the last joint. Between tendon and shin bone he made a slit, fastened the buckle of this bridle in it, threw the free end over the branch of a tree and we both pulled until the animal was swinging in the air. Quickly, he opened the belly, removed layer after layer of fat, scoured away the offal and pulled the lungs, the liver and heart from the thorax.

(p. 383)

The dexterity with which the ranch-hand proceeds is underscored by the feeling of inadequacy that the narrator experiences while observing him proceed with the operation: " – Is this what you brought me for? – I asked, standing stupidly by, ashamed of my own hands which hung idle like so much tripe" (p. 383). The manner in which the boy is reduced to the status of mere observer by virtue of his ignorance reinforces his passivity, but also underlines the physical involvement and mental absorption of his companion in his task, his being at work. The extraordinary accumulation of details belies the fact that what is being described is a relatively secondary activity, one that is just ancillary to the long cattle drive in which the pro-tagonist is engaged at that juncture. But it is precisely through the accumulation of descriptions of this sort, however, that the text manages to convey the larger horizon of human activity in which the characters are thoroughly immersed in *Don Segundo Sombra*. Later on, for example, the gathering of wild cattle is depicted as the summation of a number of discrete operations that are enumerated in series: "The barbaric tournament began. Since there were enough of us, we divided up the work. On one side, the steers milled around the tame ones that were used as decoys; on the other they were guided toward an open field where they were roped, thrown, dehorned, gelded, or – if too sick – butchered and then skinned" (p. 432).

This inordinate attention paid to work and its description as a discipline through the use of a technical rhetoric, is made more puzzling by the fact that in the novel work is conceived as possessing a dimension that can only be described as moral. In *Don Segundo Sombra* work is inscribed in an ethical universe, where it is divested of all economic ramifications. In this mystified modality, human activity is capable of redeeming even the beasts that it touches, as the following description of a herd of wild cattle illustrates:

I watched the rodeo. I had never seen such a collection of creatures. What amazed me was the great number of crippled beasts; some with fractures that had mended by themselves, others with huge scars where worms had devoured the flesh. *No human hand had ever touched these animals.* If a horn grew into an eye, there was no one there to cut it. The ones with worms died eaten, or survived with whole pieces of their bodies missing. Where the hoofs had spread they kept on spreading, until they were as convoluted as a huge tripe. (p. 430, my emphasis)

Although nature is not an antagonist in *Don Segundo Sombra*, from the perspective of this ethical dimension it serves as a backdrop against which to highlight the transcendental quality of human work. This function allows us to understand the purpose of the seemingly digressive experience at the *cangrejal*, the crab-infested marsh, where a scene of collective cannibalism is described in graphic detail: Left to its own devices, without the redemptive intervention of man through work, nature consumes itself in a frenzied, unending vortex of annihilation.

In keeping with this ethical mystification of work, there is in the text a very marked disregard, if not plain contempt, for money. Money, the detritus that marks the consumption of work by an economic circuit, is essentially absent from the novel. When it is earned, it is the result of chance – a horse race, a reckless bet, for example – and when it is lost, it is hardly mourned. Even that is taught to the boy by don Segundo, who whimsically places a bet on a drunkard's advice, and is never seen receiving wages for his work. Usury, the engendering of money by money, is inexplicably and pointedly taken as a personal insult by the protagonist during the betting preceding a cockfight contest. And finally, when the boy discovers his true identity as the son of a landowner, he believes with shame that people look at him "as if my face were covered with gold coins" (p. 491).[21]

This mystified conception of work that is characteristic of *Don Segundo Sombra* is ultimately attributable to the pedagogical enterprise that dominates the novel. Work in this register is not an economic activity but an educational program; not a commodity that circulates but the curriculum of a pedagogical project. From this point of view, one could say that the human activity described in the text is less that of men at work than that of a discipline finding its actualization in the world through the men that employ it. Don Segundo is the repository of this knowledge, and the boy presents himself as the perfect disciple, a model of concentration, assimilation and obedience. What the boy receives in return for his work is not money, but instead the knowledge that he has acquired in the process of performing his assigned tasks. This pedagogical interpretation of work is further strengthened by his denunciation of the formal education he received in elementary school as useless, since it only taught him to read and count, activities that are of no use to him as a gaucho.

This concerted repudiation of economics was previously remarked on in Güiraldes' response to the question of national identity posed by *Martín Fierro*. Nevertheless, the same movement of denial and recovery in a different register that was seen in that earlier text obtains in *Don Segundo Sombra* as well. For I believe it can be shown without much difficulty that the novel is organized through the employment of the metaphor of "taking stock" as a structuring conceit. Güiraldes' text is evidently orchestrated around three such moments – chapters I, X and XXVII – three scenes where the protagonist finds himself beside a body of water and proceeds to summarize the experiences that have brought him to that point. But these instances are truly a recounting in more than one sense of the term: in them evocations become enumerations; assets that are presented as counterbalancing previous liabilities. In chapter X, for instance, the boy makes a tally of everything he has learned during five years of apprenticeship under don Segundo:

It was he who guided me patiently to the knowledge of the gaucho. He taught me the wisdom of the herder, the cunning of the tamer, the handling of the lasso and the bolas, the difficult science of training a horse to divide up a herd and to contain a stampede, how to train a string of ponies to stop in unison on the open pampa so that I could catch them whenever and wherever I wanted. Watching him I learned to make thongs and straps to produce my own bridles, reins, cinches and saddle pads, how to form lassos, and how to place both the rings and the buckles.

Under his tutelage I became a doctor to my own horses: I learned to cure sore hoof by turning the horse on his track, distemper by the dog method or with a halter made from the stem of a plant, weak kidneys with a plaster of putrid mud, lameness by tying a hair from the tail on the sound leg, hoof growths with a hot whetstone; and boils, growths and other afflictions through several different means.   (p. 390)

This account refers to an earlier list, where the young boy had enumerated the skills he lacked at the time, just after embarking on his apprenticeship: "I had to learn to butcher, to rope both riding and standing, to tame, to run the rodeo, to make bridles, reins and hobbles, to shear a sheep, to clip a horse, to skin a cow, to brand with an iron, to throw the bolas, to trim hoofs, to cure distemper, spavin, hoof growths and heaven knows what else" (p. 383). Later on, in chapter XXVII, seated next to a pond, the protagonist summarizes the previous three years – years in which he has transformed himself into a landowner. His account begins with a sort of inventory of his new properties "Three years ago I had stopped being a simple herder and had come into my domain ... My domain! I could look round, all around, and say to myself: All this is mine" (p. 494). This urge to take stock, to inventory, as it were, reappears throughout the text, as the following passage exemplifies: "What else could I wish for? Three ponies ... a complete outfit with a set of reins, bridle hobbles, lasso and straps; a change of clothing in case the weather turned wet, and a good poncho" (p. 372).

But if the novel is structured around three such distinct instances of taking stock, one must also realize that what is ultimately being inventoried, what is being accounted for, is knowledge. The intersection of the economic metaphor with the pedagogical program suggests that knowledge in *Don Segundo Sombra* is necessarily implicated in a transaction of some nature, a circumstance that should come as no surprise since any depiction of apprenticeship is invariably teleologically motivated. First of all, the boy acquires a sense of identity as a result of his education; upon completion of his apprenticeship under don Segundo he *literally* discovers who he is. This circumstance is underscored by the fact that it is here that, for the first time in the narrative, he is given a proper name. Concurrently (and more significantly), his education *entitles* him to land and property as well. The link established by the novel between pedagogical experience and the acquisition of property is explicitly established by the remarks of don Leandro, the young man's legal guardian after his father's death, during their first interview: " – You have seen the world now and you have become a man – better than a man, a gaucho. He who knows the problems of this land because he has lived through them is tempered to overcome them ... Your property awaits you and if you should need me I will be by your side" (p. 492). Thus, the change in the protagonist's status is explained and depicted as the outcome of a process, the acquisition of a certain knowledge whose possession legitimizes the young man's ownership of the land.

Yet, from the perspective of its legitimizing capability with regard to property, this knowledge is understood to be necessary, but also hardly sufficient. In other words, if knowledge were the overriding criterion of legitimation, the pedagogical project would constitute an impossibility, since the pedagogue (don Segundo) would be from the outset in a position to claim what the student must yet undergo a process to deserve. Hence, the pedagogical enterprise injects a spurious sense of temporality into a world view that is ultimately essentialist; the necessary criterion for ownership, the genealogical one, had to exist from the beginning in the boy. This explains why he experiences his newly-found identity as a confirmation of what was a mere intuition in the past. In *Don Segundo Sombra* the genealogical determinant is attenuated by the progenitor's almost complete absence from the narrative: the father impinges on the protagonist's life only after his demise, and in the form of a delayed recognition of an illegitimate offspring. This distancing strategy notwithstanding, the land belongs to the boy by virtue of his ancestry and not because of the apprenticeship he has completed as a gaucho.

Work, therefore, has this clearly ideological function in the novel, that of serving as the putative instrument through which the boy *becomes* entitled to his new status. In this respect *Don Segundo Sombra* appears to advance the proposition that patrimony is something that must be actively earned, not merely inherited, thereby transposing ideologically the question of the legitimacy of ownership from a genealogical to an ethical plane. This is an important message, one that perhaps becomes most intelligible when placed in the Argentine context of the times. For one can envision that Güiraldes' attempt to shift the grounds – so to speak – for the legitimation of ownership of landed property constitutes a response to a crisis of legitimation within that privileged social group: At a time when historical and social transformations in Argentina were challenging the prerogatives of the landowning class, Güiraldes produces in *Don Segundo Sombra* a statement that legitimizes in a different register the claims of that class. In the most direct way, what Güiraldes' novel accomplishes is the transformation of the principle of legitimacy from passive to active: the criterion for ownership will not be any more the passive reception of a name and a title as dictated by genealogy, but the *activity* of earning that status through personal involvement in the affairs of the property. This involvement is projected in *Don Segundo Sombra* as the apprenticeship that must be undertaken by the young protagonist before he can rightfully claim what has been his all along in any event. This is the juncture where the pedagogical enterprise intersects with the economic metaphor of taking stock that structures the novel. For the boy earns the right to his claim by literally re-counting at several key moments the knowledge he has acquired in his years under the tutelage of don Segundo. One can perhaps speculate that Güiraldes' "solution" stems from his understanding of the historical crisis faced by his class as a function of the distancing by owners from their properties that had, by his time, become the norm. In this regard Güiraldes' much touted personal participation in the toils of the men in his *estancia* could be understood less as an instance of romanticized role-playing than as a programmatic praxis for the rehabilitation of the prerogatives of an embattled class. Hence, the economy of knowledge just discussed can be interpreted as the expression of an ideological intention at work in the writing of *Don Segundo Sombra*. But this realization also opens the way for an understanding of another level of the text where the metaphoric association of economics and epistemology finds its definitive expression and force.

Writing knowledge

Two months after the publication of *Don Segundo Sombra* in 1926, Güiraldes received a letter from a reader that contested the account he had given in his novel regarding the gaucho technique for healing a lame horse. The author's response, of which only a fragment is cited below, was an involved, technical defense of his description:

The correction that you propose regarding the method of healing a horse's lameness seems to me mistaken. You people in the Tucumán province tie up or perforate the ear on the opposite side of the lame leg so that when the horse scratches himself with the good hind leg, he is forced to use the weak one, thereby hastening the correct realignment of the affected joint. We, in turn, use the same logic. We tie a string of hair from the tail to the good leg thereby making it swell; the pain makes the animal use the affected leg, which he otherwise would have favored. Making use of the lame leg facilitates the return of the bones or tendons involved to their normal position.[22]

The intricacy of Güiraldes' answer allow us to understand the extent to which knowledge is implicated not only in the ideological formulations advanced by *Don Segundo Sombra* and discussed above, but also in the legitimation of the novel's own writing as an autochthonous literary text. For as I showed in a preceding chapter, the project of writing an autochthonous work, that is, the attempt to *produce* a literary text that purportedly encompasses the essence of a culture's specificity, is an enterprise that cannot transcend the contradiction inherent in its own formulation, that is: how can one engage in the *deliberate* creation of a text that simultaneously claims to arise *spontaneously* from its cultural milieu? Hence, in order to validate its claim to being a work that is expressive of such an essence, the "autochthonous" text incorporates a discourse that underwrites its presumed propriety as an indigenous creation. This situation has its resolution in a narrative that on the one hand presents itself as the unmediated representation of that essence, and on the other resorts continually to strategies of textual self-legitimation. This critical intention is represented by a discourse introjected in the work that seeks to name, to comment explicitly on the adequacy of the relationship between signifier and signified in the text – between the autochthonous and the work that embodies it. Paradoxically, this can only be achieved through a relentless underscoring of the work's own textual procedures. The outcome, then, is a narrative that obsessively calls attention to its signifying practice, to its own labor of signification. It is in the context represented by this discursive problematics that the economy of knowledge present in *Don Segundo Sombra* can be shown to acquire its full significance.

For example, in the final chapter of *Don Segundo Sombra* the narrator explicates (the verb is carefully chosen here) in a heavy-handed fashion the overarching plan of the novel's composition. Sitting beside a small pond, the young man, now in full enjoyment of his property, engages in the following meditation: "As it should be evident by now, in my life water is like a mirror in which the images of the past parade by: At the edge of a brook I examined my childhood long ago. Later, at the ford of a river where I had led my horse to drink I summarized five years of life as a gaucho. Finally, now by the margin of a pool on my own property I mentally reviewed my diary as an owner" (p. 495). The three moments that the narrator describes correspond respectively to chapters I, x, and

XXVII of the novel, that is, the three instances of tallying that as we saw earlier sustain the metaphor of "taking stock" that structures the text. Hence, what the passage undertakes is a recursive maneuver, an *accounting* of the way in which *accounting* serves as a structuring metaphoric conceit for the text. The imagistic association of the specular qualities of water to the autobiographical component of the narrative could be regarded simply as an allusion to the narcissistic dimension of the enterprise. Yet, in the context of our discussion, it functions also as an emblem for the novel's explanation of its organizing structure through the use of that structuring metaphor itself.

As if this were not enough, the narrator resorts to what is perhaps the most literal and explicit technique of textual self-referentiality, the *mise en abyme*. Its presence in the novel is, surprisingly, an aspect of the work that has hardly received any attention in the otherwise exhaustive critical literature on *Don Segundo Sombra*. In chapter XVIII, injured and tired after a fierce encounter with a bull, the delirious protagonist has a mysterious vision:

We were at Galván's ranch, under the paradise trees and the proprietor put a hand on my shoulder and said:
– "You have seen the world now and you have become a man – better than a man, a gaucho. He who knows the problems of this land because he has lived through them is tempered to overcome them. Go ahead. Your property awaits you, and if you should ever need me I will be by your side . . .
Near us a rosebush bloomed and a dog was sniffing my boots. I had my hat in my hands and I felt happy, yet sad. Why? Strange events had come to me and I felt as if I were somebody else . . . somebody who had achieved a great thing, but at the price of death. (p. 440)

No explanation or interpretation is advanced by the narrator regarding this hallucinatory experience in the context of the ongoing events in the novel. Nonetheless, much later, in chapter XXVI, when the young boy has an interview with his new guardian and tutor, the fragment cited above is transcribed almost to the letter:

– You have seen the world and have become a man – better than a man, a gaucho. He who knows the problems of this land because he has lived through them is tempered to overcome them . . .
What was the meaning of those previously heard words? I had already lived this in a world of dreams.
Near us a rosebush was in bloom and a dog was sniffing my boots. I had

my hat in my hands and I felt happy, yet sad. Why? Strange events had
come to me and I felt as if I were somebody else . . . somebody who had
achieved something great, but at the price of death.

– You will leave us when you will. Your property awaits you, and if you
should ever need me I will be by your side . . .   (p. 492)

Again, no explanation is offered for this reiteration, one that
problematizes the assumed immediacy of the first event by treating
it as a previous text that is transcribed almost to the letter. Yet, it is
clear that the repetition functions as an introjected commentary by
the text on its teleological design, given that the scene that it depicts
is the pivotal one in the protagonist's transformation. The fact that
its first occurrence is entirely unmotivated in the narrative only
makes more evident the forceful attempt by the text to establish and
call attention to its own teleological organization.

The critical consciousness that operates in the text also manifests
itself in the scrupulously dual linguistic nature of the narrative. This
linguistic dichotomy, perhaps the most distinctive stylistic trait of
Don Segundo Sombra, has given rise to a number of interpretations
that essentially reflect the concerns of the two traditional critical
perspectives on the novel. Thus, the presence in the text of two
mutually insulated and self-consistent linguistic registers is understood variously as a successful stylistic device or, on the other hand,
as an attempt by Güiraldes the landowner to inscribe in the novel
his sense of class superiority.[23] I believe, though, that there is an
alternate interpretation for the dual linguistic quality evinced by
Don Segundo Sombra.

Consistent with the idealized conception of the world of the
gaucho that the novel advances, the protagonist's realization of his
familial background, his being the son of a landowner, is experienced and described by him as a fall from essence. This fundamental
loss is explicitly conveyed by the observation made by the dejected
narrator upon being informed of his real identity: "Don Segundo
and Pedro were saddling as well. We made the same motions, and
yet we were different. Different? Why? Suddenly, in the comparison
I had discovered the source of my sadness: *I was no longer a gaucho*"
(p. 489). This interpretation of the narrator's new situation as a fall
from an ontologically privileged state is underlined in the last scene
of the novel, when don Segundo takes leave of his former protégé:
The boy and don Segundo *must* part ways, since the world that the
latter represents is now forbidden to him. In his new fallen state, the

boy grudgingly learns bookkeeping, recognizes the authority of maps to demarcate property, and develops the literary inclinations that will lead him to the composition of the narrative. In this fashion, the act of writing the novel is presented as necessarily following a plenitude of experience, a state of ontological grace. Hence the longing tone that some critics have explained by interpreting the novel as Güiraldes' elegiac song for the gaucho.

Nevertheless, if *Don Segundo Sombra* affects an air of nostalgia or resignation it is not just because it is a dirge for the gaucho that the protagonist once was; this quality is also a consequence of the narrator's rejection of writing, the only means of which he can now avail himself for action. Indeed, in the one instance where the narrator alludes to the act of writing itself he affirms the disconnection between writing and his lived experience as a gaucho: "In the meantime my new character and my new tastes acquired shape. I experienced my first yearnings for literature. I developed a taste for knowledge. *But I should not mention all of that in these simple pages*" (p. 496, my emphasis). Moreover, these new literary interests are extrinsic, appendages to a self that still prefers the directness of gaucho experience over the artificiality of cultured life: "Don Leandro's lessons, the books and a few visits to Buenos Aires with Raucho slowly transformed me into what is referred to as an educated man. Yet nothing afforded me the potent satisfaction that I had felt during my life in the pampas" (p. 496). *Don Segundo Sombra* presents us then with a text whose written nature is itself the mark of a state of fallenness from being. Even the famous final line of the novel: "I left, my life-blood flowing away," could be interpreted as a confirmation of this assertion; in a short piece published some years earlier in the review *Proa* – significantly entitled "Grafomanía" – Güiraldes had already established this figural equivalence between bleeding and writing: "[Writing] is a small hemorrhage that does not weaken me and that I find every day in a ledger that invites me to unwind my mental energy. The last trace of yesterday's hemorrhage is the first trace of today's."[24] Hence, the very moment when the boy takes leave of the privileged world he knew is described with a figure that is also allusive to the beginning of his writing career, as Güiraldes' metaphoric association suggests.

In *Don Segundo Sombra* the mastery of written discourse, represented by the composition of the novel, is understood to be the final phase of a long process of renunciation and domestication of the narrator's former self. The remarkable fact is that the distance between original communion and subsequent alienation is rigorously measured in the novel linguistically as well. This is the source for the dichotomous stylistic structure of *Don Segundo Sombra*: whenever the boy *speaks* as a gaucho, there is an attempt to transcribe his speech using a strictly phonetic criterion. However, the narrator's account of his thoughts at the time, already removed from action, is expressed in the rigorous orthographic modality dictated by the narrative situation that is only fully revealed in the last chapter. The two registers maintain a precise sort of counterpoint throughout the novel: "'It don't matter, Don. You gotta live with it. Thank God I'm good again.' With determination I cut the straps that retained my fractured arm. I essayed some motions with caution and ascertained that everything was in order" (p. 450). At times, the two can even be seen to coexist in the same line of text: "Watchit – I said to him menacingly – coolit if you don't wanna meet up with a knife" (p. 449).

Spoken language is therefore the language of participation, of immediacy, qualities that are associated with the world of the gaucho. But the stylistic fissure that characterizes the novel is meant to be more than a reflection of the change in the protagonist's status: through it, the text pretends to underwrite the privileged existential world of the gaucho by continuously forcing a comparison with another linguistic register, one that it portrays as belonging to a state of fallenness, the realm of written language. But the outcome is, paradoxically, that the juxtaposition also fosters a heightened awareness of the artificial, "produced" nature of the language that is deemed privileged in the novel, by allowing it to be examined as a function of another orthographic register. In other words, if *Don Segundo Sombra* makes a claim of transparency and immediacy for the speech of the gaucho, the strategy that it deploys to represent these qualities produces the opposite result; given the linguistic confrontation explicitly sustained by the text, it becomes inevitable also to perceive the language of the gaucho as an artificially devised orthographic code, as a rhetorical technique. In its careful discrimination between two distinct linguistic domains this aspect of *Don Segundo Sombra* is reminiscent of the structure of the glossary, a recurrent textual feature in the *novela de la tierra*. One could say that if *Don Segundo Sombra* does not append a glossary to its text, the latter insinuates itself in the work in the duality of its linguistic nature.

The result is a text that calls attention to the artificiality of a language that it also advances as the mark of immediate and unreflexive participation in experience. This linguistic dichotomy in the text is reinforced by the fact that a pervasive use of simile is the most salient tropological attribute of the narration.[25] As is well known, the simile proposes a relationship of similarity that it also recognizes as impossible to resolve in an identity; in *Don Segundo Sombra* the simile is used to convey the homogeneity of the gaucho's universe by establishing correspondences between the various elements of that world. Thus, one finds throughout the novel examples such as the following: "Meanwhile, the storm had gone through like a hawk swooping over a hen house" (p. 482); "We went to work on the fallen horse like buzzards on their prey" (p. 483); and "She was covered with freckles, like a *tero*'s egg" (p. 408). Nevertheless, the persistent use of simile in *Don Segundo Sombra* has an effect analogous to the one just seen in the analysis of the novel's dual linguistic structure: by its particular qualities as a rhetorical figure it brings attention to itself, to its transparent *attempt* to conjoin the heterogeneous elements that it purports to bring together.

Through these instances, one can detect the presence of a critical intention that operates throughout the novel in an effort to guarantee the unmotivated nature of the text. Nonetheless, the result is a narration that is continually exposing its own underpinnings, its own process of production. One begins to suspect then, that if work is so persistently focused upon in *Don Segundo Sombra*, it is because it stands as a figure emblematic of the text's production of itself. This affirmation of the work-value of textual production manifests itself in *Don Segundo Sombra* as the mastery of a specialized, involved knowledge that must be dominated if the novel is to be an effective textual entity. The possession of this knowledge is put in evidence in the text through the precise description of a discipline in all its intricacies; with each detail, however insignificant, the novel shows a mastery that certifies its identity with itself, its integrity as a textual construct. By means of this strategic maneuver, the legitimacy of the writing is underwritten through the assumed internal coherence of a *métier* conceptually mastered and described in utmost detail. In this fashion, the text endeavors to guarantee its own labor of signification through the narrative's painstaking description of work conceived as a systematic, exact body of knowledge that acquires in the novel the status of a discipline.

This may account for the fact that, conversely, work is very often described in *Don Segundo Sombra* with figures derived from the act of writing. With this in mind one notices that the *pampas*, the space where human activity deploys itself, are characterized as an unmarked, boundless surface throughout the novel, as a sort of *tabula rasa* that elicits the image of the blank page: "We would see what the unmarked paths and plains [*el campo sin huellas*] had in store for us" (p. 372). Hence, it is not surprising to find a number of descriptions that refer to the ongoing action as a kind of writing: "The deserted scene where the rodeo had taken place was a strange sight. In a large circle around the center post the ground was black with dung and urine, and had been churned by the cattle's trampling into a slimy mud that bore the imprint of thousands of hoofs" (p. 434). By the same token one also encounters the following quotation: "The spurs clicked in unison, marking the ground with their suspension points [*trazando en el suelo sus puntos suspensivos*]" (p. 374). And later in the novel the same figural identification reappears: "As soon as the first animals stepped into the rodeo I launched at them to impress [*para imprimirles*] on them a rotational motion" (p. 435). In the end, this metaphoric linkage becomes representative of the homology between writing and work that purports to legitimize the propriety of the autochthonous discourse in the novel.

Work has, therefore, a double function in the novel: it is, as I established earlier, the means through which the boy "earns" the prerogatives of his new status as landowner. But it is also the instrument that underwrites the text's writing by evincing the mastery of a knowledge conceived of as a discipline. This explains why work is presented in the text as knowledge, but also why knowledge is metaphorically amassed, tallied as currency as the novel progresses. It is this triangle of knowledge, property and writing that makes *Don Segundo Sombra* such a powerful work, for it is in the complex, delicate interaction between the three vertices that the ideological and literary effectiveness of Güiraldes' novel resides. Perhaps it is only after arriving at this realization that we may be in a position to understand the nature of the rift between the two traditional critical perspectives on *Don Segundo Sombra*. One can propose that the divergence is expressive of the different emphasis each view places on the relationships between writing and one of the other two terms – property and knowledge – but at the expense of the third. Thus, Güiraldes is perceived as either a landowner in defense of his class privileges or as a knowledgeable literary portrayer of the gaucho. On the other hand, this is why the criticism on *Don Segundo Sombra* is condemned to repeating the novel, since the text already brings inscribed within itself a discourse of classist and literary legitimation based on the acquisition of a precise body of knowledge. This explains also why the best hope for a demystifying confrontation with Güiraldes' text lies in reading it in the most literal way possible. Seen in this light, the novel's plot could not be more transparent: in its most essential outline *Don Segundo Sombra* is the narration of how a boy simultaneously becomes both a landowner and the writer of an autochthonous text.

By focusing on the preeminence of work in the novel we arrive at the conclusion that the text establishes a circuit of exchange where the three terms previously mentioned – knowledge, property and writing – become elements in a transaction. Ultimately, *Don Segundo Sombra* is the written record of this tropological exchange. Only now does the metaphor of "taking stock" that rules the novel acquire its full significance. It alludes to the economy of signification that operates in the text, to the manner in which the text moves to guarantee its own discursivity. Through this metaphor writing is likened to an economic operation, a final balancing out that should leave neither a surplus nor a deficit of signification. But there is, of course, a surplus that cannot be accounted for: the metaphor itself. Its obtrusive, continually remarked-upon presence in the text undermines the organicity and self-identity that the text would like to project. The novel's overt attempt to impose closure on its signifying practice is finally thwarted by the conspicuous presence of the powerful metaphor that it sets in place for that same purpose.[26] From this perspective, the contradictory rhetorical structure of Güiraldes' answer to *Martín Fierro*'s survey on the nature of the autochthonous could be construed as an anticipatory formulation of the writing of *Don Segundo Sombra*; in both texts, economics is explicitly rejected as a relevant category for any definition of the autochthonous, only to be reintroduced as a master trope in the text's rhetorical organization. In this way, the novel's desire to obliterate the process of its own production through the dismissal of all economic considerations is subverted by the conspicuously economic metaphor that structures the text's tropological design.

In one of those passing references that have become almost a *modus operandi* with him, Borges once described the composition of Güiraldes' major novel in the following manner: "Before Adelina [Güiraldes' wife] transcribed them to the typed page I had many a chance to see the drafts of *Don Segundo Sombra*. Güiraldes wrote his novel in one of those large accounting ledgers with hard black covers, with pages divided into Credits and Debits, that are commonly employed for bookkeeping in cattle ranches."[27] The omnipresent vertical line bisecting the horizontal trace of Güiraldes' writing is an image that must be credited to him, even if, in the end, the balance will necessarily be outstanding.

4

Doña Bárbara

Doña Bárbara stops and listens:
– All things return whence they came.
    Rómulo Gallegos, *Doña Bárbara*[1]

When the first edition of *Doña Bárbara* appeared in 1929, the Venezuelan strong-man, don Juan Vicente Gómez, received alarming reports indicating that the novel was a not-so-veiled indictment of his dictatorial regime. In order to ascertain for himself the accuracy of this accusation, the dictator had the novel read to him by his Minister of Education while enjoying a longed-for vacation on the plains. With nightfall encroaching on the open-air reading scene, an aide suggested the postponement of the reading until the next day, but Gómez, enthralled by the very engaging plot of the novel, vehemently objected. Instead, he had his limousine brought to him, and under the headlights of the automobile the recitation continued well into the night. When it was all over, the dictator broke the silence to say: "This bookworm [*bachiller*] really knows how men work." Soon afterwards, he summarily invested Gallegos with the title of Senator for that region the author had shown he knew so well.[2]

If I have begun the consideration of *Doña Bárbara* with this unusual anecdote, it is because Gómez's phrase could have been penned, *mutatis mutandis*, by countless critics and historians of literature. They too have shared in the dictator's admiration for Gallegos' intimate knowledge of *llano* life, and they, in turn, have granted Gallegos a niche in Latin American literary history. Predictably enough, Gallegos himself furnished ample evidence supporting the accurately mimetic quality of his work in several articles and conversations where he described the genesis of his novel. If the title of one of these – "Cómo conocí a doña Bárbara" – is indicative of the immediacy that Gallegos claims for his writing, the first sentence leaves no room for doubt: "It may not please many of the novel's readers to be told that its characters actually lived in the real world."[3] In the remainder of the essay Gallegos describes a voyage he undertook to the Apure valley in 1927, two years before the publication of *Doña Bárbara*, where in a reverse stroke of Pirandellian good fortune the author stumbled on his characters. The following remark is emblematic of the piece as a whole: "[In San Fernando] I met María Nieves, a herder of the Apure, a river whose alligator-infested waters he used to swim across . . . With name and all I wrote him into my book, and I am told that when anybody tried to banter with him he used to retort: – Be respectful, my friend, for I am in *Doña Bárbara*."[4]

Yet, in another article, Gallegos had endeavored to anticipate and neutralize a predictable objection to this allegation of radical mimesis: the observation that the characters of *Doña Bárbara* are predominantly allegorical. In this piece Gallegos freely admitted the symbolic nature of his narrative, and then proceeded to solve the dilemma with elegant simplicity: his characters were already symbols when he first came upon them during his voyage. Speaking in broader terms about his novelistic production, Gallegos would later remark: "The creative impulse always comes to me after encountering the significant character in the surrounding reality. For if anything is to be a symbol of a form of existence it must exist in itself . . . in direct communication and consubstantiation with the vital environment that produced it and surrounds it. Symbols that are only fed by the author's concepts and imaginings turn into simple puppets from the outset."[5] As a corollary to this insistently mimetic conception of literary representation, Gallegos argued on a number of occasions that he was not an artist, a creator, in the conventional sense of the term.

Gallegos' postulation of symbolic figures that can nonetheless be readily found in the world constitutes also a concise formulation of the conflation of mimesis and abstraction that has traditionally informed critical examination of *Doña Bárbara*. In this fashion one can understand, for instance, how the extensive allegorical dimension of the text was for a long time not considered at odds with what was regarded as the novel's remarkably faithful representation of life on the Venezuelan plains. In more recent times, however, the appreciation of the mimetic fidelity evinced by the novel has waned, forcing critics to come to grips squarely with the text's pervasive allegorical nature. The result is that the novel's standing has been thoroughly compromised by the general disregard bordering on contempt that seems to be the modern fate of most allegorical constructions. Writers in general have been harsher than most critics in this repudiation of Gallegos' most important work. For example, Carlos Fuentes, in a sweeping evaluation of novels similar to *Doña Bárbara*, asserts that the Latin American novel of the "Boom" arose from "the realization that reality is not that simple, Manichean dualism that Ciro Alegría, Jorge Icaza and Rómulo Gallegos depicted for us,"[6] an observation that is repeated approvingly by Gabriel García Márquez.[7] And speaking about cultural contexts in Latin America, Alejo Carpentier echoes the commonplace accusation that Gallegos' novel tried to reduce Latin American reality to facile and simplistic categories: "We are a product of several cultures, we speak several languages and we are the result of differing processes of transculturation. We must find solutions to vast and pressing problems that cannot be resolved with one or two *Doña Bárbaras*."[8]

But regardless of the contemporary disregard for the novel, *Doña Bárbara* enjoyed until the early 1950s an almost unanimous acclaim in critical circles. It is the case that until the advent of the so-called "Boom," it was *the* representative Latin American novel, widely translated and read throughout the world. *Doña Bárbara* benefited from the fact that it was not subjected to the kind of ideological scrutiny that was accorded *Don Segundo Sombra* from the start, probably because Gallegos' middle-class provenance was not as suspect in his case. This is particularly remarkable when one realizes that there is a patently ideological message in *Doña Bárbara* that is virtually identical to the one advanced by Güiraldes' novel: both texts endeavor to shift the grounds for legitimate ownership of the land from a legalistic/genealogical plane into an ethical realm, where personal involvement and the direct assumption of the responsibilities of ownership become the primary criteria. This is, of course, the entire project of reclamation and final redemption represented by Santos Luzardo in *Doña Bárbara*. One can understand this appeal to action in both countries, plagued as they were at the time by absentee ownership of large tracts of land, and both undergoing economic transformations that made the agrarian order of the past seem more secure. But as Carpentier has mordantly remarked, the ending of the novel, with its reconstitution of the original extension of Altamira through the disappearance of doña Bárbara's ranch El Miedo, is a decided affirmation of the landowner's prerogatives and world view. From this perspective, Carpentier suggests, the reformist, future-looking rhetoric of the novel's message is not consistent with the outcome of the events depicted in the text:

Santos Luzardo, who comes from the University of Caracas, a lawyer by training represents Civilization against Barbarism. He arrives in the plain, struggles with the Barbarous Doña Bárbara, and after a momentous conflict in which doña Bárbara is defeated . . . what has really changed here? Has there been any progress? No. The former property of the Luzardos returns to its original boundaries; the owner goes back to his manor and all the progress that has come with Santos Luzardo from the University of Caracas is a spool of barbed wire.[9]

That *Doña Bárbara* was not read in this manner until very recently only confirms the unanimous critical approval that the novel enjoyed for many years; Gallegos' text was regarded by critics of all persuasions as a truly autochthonous literary work. For this reason *Doña Bárbara* is perhaps the text in which the critical continuity that exists between the autochthonous work and its criticism can be most directly perceived. Indeed, on account of this collapse of critical distance, the commentary on the novel sometimes bears an uncanny resemblance to Gallegos' style. Take, for instance, the following fragment from a critical text, where the author speaks about the novel's setting: "The drama of the plain encompasses both the landscape and the beings that inhabit it: from drought to flood and from flood to drought: from a crime to its revenge, and from it to yet another crime: love and hate, life and death in a single vortex."[10] Turning now to Gallegos, one finds in *Doña Bárbara* a passage that obviously serves as source for the critical elaboration: "Death is a pendulum that swings over the plain, from flood to drought, from drought to flood!" (p. 793).

Ultimately, this continuity is dictated by the fact that, as was also the case with *Don Segundo Sombra*, *Doña Bárbara* exhibits an awareness of its own procedures that to a large extent anticipates and overlaps the critical commentary on it: the novel establishes a critical discourse on itself that is subsequently appropriated by critics as their own. Hence, the categories and relationships that the novel postulates as embodying the autochthonous are unproblematically assumed and brought forward by the critics who engage the text. The unquestioning confirmation of the ontologico/literary claims made by *Doña Bárbara* that one can see in the criticism on it arises from this shared critical discursive space where the novel expatiates critically on the nature of the autochthonous. For this reason, it would be instructive to examine in more detail how this space is articulated in Gallegos' text.

Just as in *Don Segundo Sombra*, there is in *Doña Bárbara* the creation of a horizon, a web of assumed relationships that avowedly constitute the autochthonous. But unlike in Güiraldes' text, where the synecdochical relations had to be abstracted from the ongoing narrative on account of the first-person narration, in *Doña Bárbara* the task is made simpler by the narrator's incessant expounding on the existence and propriety of those very assumed relationships. In the following passage, for example, there is an attempt to show how the geography of the *llano*, in its role as stage for human activity, suffuses all aspects of life on the plains: "The Plain makes men crazy and the madness of the inhabitant of this wide and free land is to be always a plainsman. This madness appears . . . in work: in both taming and in wrangling, which are less forms of work than challenges. During the leisure hours it surfaces in the shrewdness of the tale, the ingenuity of the anecdote and the sensuous melancholy of the ballad . . . In friendship and in hatred . . . the Plain, always the Plain" (pp. 556–57). It is in fact this capacity that the plain has to absorb everything that dictates one of the most tenacious conflicts in the novel: the frequent wavering of Santos Luzardo in his confrontation with the inescapable hold that nature has on all things. Geography in *Doña Bárbara* has, to be sure, its destructive side, but this aspect of it is depicted as the downturn of a cycle to which both men and animals are perfectly attuned. This is why geography in the novel is always described with a vocabulary that reflects organicity rather than strife, even when its dangers are emphasized:

This was the beautiful and vigorous life of the wide rivers and vast savannas, where man always goes along singing in the face of danger. The Epic itself. The wild Plain under its most imposing aspect: winter demanding the last bit of patience and daring; floods making risks a hundredfold greater, and making the immensity of the desert all the more apparent from the small stretches of high land; but also accentuating the immensity of man's stature and the powers he possesses when, without anybody's help, he nonetheless resolves to confront whatever may come.

(p. 699)

The relationship that links geography and human activity finds its most synthetic expression in the symbolic figure of the centaur. Regardless of the negative attributes with which Lorenzo Barquero endows it, the centaur proposes on another level the idea of a harmonious combination of man and beast where man is bound to nature in the collaborative enterprise of work. As the reader will remember Santos Luzardo's reclaiming of his diminished patrimony begins formally with the taming of a horse, in a scene that is also described as Luzardo's reconstituting of a forgotten but always accessible oneness with the *llano*. This organic relationship with nature is achieved, in fact, through work: "It is indeed the case that on the Plain one does not tame a horse or lasso a bull without consequences: he who has achieved such a feat belongs henceforth to the Plain ... A plainsman remains a plainsman five generations down the line" (p. 703). Nature and human activity consequently are not at war with each other; their opposing forces are not joined in confrontation, but rather in a continuous relationship of influence and re-molding. Man's activity is geared to the order of nature, and nature in turn yields to the actions of men. In *Doña Bárbara* the reader is witness to the entire natural cycle – drought, torrential rains, storms – and the manner in which human activity inscribes itself within it.

There is also in *Doña Bárbara* the postulation of an unmediated relationship between language and the geographic milieu. The language of the men of the *llano* is endowed with a weight and coherence that has geographical boundaries as well. This explains the use of formulas such as "as the plainsman says" (p. 508) and "as they used to say around there" (p. 602). In addition, there are many instances where the narrator depicts the genesis of some popular expression as a function of natural circumstances of the *llano*. The organic relationship that purportedly links language and geography has its foremost affirmation, however, in the poetry and song of the *llanero* – specifically in the manner in which it is presented as arising from the land itself: "And thus each took as his point of departure the other's last verse, and the life of the Plain was in every quatrain: the ingenuous and sparkling muse of the man in contact with nature went from the tender to the picaresque, from the dream-like to the tragic, without pause or hesitation, as long as there were strings in the guitar and seeds in the *maracas*" (p. 676). This fragment, reminiscent of Herder's conception of the genesis of poetry, is indicative of the immediacy of the relationship between language and land projected by the text.

The synecdochical coupling of geography and language is mirrored by a similarly conceived relationship between language and work. To begin with, the speech of the characters is dominated by figures of speech from their activities as *llaneros*, as the narrator does not fail to observe in a number of instances:

He spit out the bitter saliva of chewed tobacco, and reaching for the metaphoric language of a man raised among cattle he summarized with that joking fatalism of the Venezuelan people:
– As you can see only the yearlings are left; the big cattle, that is, my wife, my sons and their wives, were ruined by parasites.   (p. 529)

– Wake up boys! A new day is here with its morning hares.
So intones Pajarote, who always gets up in good spirits; and his morning hares are – ingenuous metaphor of this herder poet – the rounded clouds that dawn reveals towards the horizon over the dark thickets in the distance.   (p. 557)

In this fashion, the spontaneous surfacing of poetry described earlier seems to subsume also the practical activities and chores of the men, turning them into material for the figurative speech of the *llanero*. Moreover, just as was the case in *Don Segundo Sombra*, the language of the men of the *llano* is saturated with terms pertaining to their *métier*, cattle-ranching. The novel submerges the reader in the particular linguistic universe associated with the manifold activities of the men. This accounts for the long and intricate passages that show the toils of the plainsmen in great detail, textual moments when the density and internal coherence of this linguistic register can come into full view. The specific and somewhat technical terms that are used to describe these activities are compiled in a glossary at the end of the novel, where they are explained in detail to the reader.

The previous fragments have put in evidence the presence of a discourse in *Doña Bárbara* that engages in a ceaseless attempt to make explicit those very relationships that define the autochthonous. This aspect of the text is a manifestation indicative of the critical intention that the *novela de la tierra* encompasses, its incorporation of a critical dimension that endeavors to legitimize the postulates that the writing also takes for granted. This persistent commentary on its own production represents the most effective questioning of the text's grounding assumptions, given its supplementary status with respect to the text. In *Doña Bárbara* this problematic discourse of self-legitimation will be shown below to be related to the prominent presence of allegory in the novel, and to the way in which it will be seen to both organize and undermine the text's system of signification.

" . . . *otra sería mi historia*"

Contributing to the sense of caducity with which *Doña Bárbara* is perceived nowadays is the fact that the novel has consistently been interpreted as yet another document depicting the stale contest between civilization and barbarism that has had such a long history as a metaphor for Latin American reality.[11] One can hardly find fault with such a conception, since the novel seems eager to provide even at the most superficial level the bases for such a response. The text has, in a sense, incorporated into itself its own reading, so that the reader is faced with what could be described as an already-read work, one that conceives of the act of reading as corroboration rather than as interpretation. In this regard, *Doña Bárbara* is a typical instance of the *roman à thèse* as described by Susan Suleiman; a work whose entire rhetorical organization is mobilized with the intention of guaranteeing the imposition of a single reading:

> The story told by a *roman à thèse* is essentially teleological – it is determined by a specific end, which exists "before" and "above" the story. The story calls for unambiguous interpretation, which in turn implies a rule of action applicable (at least virtually) to the real life of the reader. The interpretation and the rule of action may be stated explicitly by a narrator who "speaks with the voice of Truth" and can therefore lay claim to absolute authority, or they may be supplied, on the basis of textual and contextual indices, by the reader. The only necessary condition is that the interpretation and the rule of action be unambiguous – in other words, that the story lend itself as little as possible to a "plural" reading.[12]

To this end, the text resorts to all manner of redundant communication, since redundancy is employed as a strategy of disambiguation. One could say in fact that the discourse of the *roman à thèse* may be characterized by a multiplication of redundancies in an attempt to eliminate the ambiguities that could authorize a reading other than the one proposed by the text.[13] Any reader of *Doña Bárbara* will recognize only too well the presence of such an intention in the work; one could even argue that it is the principal source of the

present-day dissatisfaction with *Doña Bárbara*: the novel is perceived
nowadays as too simplistic, too static or dogmatic, all of these
adjectives that allude indirectly to the text's unyielding desire to
control its own interpretation. One can handily find throughout the
novel many instances of such moments when – as Roland Barthes
has described it – "meaning is excessively named."[14]

This is a quality that *Doña Bárbara* shares with all allegorical
constructs, although at times, Gallegos' novel verges uncomfortably
on the self-mocking (and thereby self-parodying) quality of the
caricaturesque: names such as Santos Luzardo, Mister Dánger and
doña Bárbara, El Miedo and Altamira are also accompanied by a
commentary that is continually interpreting the ongoing narrative
action as a restating of the struggle that the forces of Civilization
must wage against Barbarism. While reading *Doña Bárbara* one must
indeed strain to resist the temptation to share in the Romantic
condemnation of allegory that the following passage by Coleridge
exemplifies: "Now an allegory is but a translation of abstract
notions into picture language, which is itself nothing but an
abstraction from objects of the senses; the principal being more
worthless even than its phantom proxy, both alike unsubstantial,
and the former shapeless to boot . . . empty echoes which the fancy
arbitrarily associates with apparitions of matter."[15] The correlative
Romantic insistence on the alleged superiority of symbol over
allegory has been well established and documented in the exhaustive critical bibliography on the subject.[16] Echoing this view, from
the later part of the eighteenth century onwards allegory has been
persistently understood to be anachronistic or otherwise dismissed
as non-poetic or overly rational. Borges' synopsis of Croce's views
on allegory provides us with a more recent example: "Croce
recognizes no difference between content and form. The former is
the latter and the latter, the former. For him allegory is monstrous
because it seeks to unite two contents in a single form: the literal
(Dante, guided by Virgil, reaches Beatrice), and the figurative (man
finally arrives to faith, guided by reason). He thinks that such a
manner of composition entails arduous enigmas."[17] Hence, it must
be realized that to decry, as most contemporary critics do, the
allegorical nature of *Doña Bárbara*, is to share in an attitude that is
subsumed by what is now a commonplace gesture in literary
modernity. One cannot expect that such a view will afford any new
insights into a novel whose appreciation by critics already suffers

from a disregard born of excessive familiarity. Moreover, as we
shall see, the presence of allegory in *Doña Bárbara* is not as
uncomplicated as the text itself, and its critics, would lead one to
believe. For alternatively, one could interpret the novel's constant
recourse to interpretation in a way that would suggest the presence
in the text of a certain anxiety with respect to the status of its own
meaning. In a book that studies the occurrence of similar interpretive moments in the narrative of Realism, William Stowe has
summarized this very dynamics in the following fashion: "The text
deemphasizes its need for interpretation, by systematically interpreting itself. This self-interpretation, however, may be read as a
device designed by an anxious author to convince the reader that
the meaning of the text is all on the surface, and therefore as a sign
that there is a more repressed, perhaps even unconscious meaning
to be found beneath the surface."[18] I would like to re-formulate
Stowe's suggestion and propose that the introjection of a persistent
interpretive discourse in *Doña Bárbara* could be taken as expressive
of the text's unease regarding the possibility of ever making itself
unambiguously, perfectly clear. Hence, the meaning whose sup-
pression is signalled by the recurrent performance of interpretation
in the novel would be the knowledge that meaning is unstable and
slippery; that it always requires for its existence the kind of
assertive overdetermination in which the text engages. As such, one
could propose that this aspect of the novel could function as a
veiled commentary on signification in a general sense, as well as on
the specific manner in which it is practiced in *Doña Bárbara* itself. In
order to ascertain the relevance of this remark I propose to explore
in more detail the issues and difficulties raised by the very presence
of allegory in Gallegos' text.

The allegorical structure of *Doña Bárbara* can be confidently
reconstructed from almost any random fragment of the novel, so
pervasive and systematic is the interplay between the two interpretive planes of the text. Santos Luzardo is a figure that refers to a
homogeneous semantic field that encompasses all the values and
conventions of civilization – the city, progress, inventions and,
perhaps above all, the law. Conversely, doña Bárbara is associated
with elements that fall under the rubric of barbarism – violence,
lawlessness, insalubrity and backwardness. The confrontation
between Santos Luzardo and doña Bárbara finds its ulterior
meaning in that other register where the two primordial impulses

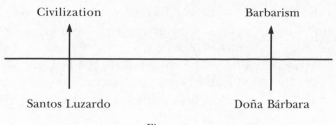

Figure 1

battle each other in what can only be described as a Manichean conception of Venezuelan or perhaps even Latin American reality. There have been – it should be noted – some recent critical attempts to soften the rigidly antithetical character of the relationship between the two forces by pointing, for example, to the way in which Luzardo shows his appreciation at times for the barbaric, unreconstructed state of the *llano*, or the manner in which doña Bárbara succumbs momentarily to noble impulses.[19] Nonetheless, these moments do not, I believe, throw into question or otherwise challenge the essential doctrinaire intention of the novel, although the wavering they represent can perhaps be recovered and explained by the argument that will be developed below.

The allegorical structure of *Doña Bárbara*, then, could be schematically represented as in Figure 1. Santos Luzardo and Doña Bárbara share a given manifest plane that alludes in turn to another level where their actions acquire a transcendent meaning as a confrontation between Civilization and Barbarism. Of particular interest in this schematic rendition is the interpretive dimension established by the backwards glance of the manifest content to the latent form that defines and endows it with a fullness of meaning that it does not possess on its own. Such is the level constituted in *Doña Bárbara* by the obtrusive commentary that seeks to evince and explicate the allegorical nature of the novel, a gesture that sometimes acquires rather ludicrous complexions. This aspect is already synthetically inscribed in the onomastic structure of the text, with names like doña Bárbara and Altamira; but it also finds its representation in fragments analogous to the following: "It was the same tendency to heedless action that had caused the Luzardos' demise, except that he subordinated it to an ideal. To struggle against doña Bárbara, the personification of the prevailing circumstances, would mean not only to save Altamira, but also to contribute to the destruction of those forces that held back progress on the plain" (p. 511). This discourse of legitimation exists in the novel to propose a concordance between the two levels of the allegorical narrative; its purpose is to establish the fact that the interpretive operation that it describes is an essential component of the novel, one without which the latter's meaning would be incomplete.

Nonetheless, an attentive reading of *Doña Bárbara* reveals that the presence of allegory in the text is not just circumscribed, as in the previous quotation, to the overarching conceit that relates Luzardo and doña Bárbara to Civilization and Barbarism respectively; on the contrary, allegory can also be seen to function in the novel as Gallegos' principal rhetorical device for the composition of the narrative events themselves. In other words, the doctrinaire allegorical intention of the novel dictates that there must be a struggle between Santos Luzardo and doña Bárbara, which in turn must be interpreted as alluding to the conflict between the abstract concepts of Civilization and Barbarism; I have already remarked on some of the strategies used by the text to guarantee such an interpretation. And yet, one can further establish that allegory is simultaneously used by Gallegos *also* as a means of depicting the very struggle between doña Bárbara and Santos Luzardo that constitutes the novel's argument. Consequently, allegory in *Doña Bárbara* is not just an interpretive intention projected into the text, but also a narrative technique extensively employed to construct the events depicted in the novel.

There is a large number of instances throughout the work that can be produced to substantiate this observation. One of the highlights of *Doña Bárbara* is the scene where Pajarote and María Nieves, two of Luzardo's men, ambush and kill the Tuerto del Bramador, an enormous and fierce alligator that had terrorized both men and livestock in the region for countless years. The account of this significant episode begins with the text's unequivocal identification of the terrible beast with doña Bárbara: "Its habitual hunting grounds were at the entrance to the Bramador channel, now in doña Bárbara's property; from there it lorded over the Arauca and all its tributaries . . . The channel was its safe haven since doña Bárbara, mindful of the animal's reputation as a bewitching beast, had expressly forbidden that it be attacked" (p. 658). Luzardo's peons, hiding under an elaborately camouflaged canopy, finally manage to get close enough to the unsuspecting reptile; a struggle ensues:

The muddy waters boiled, an enormous mass thrashed convulsively around, and a fearful tail rose again and again in the air with a terrific splash each time it struck the water. Finally the alligator turned over and lay still, its gigantic white belly floating upwards and its sides spewing blood. Then Pajarote and María Nieves rose from under the water to exclaim:

– God Almighty!

And a roar of applause came from those on shore:

– Goodbye to the Terror of the Bramador!

– And such will be the fate of all spells from El Miedo, because now we have the spell-breaker here. (p. 659)

Given the identification of the beast with doña Bárbara explicitly advanced at the beginning of the scene, the contest between Santos Luzardo's men and the alligator is depicted by the text as alluding allegorically to the struggle between Luzardo and doña Bárbara: In this scene, the two novelistic antagonists confront each other by proxy, so to say. The propriety of this interpretation is, of course, vouched for by the last recorded voice in the fragment just cited; through it, the validating commentary that is typical of allegory is introduced into the novelistic scene as an anonymous voice coming from the group of men that have just witnessed the events described.

An identical allegorical construction can be seen at work in the presentation of many other narrative events as well. One such instance is especially significant, since it concerns one of the few times in *Doña Bárbara* when the two protagonists are in each other's presence. Soon after his arrival in Altamira, Santos had proposed to doña Bárbara that they should both contribute their men in order to have a rodeo to sort out the stray cattle on their properties. Doña Bárbara, sensing an opportunity that could be manipulated to her advantage, agrees to Luzardo's request. Once the rodeo has started, Santos finds himself in pursuit of a formidable bull, "the white-faced one that has been giving us trouble for two years – Pajarote announced" (p. 645). Remembering the skills he acquired as a child, Santos ropes the animal and, after a brief struggle, the bull is forced into submission, castrated and branded with Altamira's iron. Here one of Luzardo's men interjects: " – This one won't bother us again," to which Pajarote confidently adds: " – I guess the big devil must be a loyal Luzardero and didn't want any other brand on him but the one his mother had. He was just waiting for the owner to come home to surrender himself to him. That's why we could not rope him during the last rodeo" (pp. 646–47). Pajarote's story regarding the men's inability to tame the bull in the past, and the contrast it establishes with Luzardo's triumph in the present, attests to the allegorical nature of the entire experience. Once again, the interpretive commentary provided by one of the characters at the scene demands that the event be understood as an allegorical repostulation of the contest between Santos Luzardo and doña Bárbara.

Another well-known passage evinces an analogous recourse to allegory as a narrative strategy. Upon his return to Altamira, Santos had been anticipating his encounter with the overseer Balbino Paiba who, in confabulation with doña Bárbara, had worked for years to erode Luzardo's land and property. When the awaited interview finally takes place, Santos foils Paiba's scheme to intimidate and humiliate the owner into recognizing his authority at the ranch. In the meantime, and within earshot of Santos' verbal manhandling of the ex-overseer, some of Luzardo's ranch-hands are attempting to subdue and saddle a horse that one of them will ride for the first time. The parallelism between the two situations does not go unnoticed by the men:

Pajarote, turning to María Nieves and Venancio – who were in the corral awaiting the climax to the little drama although apparently busy preparing lengths of rope to hobble the colt – shouted meaningfully:

– Come on, cowboys! Haven't you got that bronco hobbled yet? Look how he's shaking with rage. You'd think he was afraid. And he has only seen the hobble so far: what will he do when we've got him pinned to the ground?

– We'll see pretty soon. Let's see him try to throw off this hobble as he did the others! – added the two peons laughing at the double meaning [*doble intención*] of their friend's words, which referred as much to Balbino as to the colt. (p. 560)

As in the previous situations discussed, the narrative endeavors to call attention to the necessity of an interpretive operation to be performed on the event depicted; the reference to the existence of a "double meaning" to the words proffered by the men underscores in no uncertain terms the allegorical design of the novelistic passage. The same figural strategy reappears in the account of how Melquíades, alias El Brujeador, doña Bárbara's henchman, is tricked by a horse that he had been stalking for an entire night:

Some nights later, in his task of stealing Altamira's troops of mares the Brujeador pursued one that gave him plenty to do, because the stallion that led it ran for the open prairie, avoiding the thickets and moving at a steady gallop. Besides, there was a dense fog that made it impossible to see more than a short distance ahead. When daybreak came, the band of horses was in exactly the same place where Melquíades had raised it . . . This was the first time that the Brujeador had been fooled by a horse, and since this seemed to him a bad omen, he referred the incident to doña Bárbara.

. . .

– You too, Melquíades? You say the stud turned you in circles without you noticing it? I can tell now there is a real man in Altamira that is not afraid of the phantoms of the plain! (p. 717)

In this case it is doña Bárbara herself who provides the commentary that identifies the latent meaning of the story she has just heard, all the more unnerving to her since that meaning is expressive of the weakening of her power in the face of Luzardo's return.

But perhaps the most instructive passage from the perspective I wish to elucidate is the famous chapter in which Santos' attempts to educate Marisela are detailed. There can be little question that this section makes explicit a homology established in the novel between Santos' efforts to reform doña Bárbara's daughter and his overall project to civilize the plains. Luzardo's pedagogical enterprise with respect to Marisela only finds its complete meaning in its allusion to a similar constructive molding of the forces of the *llano*: "'In this as in many other things your instincts lead you swiftly and correctly' – Santos concluded, satisfied with the qualities of the girl's nature, strong and malleable at once; for he perceived in Marisela a personification of the country's soul, open, like the landscape, to any project of reform" (p. 624). This allegorical complementation explains the attention devoted in the novel to the depiction of Luzardo's educational program. And yet, Santos' efforts are themselves allegorically mirrored, at yet another level, in the simultaneous narrative that describes the taming of the mare La Catira by one of his men, a comparison that is clearly announced in the plural in the chapter's title – "The tamers" ["*Los amansadores*"] – and carefully sustained throughout the section. This proliferation of allegorical relations is, as I have endeavored to show, characteristic of the entire text of *Doña Bárbara*. I would like to address at this point its implications for the status of allegory in the novel.

If the previous collection of narrative instances is examined it can be established that, regardless of the difference in their manifest content, they all point in the final analysis to the same latent subtext: the conflict between Santos Luzardo and doña Bárbara. Therefore, the confrontation between Luzardo and his antagonist is represented in the text indirectly, through the accumulation of allegorically structured scenes such as the ones that have been cited – that is to say, narrated events that have in turn as their latent meaning Santos' weakening and defeat of doña Bárbara. Nevertheless, this realization brings with it significant implications regarding the function of allegory in the novel, since, as it was ascertained during the discussion of the doctrinaire message advanced by *Doña Bárbara*, the struggle between Luzardo and doña Bárbara is *itself* the vehicle through which the larger strife between civilization and barbarism is enacted. Earlier we had seen the text submitting the existence of a univocal, direct and unambiguous relationship between its two allegorical levels, with the confrontation between doña Bárbara and Santos Luzardo serving as a surface restating of the primordial yet latent conflict between the forces of Civilization and Barbarism. Yet, the analysis of the passages above reveals that what was originally postulated as manifest meaning has become *itself* the latent content to a different allegorical register in the same text, susceptible in turn to further allegorical treatment, as the Marisela/La Catira episode shows. Thus, the diagram depicting the original allegorical relationship would now appear as shown in Figure 2. The profligate, built-upon presence of allegory in *Doña Bárbara* creates, then, a sort of monstrosity: a level of the text that functions both as manifest *and* latent content simultaneously, depending on which allegorical plane or perspective one wishes to assume. In the end, this iterative employment of allegory necessarily has the effect of weakening the adequacy and propriety of the original allegorical formulation, since it casts doubt on the finality and immobility of the latent sign whose function is to complement the meaning inscribed in the manifest level; that is, there can be no guarantee that the presumed final stopping point of the allegorical chain thus established will not become itself a manifest level to a "deeper," yet more fundamental content. This development points to the impossibility of arresting at any one privileged place the backwards glance of allegory and achieving the plenitude of meaning ostensibly promised by the interpretive displacement of the allegorical movement. One has

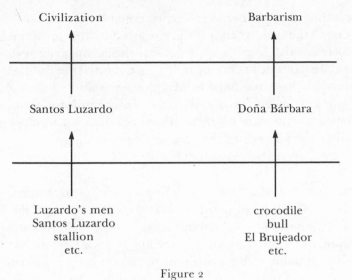

Figure 2

instead a succession of similar authenticating gestures whose coexistence in the same text only serves to undermine the singularity and hence the validity of the relationship that they purport to demonstrate.

This dynamics that puts into question the text's own signifying procedures may account not only for the excessive use of commentary in the novel, but also for the anxiety manifested by the recurrent description of interpretive performances in *Doña Bárbara*. Thus, for example, the village idiot Juan Primito "reads" in the changing predilections of his imaginary vultures – the *rebullones* – the transformations in doña Bárbara's mercurial moods and desires; she in turn strives to interpret the meaning behind the words of El Socio, the sinister supernatural presence with whom she supposedly communicates. Likewise, the viability of Santos' civilizing project – and his soul – are saved decisively by Marisela's meticulous interpretation of Santos' own account of the death of doña Bárbara's hired assassin, El Brujeador, whereby she demonstrates convincingly to Luzardo that he could not possibly have fired the bullet that accomplished the deed. Hence, the awareness that meaning is constantly in danger of slipping translates itself into an obsessive recourse to scenes where interpretation is featured as a legitimizing operation in the novel.[20]

One of the most salient examples of the problematic status of interpretation in *Doña Bárbara* is represented by the glosary that is appended to the text, where peculiar terms that appear in the novel are gathered and defined. This is not surprising, since the glossary is representative of a desire on the text's part to interpret itself, even in the reduced scope envisioned by the glossary's limited dimensions. In the glossary, the novel takes itself as its own interpretive object in an attempt to translate itself, to illuminate its own formulations. Hence, one can discern in the glossary's intention an activity that recalls the allegorical commentary that is so prevalent in the novel.[21]

Upon first consideration, the glossary seems to entertain an uncomplicated relationship of elucidation with respect to the main body of the novel. Indeed, without it one would be hard-pressed to understand lines such as the following: " – Apuren muchachos, reclamaba Antonio – . Y los que tengan caballos chucutos crinejeen de una vez, porque vamos a llegar picando" (p. 672). A swift consultation of the glossary reveals that the speaker, a ranch-hand, is alluding to a commonplace operation pertaining to the dressing of a horse before driving a herd of cattle. But the apparent transparency of the glossary's function and location *vis-à-vis* the text it accompanies soon begins to give way to a more complex interaction between the two. In order to understand better the nature of this development I must digress for a moment into a synoptic view of the historical transformation of the glossary into its present-day format.

Glossography had its beginnings chiefly in the context of Medieval hermeneutical endeavors. Scholars and commentators, in the course of reading the manuscript texts of classical authors, the Bible and early Christian and profane writers, on encountering obscure or ambiguous terms would write above them, or in the margins, interpretations or explanations in an attempt to clarify or define the term in question. The interpretations written above the lines were called interlinear, and those executed in the margins of the manuscript marginal glosses. Later on, from these glossed manuscripts glossaries were compiled; that is, the obscure words together with their interpretations were excerpted and collected in companion volumes in the order in which they appeared in the manuscript, with the name of the author or the title of the book whence they were taken placed at the heading of each volume. After some time, the glosses came to be ordered in alphabetical sequence, according to the first letter of the word interpreted, but still arranged in order to conform with the internal divisions of the glossed original. A final operation collected all the available glosses in alphabetical order to create those vast catalogues that the Medieval mind treasured so highly.[22]

If this brief excursus into an account of the successive stages in the development of the glossary has been deemed necessary, it is because the historical description of glossography as a hermeneutical enterprise brings to the fore the intermediate stages that the final version of the glossary suppresses or does not show readily. That is to say, the creation of every glossary repeats, at least in principle, the major stages of this itinerary: the singling out of words in the original, their compilation, the final alphabetical rearrangement and transposition of the chosen terms into a separate text. This recapitulation of glossarial phylogeny (so to speak) that obtains in the compilation of every glossary, allows us to conceptualize a glossary as the outcome of a sequence of textual transformations that leave their faint individual traces in the finished version of the glossary. Accordingly, one could assert that there is a temporal dimension to the spatial arrangement of exclusion that separates the text of *Doña Bárbara* from the glossary that follows it. Hence, the glossary's external location with respect to the body of the novel is meant to signal also that the interpretive operation that it represents occurs *after* the text as well. The presence of the glossary in *Doña Bárbara*, then, proposes the idea of Gallegos as both author and exegete of his own work, a division that congeals as it were the text of the novel, and places it outside of, and yet at the origin of an interpretive chronology where the glossary's commentary supposedly unfolds itself. Nonetheless, this temporal "fable" of the glossary's interpretive function is dismantled by the fact that Gallegos has projected into the novel his supposedly *a posteriori* role as interpreter of the text by including in the body of the novel traces of the "composition" of the glossary: In fact, he inscribes glosses in the text in much the same way in which those early Medieval glossators wrote theirs in the interstices of the manuscript they were elucidating. The presence of this annotating function can be felt throughout the entire text of *Doña Bárbara*. Take, for instance, the following scene, where a ranch-hand informs Santos Luzardo that some stray, unmarked cattle have been captured: " – Today we *rounded up* [*cachilapiamos*] about fifty head of cattle in a single round-up – Sandoval said to him." At this point there is a break in the narration, a textual opening that is employed for the insertion of an involved, technical commentary on the practice alluded to:

Cachilapear, that is to say, lassoing unbranded cattle found within the limits of the ranch, is the favorite sport of the Apure plainsman. Given that the lands in those limitless prairies are not enclosed, the herds are free to wander, and ownership of the cattle is acquired by every ranch owner either in the round-ups undertaken in concert with neighbors in which each gathers and brands whatever yearlings or unmarked steers he collects; or outside of these, at any time, by the natural right of the noose. This primitive form of acquisition . . . somewhat resembles old-fashioned rustling, and that is why it is not so much a form of work as a diversion for the men of the open plain, where might still always makes right. (p. 591)

Later in the novel, doña Bárbara agrees to cooperate with Luzardo in the rounding-up of cattle in a scene that was alluded to earlier. Once the two groups have assembled, Antonio, *mayoral* of Altamira, invites his counterpart in El Miedo – the villainous Balbino Paiba – to accompany him in the labor. Thinking himself one notch above Luzardo's man, Paiba declines the offer: "Thank you, don Antonio. But I will stay right here with the *Whites* [*el blancaje*]." Once again, the urge to annotate takes over the text: "The plainsman uses this term to refer to a gathering of the ranch owners who are present at the rodeo not to participate in the proceedings but in order to look after their affairs when the gathered cattle are ready to be apportioned" (p. 641). Instances like these, varying in length and abruptness, can be readily found in the text; the format is almost invariably the same, that is, with the glossing commentary closely following the written representation of the word that is singled out for explanation. Hence, for example:

– I have hardly been able to round up forty stray head this year. And by the way, would you be willing to buy them from me? I am in need of some money and would give you a good deal.
– Are the old brandings *well disguised* [*cachapeados*]?
Cachapear, that is, to make the original brand in a steer disappear in order to sell it as one's own, was one of Balbino Paiba's foremost skills. (p. 766)

Sometimes, though, one finds less conspicuous instances of the phenomenon:

– Melquíades, maybe you can drive some wild animals for me to the corral at La Matica . . .
The corral at La Matica was the place where Balbino kept the cattle that

he skimmed from doña Bárbara, and this sort of theft, because they were the acts of the mayordomo, were called in El Miedo: *mayordomear*.

(pp. 713–14)

Culling all these instances, one realizes that if the glossary's explanatory authority depends on its external status with respect to the novel, then that authority has been undermined by the evident incorporation of the glossary into the body of the novel. By this stroke, the glossary becomes an excess, an unnecessary repetition, a surplus; another attempt at interpretation that resolves itself in the production of yet another text. In addition, a careful examination of the glossary shows that it can never be the pristine aid that it purports to be; its supposed explanatory function is further called into question when one realizes that the imaginary line between the two linguistic columns is no guarantee that the two linguistic registers on whose separation the glossary's effectiveness resides will not commingle. For at times the explanation of a certain term will include words that are themselves defined somewhere else in the glossary, so that the ultimate meaning of a given word will be clouded over by the iterative accumulation of translation upon translation. The following sequence is illustrative of the self-referential quality that I am referring to:

Chischeo:　Onomatopoeia for the sound made by the *maracas*.
Maraca:　Percussive musical instrument, made with a round gourd, that has *capacho* seeds inside.
Capachos:　Seeds from the plant of the same name that serve as rattles for the *maracas*.　　　　　　　　　　(pp. 800–3)

This particularity gives the glossary a circularity and density of its own that belies its apparently uncomplicated status *vis-à-vis* the novel. Thus, the attempt to make the text more accessible, more pristine, only succeeds in producing yet another text, itself in need of commentary since by using the very terms it endeavors to define it retreats into a circular opacity of its own. This situation is analogous to the one identified before during the discussion on the proliferation of allegory in *Doña Bárbara*, where the attempt to postulate a univocal relation between signs was undermined by a succession of similarly conceived allegorical operations, each one of them capable of alluding to yet another level of signs, to another text.

Ultimately, it could be argued that the dismantling of the allegorical intention of *Doña Bárbara* can be understood as a function of the very allegorical nature of the text. In a well-known essay Paul de Man has proposed that the essence of allegory is such that it can be taken as a demystifying commentary on signification in general. What we have in allegory, he says, "is a relationship between signs [that] necessarily contains a constitutive temporal element; it remains necessary, if there is to be allegory, that the allegorical sign refer to another sign that precedes it. The meaning constituted by the allegorical sign can then consist only in the *repetition* of a previous sign with which it can never coincide, since it is of the essence of this previous sign to be pure anteriority."[23] And yet, this predicament sets the stage for an endless repetition of this authenticating gesture, expressive of allegory's desire for concordance. Joel Fineman has acutely observed in this regard that allegory, "distanced at the beginning from its source, will set out on an increasingly futile search for a signifier with which to recuperate the fracture of and at its source, and with each successive signifier the fracture and the search begin again: a structure of continual yearning, the insatiable desire of allegory."[24] This explains why exorbitance and surfeit always seem to constitute the hallmarks of all allegorical formulations.[25] The breach that is posited by allegory is an acknowledgement of the unbridgeable difference that haunts all attempts at signification, an admission of the essential tension inherent in all signifying practices. What makes this demystifying dimension of allegory particularly compelling is the paradoxical fact that it obtains in a discourse obsessed with describing the propriety of the relationship between the two elements that constitute it as a sign. This is the case because allegory exists in the midst of a dialectics of revelation and concealment: the knowledge about signification that allegory embodies offers itself in the form of an assertion of propriety that the very presence of allegory denies. In *Doña Bárbara* the legitimacy of this claim to propriety – embodied in the doctrinal allegorical message of the novel – is weakened by the repetitive and consecutive use of allegory, a practice that allows surplus and excess to exhaust and dissipate the strength of the original formulation. The veritable proliferation of allegoresis in the novel brings implicit with it the understanding that in allegory anything can stand for anything else, provided there is a discursive will that suppresses the knowledge represented by that very insight.[26]

What is even more significant is the fact that the text's erosion of its allegorical authority seems to undermine also the hierarchy of

values inherent in the doctrinaire statement of the novel; that is, the
narrator's ideological identification with Santos Luzardo and, by
extension, with the forces of civilization. For if we heed the text's
commentary on its own failed signifying practice, we see that doña
Bárbara is a more appropriate symbol for the knowledge that is
enacted by the text. If Santos is identified with the impulse towards
the open future, progress and modernization, doña Bárbara is
represented as the exact opposite: a woman whose present is entirely
dominated and explained by a brutal event in her past: the ravishing
of a young girl by a crew of drunken river pirates. This characterization of doña Bárbara is reminiscent in the novel of the backwards
glance of allegory towards that previous latent content that endows
its surface formulation with meaning. And yet, the demystifying
quality of allegory is also reflected in the nature of Doña Bárbara's
relationship to that critically significant moment in her past. For
every time doña Bárbara attempts to evoke that fateful event, she
encounters not the painful shudder of lived experience but quite
literally, another text. Her attempts at recreating that primordial
scene invariably take the form of a quotation – citation marks and all
– from that earlier text that tells of her savage rape. Thus, for
instance, when she first learns of Luzardo's return she tries to
deceive her lover Paiba into thinking that her mysterious powers
allow her to see Santos in the bottom of a glass of water; in the
middle of this ruse, she falls unexpectedly silent:

In the meantime, doña Bárbara had placed the glass of water back on the
table without drinking from it, overcome by a sudden recollection that
threw a cloud over her face:
"It happened on a river boat . . . Far away, beyond the profound silence,
the hoarse roar of the Atures rapids could be heard . . . Suddenly the *yacabó*
shrieked . . ."

. . .

The lamp began to flicker and finally went out. Doña Bárbara remained
seated at the table, her harsh and gloomy thoughts still fixed on that fateful
moment of the past:
"Far away, beyond the profound silence, the hoarse roar of the Atures
rapids could be heard . . . Suddenly the *yacabó* shrieked . . ."   (p. 545)

Much later, when she is endeavoring to mend her ways that Santos
might love her, she has a similar recollection: "It was as if the city
wished to remind her of previous deeds that she was endeavoring to
forget. It seemed to be whispering in her ear: "To be loved by a man

such as Luzardo one cannot have a past." And her own story came to her, as usual, from its very beginning: 'It happened in a river boat that traversed the mighty rivers of the rubber fields . . . '" (p. 790).

Doña Bárbara's tragic irredeemability in the novel stems not so much from an intrinsic malevolence as from her repeated but failed attempts to collapse past and present in the figure of Luzardo: "For an instant, while facing the water landscape, Santos' image had blurred in her mind with the imprecise picture of Asdrúbal that she still retained; one seemed as distant as the other, shadows that receded while dissolving in the uncertain light of a fanciful world" (p. 793). For this conflation to take place, however, history would have to be abolished and, as the previous quotations assert, this is an impossibility, not only because she does have a history, but also because there is an inescapable temporal predicament to allegory that can never be resolved in simultaneity. It is significant in this regard that doña Bárbara's insight that "all things return whence they came" – a concise expression of allegorical propriety – occurs in the novel simultaneously with her probable self-immolation and effective disappearance from the text.

But doña Bárbara is also representative of the novel's surreptitious knowledge regarding signification because she is described as motivated by pure, uncontrolled desire. This is why as she herself expresses it, the concept of limit is so hateful to her: "Nothing could please her less than this news of a boundary. When her ambition for more territory was mentioned she would answer mockingly: – But I am not half as grasping as I am depicted. I am just satisfied with a bit of land, enough so that I can always be at the center of my property, regardless of where I might be" (p. 606). Doña Bárbara's statement appeals rhetorically to a concept of property based on the structuring idea of a center and the circumference determined by it; nonetheless, her peculiar version of property defines this center as movable, and its displacement ruled by boundless, unreflecting desire, as expressed by the phrase "regardless of where I might be." Hence, property in this scheme becomes an impossibility, not only because the very grounding idea of the concept of property is destroyed, but because property ceases to have any meaning when it encompasses everything. Or better yet, property becomes a matter of will, an unending succession of congealments of the circumference that is defined by this perpetually displacing center.[27] This description recalls the earlier discussion of the problematic presence of allegory in *Doña Bárbara*, where the propriety postulated by the allegorical structure of the novel was undone by the excessive recourse to allegory in the text: just as is the case with property, meaning too ceases to have any meaning at all when anything can mean anything else.

It is thus that in doña Bárbara's violent, poignant nature we can perceive an emblem of the novel's contradictory comments on its own economy of signification. Doña Bárbara's doomed project to bring together present and past is reminiscent of allegory's desire to guarantee the necessity of the relation between signifier and signified; in her failure one can see an awareness of the temporal problematic and self-demystification that is constitutive of all allegorical constructions. In this fashion, doña Bárbara, the embodiment of negative attributes in the novel, is at the same time the best representative of the text's own dialectics, a circumstance perhaps foreshadowed from the outset by the title Gallegos chose for a text that also demands to be read as an apology of the forces of civilization.

Given that this is a knowledge that is constitutive of allegory, any reading that purports to demystify an allegorical text is bound in turn to be mystified by it. Such is the case, for instance, with a recent masterful and masterly reading of *Doña Bárbara* by Roberto González Echevarría.[28] In it González proposes that the struggle between Santos Luzardo and doña Bárbara stands for a conflict between two kinds of writing: one founded on propriety and legitimacy (Santos Luzardo), and the other – identified with doña Bárbara – unbounded and disseminatory:

As a lawyer, he [Santos Luzardo] specializes in the encoding and interpretation of language in its relation to reality. In a very significant way he is a writer and a reader. Doña Bárbara is also a reader, since her supernatural powers enable her to read the future, not in documents but in the signs she discovers in the reality around her. She is a writer as well: she reiterates a number of times in the novel that she has rewritten the Law of the Plain and that the property titles, not to mention boundaries and cattle brands, have been rewritten according to her whims and to her desire to monopolize everything.[29]

The result is, as González would have it, that *Doña Bárbara* can be interpreted as "a tragic fable about the contradictory nature of writing."[30] Nevertheless, the evident *allegorical* nature of this reading makes it impossible to dismantle radically the authority of allegory in *Doña Bárbara*; in interpreting Gallegos' novel as an allegory about the inadequacy of the novel's allegorical intention, González's reading has merely accomplished yet another allegorical restating of the confrontation between Santos Luzardo and doña Bárbara, identical in status to the others that I have cited above – regardless of its metatextual position *vis-à-vis* the novel.[31] In other words, by incurring in the very proliferation of allegory with which – as I have suggested – the novel undermines its own allegorical pretensions, González's critical performance exemplifies the inevitable belatedness of criticism with respect to the self-demystifying capacity of the allegorical text.

That this should be the case should come as no surprise: If at a superficial, ideological level *Doña Bárbara* attempts to reduce its interpretation to a single meaning, in its unceasing allegorical transformation it anticipates every effort to read and interpret it, given that every interpretation can be construed as an attempt to produce another narrative, another story that will stand for the text it confronts. "It is not often realized," Northrop Frye has said, "that all commentary is allegorical interpretation, an attaching of ideas to the structure of poetic imagery. The instant that any critic permits himself to make a genuine comment about a poem . . . he has begun to allegorize."[32] Or in the words of Fredric Jameson, "interpretation proper . . . always presupposes, if not a conception of the unconscious itself, then at least some mechanism of mystification or repression in terms of which it would make sense to seek a latent meaning behind a manifest one, or to rewrite the surface categories of a text in the stronger language of a more fundamental interpretive code."[33] In this fashion, Gallegos' novel incorporates the proleptic knowledge of its interpretation, its inevitable future transformation into something else through an act of critical will. Hence, the text of *Doña Bárbara* confronts the reader with an anticipation of his or her critical performance that threatens that performance with an intimation of its superfluousness. That is why it becomes necessary for us to misread *Doña Bárbara*, to denounce it as simplistic, to be oblivious to the knowledge that it advances, if we are to insist on interpreting it at all. For in the end, even the most rigorous critical performance will only manage to establish the insight that was present in the work in the first place, and only as the outcome of yet another interpretive transformation of the text. And by then, of course, it would be – as it is for us now – entirely too late.

Read from this perspective, *Doña Bárbara* becomes a truly gripping text, undeserving of the accusations leveled at it by modern interpreters. One can only hope that this new examination of the novel will provide an incentive for a comprehensive revalorization of Rómulo Gallegos, perhaps the most neglected of Latin America's major writers of the recent past.[34]

5

La vorágine

– I can furnish proof, if you so wish.
– All good prose has some verses – argued Rivera.
– True; but not entire stanzas.
– But there are no stanzas in *La vorágine*.
– There are; not good ones to be sure, but they are there.
– I bet you a dinner for ten that you cannot find a single stanza – the poet Rivera said finally, certain of his claim.
  (Account of a conversation between Rivera and a friend detailing a wager he subsequently lost.)[1]

Upon first consideration, it would seem unusual for José Eustasio Rivera's novel *La vorágine* to be included in the same breath with *Doña Bárbara* and *Don Segundo Sombra*. To begin with, Rivera's work does not evince the overt nationalistic inclinations of the other two novels; there is no counterpart here for the gaucho or the *llanero* as archetypal representative of national character. Furthermore, the general tone of the novel is one of great pessimism and defeat, contrary to the other two texts, where all setbacks and violent events are overcome through the affirmation of a larger transcendent order. Still, for many years *La vorágine*, along with its Venezuelan and Argentine counterparts, has been widely considered one of the paramount examples of the *novela de la tierra*.

I would argue that *La vorágine*'s dissimilarity with the other two novels is essentially the result of a shift in sign from positive to negative in the conception of autochthony that rules the text; that is, the qualities that differentiate it from the works examined earlier are attributable to the fact that it portrays what can be described as a negative autochthonous condition. The relationships among the constitutive elements of the autochthonous discourse that have been identified before are present here as well; but instead of consonance and correspondence there is disjointedness and mutual annihilation. This becomes clear in the text's depiction of the most salient geographical locus of *La vorágine*, the jungle. If in the other novels the land was perceived as quietly suffusing all beings with a beneficent influence, in the jungle of Rivera's novel the relationship is overwhelming and pernicious: "Here: the croaking of dropsical frogs, the entangled misanthropic undergrowth, the stagnant backwaters of putrid channels. Here: the aphrodisiac parasites that cover the ground with dead bees; the disgusting blooms that throb with sensual palpitations, and whose sticky smell intoxicates like a drug; the malignant vine, whose hairs blind animals; the *pringamosa* that irritates the skin . . . "[2] By the same token, where the other novels emphasized the openness of the geographic milieu and the boundless opportunities it presents to human action, the jungle offers these same possibilities but in an illusory and contradictory fashion:

Slave, do not bewail your bondage; prisoner, do not lament your condition; you ignore the torture that is to meander freely in a dungeon such as the jungle where the ceiling is green and the walls are enormous rivers. You have not experienced the torment of shadows, when you can see the sun illuminating a faraway shore that can never be reached! The chain that gnaws at your ankles is more considerate than the leeches in these swamps; the jailer that tortures you is not as stern as the trees that watch us without a sound!   (p. 230)

The overwhelming power of nature is reflected in the exorbitant, hyperbolic tone of the protagonist's language throughout the novel. The heightened rhetoric of the poet Arturo Cova could be taken as conveying the equally disproportionate dimensions of the natural environment that it presumably reflects; however, his strident discourse is not the result of consonance between language and nature, as in the other texts, but rather of the existence of an unbridgeable disconnection between them that resolves itself in the poet's melodramatic excess. Hence, the language of nature only becomes intelligible to Cova in an instance of near-death delirium; otherwise it is a "cathedral of gloom, where unknown gods speak in half tones a language of whispers" (p. 125). The symbiotic relationship between language and geography that was present in the other novels is construed in *La vorágine* as a solipsistic monologue, where nature acts as a sort of immense echo chamber that returns to the speaker the garbled and amplified reverberations of his own discourse.

The human activity portrayed in the text, the extraction of latex from wild rubber trees, is described as being so intertwined with nature as to be almost indistinguishable from it. But whereas in the other novels discussed this closeness arose from a condition of mutual and harmonious molding between man and his environment, the relationship is now depicted as one that results in the weakening and eventual annihilation of the two parties; consequently, there is in *La vorágine* no redeeming value to the human activity depicted. Instead, the latter becomes another expression of the destructive interaction of nature and man, part of the jungle's natural cycle of death: while man taps the trees for rubber, nature simultaneously saps his stamina and rationality. This pernicious association is explicitly conveyed by the following passage, where the mutually debilitating relationship between man and tree is described: "While I spike the tree with the spigot so that its sap, like tears, may run into the cup, the swarm of mosquitoes that defends it sucks my blood and the haze of the forest clouds my eyes. Thus the tree and I, each tormented in different ways, cry unto death and will combat one another until the end!" (p. 231). Man's interaction with the jungle through his work is invariably presented in this fashion in *La vorágine*. In this exchange nature is always victorious on account of its inexhaustible ability to replenish itself, while men engage in a feverish and senseless activity of exploitation that ravages them physically and in the end also corrupts them to the core.

Finally, the relationship between human activity and the linguistic element of the text is articulated – as in *Doña Bárbara* and *Don Segundo Sombra* – through the use of a specialized vocabulary related in this instance to the exploitation of rubber. In order to attain the novel's avowed intention to serve as an indictment of the Amazonian rubber industry, Rivera portrays in detail all aspects of the rubber operation: the extraction of latex, its processing and transportation, the dishonest accounting practices of the entrepreneurs that create indentured and inherited servitude for the Indians, the sadistic punishments inflicted on the unfortunate workers. As a result, the novel incorporates the precise lexicon associated with that human operation, which is thereby projected as a closed linguistic universe. Most of these words appear underlined or in quotation marks in the text, a practice that anticipated the eventual formulation of the glossary that is now commonplace in most editions of the novel. By effecting a careful recreation of the precise terminology associated with a given economic activity, *La vorágine* repeats a gesture that was seen in the novels analyzed previously as well: the creation of a self-contained linguistic space that is identified with the boundaries of a homogeneous autochthonous order.

Moreover, *La vorágine* expanded the textual recreation of what was perceived to be the autochthonous reality of Latin America through its geographical displacement to the jungle regions. This projection of the autochthonous to a continental context explained its weakened nationalistic tone when compared to the two other novels examined. Nonetheless, Rivera's text represents an instance of the discourse of the autochthonous insofar as it mobilizes the synecdochical relations on which this discursive modality is predicated. In this case, however, autochthony is considered a negative referent, a characterization that could be traceable to the author's declared purpose in writing *La vorágine*: the denunciation of the terrible abuses of the rubber industry in the Amazon region. If the sequence of our consideration of the three novels has contravened the order in which they were published, it is because the backward glance to Rivera's novel allows for a better understanding of the inclusion of *La vorágine* in the group of "three exemplary novels." Conversely, Rivera's nightmarish vision of the jungle's unbridled force allows us to perceive the covert presence of this characterization of nature in the other two texts as well. In *Don Segundo Sombra* there are resonances of this violent facet of nature in the description of the *cangrejal*, the crab-infested marsh. In Gallegos' text that same quality is condensed in the depiction of the Palmar de la Chusmita, a swamp where nature seems turned in on itself in a never-ending cycle of death. The inclusion of scenes such as these, which constitute a sort of zero-degree of nature, provides an implied background against which the all-important human activity in all three novels can be both measured, defined and valorized. The combined effect of all these factors allows us to understand the inclusion of *La vorágine* in the famous triad, while still acknowledging the differences that would make this inclusion somewhat surprising.

But regardless of these obvious dissimilarities, *La vorágine* has suffered the same turn in critical fortune as the other two novels with which it is most often associated. After an initial continent-wide success that paved the way for translations into several languages, the work has fallen on harder critical times. It has become a customary practice to offer it as the quintessential example of the kind of narrative where the overwhelming presence of nature diminishes both the importance of human characters and the literary value of the final product. Rivera himself may have planted the seeds of such a reading by going to great lengths to emphasize the non-literary component of *La vorágine*. Asked on one occasion if the novel was true to life, he answered boldly: "Almost in its entirety. I saw all those things. The characters depicted in the novel are all real and some of them even appear with their own names."[3] Rivera's comment is indicative of the investment he had in what he considered to be the novel's principal objective: the denunciation of the rubber trade in the Amazonian territory. The depiction of atrocities, the allusions to historical personages of the rubber industry and the detailed descriptions of all aspects of the rubber operation reinforced the notion that the novel's intention was to denounce the conditions under which men were forced to live and work in the jungle regions. Rivera, who as a representative in his country's legislative body had acquired a reputation as a gadfly, also encouraged the contemporary interpretation of *La vorágine* as an indictment of the government's neglect of its regulatory role in matters pertaining to the rubber trade. Moreover, the novel provoked an intense interest in the region depicted, given its implication that the government had overlooked its potential and had failed to lay legitimate claim to it. Colombia was especially ripe for the arousal of this sort of nationalistic fervor, since the scar left by the loss of Panama was still quite fresh. In fact, the area where most of the rubber enterprise in the novel takes place was, at the time of the writing, still in dispute as to whether it was a part of Colombian, Peruvian or Venezuelan national territory. In this respect Rivera was careful to suggest in *La vorágine* that Colombians were being victimized by foreign entrepreneurs in their own country, an allegation that he expressed in a rebuttal to one of his critics: "How can you ignore the patriotic and humanitarian goals that suffuse [*La vorágine*]? how can you not join in my cry of justice for so many people enslaved in their own land? . . . God only knows that when I wrote my book my only purpose was to fight for the redemption of those pathetic beings that live imprisoned in the jungle."[4] The combined effect of all these factors helps to explain why the novel was initially interpreted as a *documento de denuncia* in the narrow context of contemporary national preoccupations. Indeed, the feel-ings aroused by the novel's depiction of the harrowing lot of the rubber workers led – as Rivera once boasted proudly – to the creation of an investigative commission in Brazil that was specially appointed to study the situation.[5]

The author's claim to have witnessed or experienced most of what is depicted in the novel was founded on a voyage he made to the Amazonian jungle in 1922. Rivera, a lawyer by training, was appointed by the government to a commission that was entrusted with the task of settling a much-disputed border demarcation between Venezuela and Colombia. The commission was divided into three groups, one of which would actually undertake the journey to the disputed territory with a Venezuelan contingent. Rivera, along with an engineer and an astronomer, was assigned this significant endeavor. Two months into the journey the writer resigned from his post in the commission, in disgust over the way the expedition had been planned, and protesting the lack of cooperation from the Venezuelan authorities. Instead of returning to Bogotá, however, Rivera continued the journey on his own until he reached the town of San Fernando de Atapabo. After some weeks of restless inactivity Rivera, accompanied by two Indians, explored the little-known region of the Inírida River, drawing maps and making geographical annotations. Upon his return to San Fernando he and the astronomer, who had managed to reach the town on his own, traveled to the village of Yavita where they spent several months. Some time later they were joined by the other members of the expedition. It was here that Rivera avowedly wrote many of the pages of *La vorágine* and read them aloud to the assembled members of the entourage. This is an episode that has become a permanent aspect of the critical lore surrounding the novel, as the following account exemplifies: "After days of long trajectories through swamps teeming with leeches; driven to desperation by clouds of mosquitoes . . . flogged in body and soul, Rivera and his com-panions would sit around a smoky campfire to fend off the swarms. He would break the silence first: 'Hear – Rivera would say – what I have written today.' And he would then recite the tragedy-filled pages he had composed, which, for lack of paper, were preserved only in his memory."[6] Rivera and his companions returned to Bogotá in October of 1923, a little more than a year after they had departed. Immediately after his arrival, Rivera embarked on a crusade to denounce the highest-ranking official of the commission as well as Colombia's Foreign Minister for sponsoring what he regarded as a bogus expedition. In the middle of this turbulent personal period he rushed to revise and publish the manuscript of *La vorágine*. When the novel appeared in 1924, the entire country was taken by storm on account of its sensational revelations concerning the rubber industry of the Amazon jungle.

A knowledge of this background is necessary to recreate the milieu in which Rivera's work made its appearance and therefore understand its reception as a document of denunciation. This reading of the novel almost imposes itself on the reader; the graphic depiction of wounds, disembowelments and other barbaric acts could only have the intention of producing revulsion and indignation for the system that instituted and perpetuated them. Indeed, at times the detailed depiction of the operations of the trade forces the novel to assume the form of a sociological treatise on the rubber industry:

The working personnel is made up mostly of Indians and journeymen who, according to the laws of the trade, cannot change bosses before two years. Each worker has an account in which he is charged for the trinkets, tools and food that he is given in advance, and in which he is also credited for the latex he produces but at a ridiculous price determined by the boss. Not a man ever knows the real state of his account; and the contractor keeps the books in such a way that he is always owed more work. This new form of slavery destroys the entire life of many men and is also passed on to their heirs.   (pp. 187–88)

At a certain level, then, this interpretation of the novel is an inescapable outcome, one carefully substantiated and sponsored by Rivera himself; if contemporary accounts are to be trusted, the author even appears to have staged the *mise en scène* for his novel's reception in this vein. For it is believed that Rivera ran a notice in three newspapers in Bogotá announcing his forthcoming novel, and which read: "*La vorágine*. A novel by José Eustasio Rivera. It is about life in the Casanare, about Peruvian activities in La Chorrera and El Encanto, and depicts the slavery of the rubber trade in the jungles of Colombia, Venezuela and Brazil. Comes out next month."[7]

We now know, nonetheless, that Rivera concocted his account of the iniquities of the rubber trade using documentation that had been published many years before in some cases, and that his claim to have witnessed or experienced most of what he included in the novel was, at the very least, exaggerated. Rivera's careful weaving of second-hand factual information and fictional material has been painstakingly established by Eduardo Neale-Silva in an important early article.[8] It appears that Rivera based his account on a number of books and documents that had appeared previously and whose express purpose was the condemnation of the brutality and excesses that were intrinsic to the rubber industry.[9] Thus, the Colonel Tomás Funes who is alluded to in passing in the novel was in fact a rubber entrepreneur who, as the narrative claims, was responsible for a massacre at San Fernando de Atapabo in 1903 in which then Governor Roberto Pulido and members of his family were assassinated – an incident also referred to by Clemente Silva in *La vorágine*. The same can be concluded about the death of the French explorer Eugenio Robuchon, murdered by rubber magnates to avoid the publication of photographs he had taken during a sojourn in the rubber fields, an event that Rivera alludes to in his text.[10] Even some of the specific crimes described in *La vorágine* had been denounced previously by others. For instance, the scene where a vicious foreman douses several Indians with kerosene and then sets light to them has a clear antecedent in a 1907 deposition given by a Peruvian reporter in which he condemned the cruelty with which the Indian laborers were treated:

That year (1903) more than 800 Indians from Ocaima arrived at La Chorrera to hand in the rubber they had harvested. After weighing and storing the rubber the sub-administrator of the region where the Indians worked, Fidel Velarde, set aside twenty-five of these alleging they were too lazy at work. Víctor Macedo and his accomplice Loaíza ordered that every Indian be wrapped in a jute sack doused with oil, and they were immediately lit. Fleeing in terror, the victims ran to the nearby river with the hope of saving themselves; but they all drowned. These were the habitual amusements of Macedo and his hellish associates.[11]

Rivera incorporates the reporter's account of this incident in *La vorágine* with some minor modifications:

A drunken foreman wanted to amuse himself: he poured kerosene in a bowl and offered it to some Indians. As none of them would fall for the trick, he threw the liquid over them. I don't know who struck a match; but a moment later a crackling flame consumed the bodies of the unfortunate beings. They dashed madly through the crowd shrieking, crowned by livid fire, and plunged into the river in their final agony. (pp. 194–95)

Instances like this one can be readily found throughout the text of *La vorágine*. My purpose in calling attention to them is not to cast aspersions on Rivera's indictment of the rubber enterprise, but rather to free the representation of the rubber industry in the novel from the mimetic intention with which Rivera – and most critics – regarded it, thereby opening up the possibility of a different inscription of this representation in the text. For regardless of Rivera's public pronouncements, his avowed condemnation of the rubber industry is fashioned in the form of a poet's itinerary into the heart of the jungle, an aspect of the novel that has not been sufficiently examined.[12] I propose to begin the exploration of this dimension of *La vorágine* by engaging in an analysis of Rivera's own poetic praxis.

The poetics of the jungle

Prior to the writing of his novel, Rivera had published only one other work, the book of poems entitled *Tierra de promisión*, in 1921, three years before the appearance of *La vorágine*. This collection of poems consisted of fifty-four compositions in sonnet form divided into three groups of eighteen, ten and twenty-six poems each. The aim of *Tierra de promisión* was, as the title suggests, the poetic representation of Colombia's three major and distinct geographical zones: the jungle, the mountains and the plains. Most critics who have devoted their attention to this first work endeavor to demonstrate the differences between Rivera's vision of the jungle in it, and his subsequent depiction of that region in his famous novel: "The jungle of the first eighteen sonnets is very different from the monstrous one depicted in *La vorágine*. When he wrote the sonnets Rivera had not yet visited the Amazon jungle; this explains in part the difference between the loving, vital and serene vision of it in *Tierra de promisión*, and the tortuous one of the novel, published three years later."[13] They invoke in their arguments the poet's journey with the boundary commission in 1922–23 as a decisive turning point in his conception of the jungle. Since it is a well-documented fact that Rivera had not visited the region before he published *Tierra de promisión*, these critics discern in his earlier portrayal of the jungle a mystification that is later dispelled and denounced in *La vorágine*. Neale-Silva, for instance, proposes the following recreation of Rivera's thoughts while in immediate confrontation with the jungle:

A further reason reinforced the distaste that he now felt for the jungle: he understood now how different reality was from what he had earlier imagined it to be. Was it not he who had written with Kipling-like fascination about "the wide-vaulted jungle" in which the winds "rehearse lofty matins," where "tamed voices" and "faint piccolos" can be heard? Upon remembering his poems he must have felt annoyed and perhaps even a bit ridiculous. He had not found any of these things in the Orinoco wilderness. "Where is the poetry of contemplation here, where are the butterflies that seem translucent flowers, the enchanted birds, the singing brooks," – he asked himself. "Only in the minds of poets that have experienced nothing but a sedate solitude!"[14]

Neale-Silva's argument seems, at first, hard to contradict: Rivera's description of the jungle in his sonnets appears to be a highly romanticized version of the real one Rivera had to contend with during his journey, and which later ostensibly inspired *La vorágine*. The fragments of verses that Neale-Silva cites from *Tierra de promisión* are from the fourth poem of the jungle cycle:

> The wide-vaulted jungle rehearses its lofty matins
> as the wind begins its symphonic lilt;
> and as two branches wail like violins
> the swaying foliage heaves a profound sigh.
>
> Tamed voices murmur in their hidden retreat;
> the cane reeds produce the sound of faint piccolos,
> and while the *cambulo* blooms in garnet flowers,
> through the thicket a sapphire-colored light shimmers.
>
> Bent in the musical pause the palm tree
> offers its fans to the light breeze;
> but suddenly an awesome tremolo of concerted sounds
>
> breaks the vanilla stems! . . . and with solemn insolence
> the foliage, intoxicated with its own fragrance,
> becomes a lion that shakes his mane in the winds.[15]

> [La selva de anchas cúpulas, al sinfónico giro
> de los vientos, preludia sus grandiosos maitines;
> y al gemir de dos ramas como finos violines
> lanza la móvil fronda su profundo suspiro.
>
> Mansas voces se arrullan en oculto retiro;
> los cañales conciertan moribundos flautines,
> y al mecerse del cámbulo florecido en carmines
> entra por las marañas una luz de zafiro.
>
> Curvada en el espasmo musical, la palmera
> vibra sus abanicos en el aura ligera;
> mas de pronto un gran trémolo de orquestados concentos

rompe las vainilleras! . . . y con grave arrogancia,
el follaje embriagado con su propia fragancia,
como un león, revuelve la melena en los vientos.]

There is, to be sure, a placidness in the description of the jungle here that is the result of its intense aestheticization. But if the two tercets are examined, we observe that the symphonic harmony that was posited in the first two stanzas is shattered here without warning. The sedate, separate voices of the jungle unexpectedly come together in a burst of music whose power elicits a comparison with the ferocious strength of a lion. This transition is in keeping with the classical syntactic formula of the sonnet, where the quatrains propose an argument that is subsequently overturned or somehow made problematic in the tercets.[16] A close analysis of the other poems in the jungle cycle reveals that the procedure is repeated in every case, and that the poem above exhibits the least violent of these transitions. A far more representative example is the eighth sonnet of the collection:

On the scalding shore, bloodthirsty and astute,
a tiger flexes his terrifying steel claws;
he has left behind the hunting dogs, and he challenges
the archer with an enigmatic and feral growl.

The golden spots, bright amongst the stains of mourning,
lend a subtle sheen to his undulating coat;
the foliage is paralyzed by his bewitching eye, and his
tail is now more agile and his sides more lean.

Behind the green palm trees, extending his arm,
the naked Indian stretches the bow-string taut,
and the breeze sighs as the arrow flies . . .

The tiger roars, while his bloody entrails trail;
he is dying, and when the sun sees him lie, it sweeps
down, like a buzzard, through the towering mountains.

(pp. 27–28)

[En la tórrida playa, sanguinario y astuto,
mueve un tigre el espanto de sus garras de acero;
ya venció a la juaría pertinaz, y al arquero
reta con un gruñido enigmático y bruto.

Manchas de oro, vivaces entre manchas de luto,
en su felpa ondulante dan un brillo ligero;

magnetiza las frondas con el ojo hechicero,
y su cola es más ágil y su ijar más enjuto.

Tras las verdes palmichas, distendiendo su brazo,
templa el indio desnudo la vibrante correa,
y se quejan las brisas al pasar el flechazo . . .

Ruge el tigre arrastrando las sangrientas entrañas
agoniza, y al verlo que yacente se orea,
baja el sol, como un buitre, por las altas montañas!]

The two quatrains reveal the stasis of the confrontation between man and beast, which allows the poet to describe the undulant uniformity of yellow and black on the tiger's fur. Just as before, however, the last two stanzas produce a violent act that has the effect of subverting the standoff created in the first two: the tiger is disemboweled and it is hinted that the sun begins the process of decomposition through its being compared to a vulture. The same scheme can be seen at work in the third sonnet, where a wild duck is furtively stalked by a crocodile:

> Close to the wide murmuring river,
> on the shore with sun-scorched sands
> awaits the caiman, whose corrugated back
> resembles a miniature mountain range.
>
> He watches a shiny yellow duck
> skim the pure surface of the water,
> and he opens wide in its hard socket
> the turbid speck of emerald that is his eye.
>
> Traitorously submerged in the liquid
> shadow for a while, suddenly
> his jaws close tightly on the duck;
>
> then the scattered feathers float,
> the current sweeps them into a vast circle,
> and the reddening foam quivers.   (pp. 17–18)

[Cerca del ancho río que murmura,
en las arenas que el cenit rescalda
vela el caimán, cuya rugosa espalda
parece cordillera en miniatura.

Viendo nadar sobre la linfa pura
lustroso pato de plumaje gualda,
como túrbido grano de esmeralda
agranda el ojo entre la cuenca dura.

Pérfidamente sumergido un rato
en la líquida sombra, de repente
aprietan sus mandíbulas al pato;

entonces flota la dispersa pluma,
abre un círculo enorme la corriente,
y tiembla, sonrojándose, la espuma.]

One can appreciate through these examples that Rivera's vision of the jungle in *Tierra de promisión* is not that of the placid garden that most critics have claimed to identify, and which they in turn contrast with the author's "demystified" portrayal of that same region in *La vorágine*. Violence and death are an integral component of nature in *Tierra de promisión*, and Rivera makes them a constitutive part of the structure of the sonnets in his earlier collection.

That this aspect of the poems has escaped detection reflects the discontinuity that critics have always posited between Rivera's two texts, a chasm that is understood to reflect the author's journey to the Amazonian jungle. More importantly, though, the belief that Rivera denounced in *La vorágine* his earlier portrayal of the jungle is predicated on a collapsing together of the author and the protagonist Arturo Cova, an understandable critical lapse, since the internment of Rivera the poet in the jungle parallels that of Cova the poet in *La vorágine*. Hence, for instance, if we return for a moment to Neale-Silva's quotation, we see that in his imaginative recreation of Rivera's state of mind while in the jungle he ascribes to him the very thoughts of his character Arturo Cova in *La vorágine*: " 'Where is the poetry of contemplation here,' he asked himself."[17] This conflation of author and protagonist is one that has characterized much of the critical discourse on the novel.[18] Blinded by this resemblance critics have unwittingly foreclosed simultaneously the possibility of a reading of *La vorágine* that envisions an ironic attitude toward Cova on Rivera's part. I will attempt to establish the grounds for such an interpretation as a preliminary step in the exploration of *La vorágine* as a text where *poiesis* is a major concern.

I do not believe it would be untenable to suggest that Rivera's depiction of the poet Arturo Cova is fraught with irony. An essential component of this characterization is the use of the first-person narration, inasmuch as it allows for the unmediated presentation of Cova's unstable and contradictory being. The overwhelming effect produced by this unfiltered access to the poet's unbalanced thoughts has prompted several critics to interpret this narrative device as a shortcoming in the conception and description of the protagonist. John S. Brushwood, for instance, interprets this development as the outcome of a faulty narrative strategy – a case of too much telling and too little showing: "The trouble comes from the author's mishandling of first-person narration. The saga of Arturo Cova is supposedly in diary form. Therefore, he tells his own story. Unfortunately, his creator could not shift completely from the third-person view of the narrative. So it is that Arturo says things about himself that should be revealed by what other people say and do. That way we would be spared Arturo's overwrought explanations of his own sensitivity . . . his eternal rhetorical questions."[19] But Cova's "overwrought" consciousness *is* a character trait, and one that is consistently developed and expanded on throughout the narrative. It explicitly shows that in Cova's case the most rigorous introspection never results in self-knowledge, but in self-delusion and mystification.

Cova's propensity for compensatory daydreaming is established early on in the novel; his dreams are always out of proportion with the incident that elicited them. Thus, when his friend Fidel Franco makes him a modest business proposal, he embarks on a flight of fantasy where he pictures himself returning to Bogotá as a millionaire (p. 56). Later, thinking that the *llaneros* leave him behind when they depart for their chores because they have doubts about his masculinity, he imagines a scene where he throws a bull "with one twist of the tail, provoking the envy of the astonished onlookers" (p. 100).

Cova's obsession with the analysis of his own motivations serves no real purpose, since he is profoundly incapable of controlling his mercurial will. As he himself says in a paradoxical moment of self-definition, his only constant trait is that of change itself: "Frequently, impressions achieve a maximum of power in my excited states; but any given impression has a tendency to degenerate into its opposite after a few minutes . . . My heart is like a shore where tides ebb and flow intermittently" (pp. 62–63). This quality is plainly in evidence in his confrontation with the Madona Zoraida Ayram. His first impression of her is quite negative; he finds her almost repugnant (p. 266). Nonetheless, he subsequently manages to concoct in his mind a story where the Madona becomes a tragic figure, wandering through the jungle rivers alone and unprotected.

Consequently, a few pages later he is able to exclaim: "Without question, Madona Zoraida Ayram was an extraordinary woman!" (p. 274). Knowing that the matron customarily uses her sexual allure to achieve her ends, he nevertheless persists in his idealization even when he understands he is the one being manipulated. The final seduction scene has a preposterous tone on account of the disjunction between Cova's rhetoric and its object:

– Sir, do not pinch me! You are mistaken!
– My heart is never wrong! And upon saying this I nibbled her cheek; only once, because my teeth got covered with vaseline and rice powder.

(pp. 276–77)

Another related deprecatory aspect of the poet that is emphasized in the novel is his aggrandized concept of self. There is an underlying and unredeemed triviality in his life that constantly erodes the protagonist's appreciation of his own stature. The petty and somewhat sordid conditions under which he and Alicia left Bogotá are a case in point. This overblown self-image manifests itself most clearly in Cova's grandiloquent speech, which is usually melodramatically out of joint with the situation at hand. When the poet meets Barrera for the first time – in a scene that can only be interpreted as a sarcastic comment on the former – he addresses Arturo Cova with the same inflated rhetoric, significantly, to flatter him by extolling his literary merits: "Praised be the hand that has composed such beautiful stanzas. Delight of my soul they were in Brazil, where they induced in me a wave of nostalgia, for it is the privilege of a poet to chain together the scattered sons to the heart of the motherland and to create new subjects in foreign lands. I have demanded much of fortune, yet never did I aspire to the honor of declaring to you, in person, my sincere admiration" (p. 45). Cova is easy prey for such transparently meretricious compliments: "Although I was forewarned about this man, I must confess that I was susceptible to his adulation" (p. 45). The scene has a powerful ironic undertone since in it Cova is initially seduced by the man who will later show the most consummate contempt for him.

Moreover, Rivera has surrounded Cova with other characters that are, when confronted with him, themselves critical commentaries on his behavior and personality. There is, for instance, Clemente Silva, the aged guide, who had willingly interned himself in the jungle in a desperate search for his beloved son Luciano. Once he has ascertained his death as a fact, he remains in the forest steadfastly in order to recover his remains. His loving quest creates a direct contrast with Cova's journey, the latter motivated by vengeful desire and wounded honor, and all for a woman he acknowledges in a number of occasions that he is not even certain he loves. Once inside the jungle, Arturo unexpectedly runs into a former friend, Ramiro Estévanez, who, it turns out, had come to the jungle for reasons similar to Cova's. Nevertheless, Estévanez has acquired enough distance to understand his past mistake; the following scene ensues between them:

Finding him helpless, inept and unlucky, I described my situation to him with a certain insolence, hoping to dazzle him with my audacity:
 – Hello, aren't you curious to know what on earth I'm doing in these jungles?
 – Excessive energy, the search for El Dorado, the atavistic influence of an ancestor who was a Conquistador?
 – No! I stole a woman and somebody stole her from me! I have come to kill whoever has her!
 – Lucifer's red plumes do not suit you well. (p. 284)

Instead of recovering a lost friend and learning from his experience, Cova attempts to convince himself both of his superiority over Estévanez and of the absolute singularity of his situation.

Foremost among these critical counterparts to Cova is Fidel Franco who, as his given name suggests, has accompanied the poet in his expedition as an act of loyalty. In a scene early in the novel, two Indians had suddenly drowned while attempting to maneuver the group's canoe through some treacherous rapids. For Cova, the incident held a special fascination, since – as he envisioned it – through it Death had found a swift, new way of disposing of its victims; for him, any attempt to rescue the men would be futile but, more importantly, also aesthetically unpleasant, since it would "cheapen the astonishing catastrophe" (p. 170). Franco's cutting rejoinder on hearing the poet's reasonings is very valuable since it provides a succinct exposition of everything that is objectionable in Cova's character and trajectory:

Never had I known a rage so tumultuous and eloquent. He spoke of his life, sacrificed to my whims, of my ingratitude, of my willful nature, of my rancor; of how at La Maporita I had not been truthful to him, telling him that I was married when Alicia's every gesture revealed the precarious condition of concubine! And to guard her like a virgin, after having degraded and perverted her! And to shriek because another had run off with her, when I had initiated her in those ways by seducing her! And to insist stubbornly on pursuing her into the wilderness, . . . and to drag them into this adventure, this fatal trip, only to rejoice when friends perished tragically! All because I was an unbalanced, impulsive and theatrical fool!

(p. 171)

All these instances point to the fact that there is much in *La vorágine* to make exceedingly problematic the direct or surreptitious identification of Cova with Rivera that has been a commonplace of critical commentary on the novel. More interestingly, the story of a poet who in the end is devoured by nature is too charged with aesthetic and literary connotations not to invite an interpretation on a meta-poetical level. The fact that Cova is a poet, placed in the extended framework of the ironic characterization by the author that I have suggested, suggests the possibility of a reading of *La vorágine* as a statement on *poiesis* by counterexample. This alternative will become even more enticing when we reflect on the complicated literary horizon in which *La vorágine* was written and conceived.

Rivera belonged to a generation of writers known as the *centenaristas*, men who had come of artistic age during the decade-long celebration of Independence that has already been documented. In very ample terms, the aesthetic program of this group was defined *vis-à-vis* the immediate background constituted by *modernismo* and the reawakened interest in a national thematics that had resulted from the celebration of the *Centenario*; consequently, one can discern in their literary production a desire to achieve a fusion of *modernista* aesthetics with an autochthonous thematics. Their poetic project envisioned what they considered to be a corrective turn away from the exotic atmosphere characteristic of *modernista* writing, and towards an exploration of indigenous themes. Therefore, in matters of artistic form, the *centenaristas* did not conceive of themselves as constituting a discontinuous moment with the past. Eduardo Neale-Silva has summarized this relationship quite precisely:

In their literary production the *centenaristas* were descended from *modernismo*. Their efforts were not a negation of anything but an attempt to go beyond; this explains the ease with which they incorporated in their movement some men from the previous generations such as Grillo, Sanín Cano, Londoño and Valencia. Rivera thought of the last two writers as his literary models, and even if he had chosen themes that these men would have not cared much for, he felt nevertheless a profound affinity with them . . . Between the *modernistas* and the *centenaristas* there was no break in continuity.[20]

Rivera's first work, *Tierra de promisión* was the perfect synthesis of this poetic program; its attempt to textualize the entire geography of Colombia in a series of carefully crafted sonnets was a reaffirmation of *modernista* theories of composition adapted to the new thematic environment. Rivera, who had published separately many of his poems before collecting them in *Tierra de promisión*, became one of the most prominent figures of this poetic generation.

Nevertheless, this aesthetic compromise with the past was radically challenged at all levels by the appearance of a poetic phenomenon that transformed the literary scene to its very core: the avant-garde, the group that received in Colombia the specific rubric of "*los nuevos*," but had a counterpart during the 1920s in almost every Latin American capital.[21] Neale-Silva again provides a succinct description of the moment:

With the appearance of the *vanguardistas* the literary atmosphere lost its former serenity. A time of incomprehension and crisis had begun. The men of the *Centenario*, among them Rivera, were shocked by the insolence shown by the young artists and their lack of interest in Colombia's cultural past. *Los nuevos* were attracted to anything that expressed novelty of spirit: verbal audacity, metaphoric subtlety, agility of expression, without the need of a story, the weight of a message or the fog of philosophical lucubrations. There was, then, a veritable abyss between the formal correctness, measure and propriety of the established poets and the impudence of youth.[22]

La vorágine was written in the midst of this poetic abyss created by the appearance of the avant-garde writers. Rivera has left very few statements regarding his conception of poetics, but it seems fairly clear that he, along with other members of his generation, sensed the overwhelming challenges implicit in the *vanguardista* pronouncements and poetic praxis; at stake was not only the justification and permanence of his own poetic production, but the survival of poetry as he conceived it. In an interview where he referred specifically to *los nuevos*, his remarks clearly betray this last preoccupation: "I greatly admire their spiritual curiosity; but I do not believe that doing away with poetic form will become an adequate and lasting mode of expression for poetry."[23] The fact that *La vorágine* is the story of a poet who dies in his confrontation with nature, coupled with the radical break with poetic diction and form that was represented by the avant-garde, should perhaps alert us to the possibility of finding resonances of this conflict in Rivera's novel. I do not wish to suggest that Rivera conceived of Cova expressly as a prototype of the new poet, but rather that in *La vorágine* there is an underlying commentary on *poiesis* that arises from the challenges represented by the poetic principles and artistic practice of the avant-garde.

Tierra de promisión and *La vorágine* present us with two essentially contrasting visions of a poet's encounter with the violence and chaos of the jungle, one of which is resolved in the annihilation of the poet by nature. This confrontation between poet and nature can be understood as a sort of primordial scene of poetic writing, as an allegory of the poetic act for Rivera. In this encounter between creator and nature one could discern an allegorical reformulation of the struggle between the poetic subject and the language from which he must fashion his work. From this perspective Cova's ultimate defeat and annihilation by the forces of nature can be translated into an implicit statement on poetic creation: language is a perilous and violent entity that must be mastered by the poet, lest he be mastered by it. This implied admonition becomes particularly appropriate when placed in the historical context of the challenge represented by the poetic concepts of the avant-garde to the *centenaristas*. Through this fable of poetic origins Rivera would thereby emphasize the necessity of strict poetic diction, of elaborate poetic technique as against the seemingly haphazard principles of composition and unbridled poetic experimentation of the *vanguardistas*.

If we now return to the sonnets of *Tierra de promisión*, we can discern that Rivera had already enacted this almost ritual mastery of language in poem after poem of that earlier collection. As was shown before, the danger and violence of the jungle were subsumed and subdued in each instance under the formal exigencies dictated by the composition of the sonnets: In every case, an initial moment of balance described in the quatrains – a moment that was conceived of differently in each poem – was overturned almost invariably by a violent, sudden act in the tercets, but with this violent instant framed and controlled by the well-established and defined rhetorical and syntactic requirements of the sonnet form. It is precisely this strict, conventional set of demands made by the sonnet that has prompted Barbara Herrnstein Smith to remark in her study of poetic closure that "the sonnet is one of the most highly determined formal structures in Western poetry . . . It is also one of the few forms with a predetermined length. In other highly conventional forms, such as *terza rima* and rhyme royale, the stanzaic structure is rigidly prescribed but the number of stanzas is not limited by any rule. The sonnet, however, is obliged to conclude not only in a fixed way but at a fixed point."[24] This observation becomes even more meaningful when we take into account the reputation Rivera acquired for his fastidious craftsmanship of the sonnet form. Many critics and acquaintances have left descriptions of the monomaniacal fashion in which Rivera wrote and revised his poems time and again. His close friend Ricardo Charria Tobar asserts that "Rivera used to spend entire days and even weeks choosing one word, selecting a term to substitute for another that was not to his liking. It was not uncommon to find him in this activity, his eyes glued to the Dictionary of Synonyms."[25] By the same token, in a work devoted exclusively to the study of Rivera's sonnets, Eduardo Neale-Silva has corroborated the author's constant reworking and polishing of his poems, even beyond publication.[26] In his sonnets, then, Rivera engaged repeatedly in an attempt to accomplish a masterly domestication of the violence of nature through his wielding of a highly codified and rigorously structured poetic form. If, as I have suggested, this repeated enactment can be read as a repostulation of a primordial encounter between poet and language, then the poems of *Tierra de promisión* become the ritual performance of a statement on *poiesis* that conceives that confrontation as the controlling of an essential violence in language through the agency of the poetic act. This is the point at which one may perhaps begin to comprehend the connection that relates *Tierra de promisión* to *La vorágine*, a text where nature is a formless and violent chaos, an unchecked agent of destruction that constantly renews itself from within:

Here, at night, unknown voices, disturbing pauses, funereal silences. It is death that passes giving life. One hears a fruit fall, giving promise of a new seed; leaves come to earth with a faint sigh to become fertilizer for the roots of the parent tree. Crunching jaws are heard, devouring with the fear of being devoured. Warning whistles, dying wails, beasts retching. And when dawn showers its tragic glory over the jungles, the clamor of survivors begins anew: the buzz of the *pava chillona*; the wild boar crashing through the underbrush; the laughter of ridiculous monkeys.   (p. 239)

The contradictory relationship between the two texts is initially underscored by the fact that *La vorágine* encompasses the opposite geographical displacement from that portrayed in *Tierra de promisión*: In Rivera's poetic representation of his country, the journey begins in the jungle and concludes on the *llanos*, as if the "domestication" of nature were an enabling poetic initiation that allowed the poet to constitute himself as such before embarking on his poetic trajectory. By comparison, the poet Arturo Cova's voyage from the plains into an ever-deeper internment in the jungle ends in despair and annihilation. The same contrastive intention can be observed in the respective depiction of the river that grants access to the jungle in both texts. The juxtaposition of the two descriptions allows one to perceive immediately the coincidences and divergences between them. In *Tierra de promisión*:

> I am an abundant river that at *high noon*
> flows by the banks *reflecting the landscape*;
> and in the deep *murmur* of my audacious *waves*
> the *solemn voice* of the distant jungle can be heard.
>
> The sun floats in the mist of my light *foam* . . .
>
> (p. 9, my emphasis)

> [Soy un grávido río, y *a la luz meridiana*
> ruedo bajo los ámbitos *reflejando el paisaje*;
> y en el hondo *murmullo* de mi audaz *oleaje*
> se oye la *voz solemne* de la selva lejana;
>
> Flota el sol entre el nimbo de mi *espuma* liviana . . .]

La vorágine describes the river in the following terms: "The canoe, like a floating coffin, continued down-river, *at the time when the day lengthens all shadows*. On the current's surface one could see *the parallel banks reflected*, with their somber vegetation and hostile swarms of insects. That river, *without waves and without foam*, was *silent, deathly silent* like a presage, and it seemed like a dark path leading towards a vortex of nothingness" (pp. 129–30, my emphasis). ["La curiara, como un ataúd flotante, siguió agua abajo, a la hora en que la tarde alarga las sombras. Desde el dorso de la corriente *columbrábanse las márgenes paralelas*, de sombría vegetación y plagas hostiles. Aquel río, *sin ondulaciones y sin espumas*, era *mudo, tétricamente mudo como el presagio*, y daba la impresión de un camino oscuro que se moviera hacia el vórtice de la nada."] The river of the earlier text is a torrent whose vitality stands for creativity and poetic power, not only because the poet identifies himself with it, but also since a great deal of emphasis is placed on its sonorous quality. In contrast, the river in *La vorágine* is still a specular surface, but the reflections that it captures are those of grim vegetation and menacing vermin; it has been further degraded into an inert and mute body of water that will transport the poet to loss of meaning and death.

Nature is indeed, as countless critics have affirmed, the primordial force in *La vorágine*, but its total impact in this regard can only be gauged through its role in this fable of failed *poiesis* at the heart of Rivera's novel. Its predominant power and character in the text is such that it finally compromises the alleged denunciatory intent behind the writing of *La vorágine*, namely the condemnation of the greed and abuses of the rubber magnates. For the cruelty of men toward each other is ultimately explained in the novel as a sort of disease induced in them by the jungle, rather than as a function of the iniquitous enterprise of rubber extraction. Hence, both exploiters and slaves are victims of the jungle, impelled to fight one another as an extension of their hapless struggle with it: "There is a magnificent courage in the epic of these pirates who enslave their peons, exploit the Indian and struggle against the jungle . . . With the jungle for an enemy they do not know where to strike and thus they attack one another, mutually killing and subjugating each other when they are not battling the jungle" (p. 240). And also: "The jungle disturbs man, developing in him the most inhuman instincts: cruelty invades the soul like a thick and thorny bush and greed burns like a fever" (p. 181). This is the same influence under which Cova succumbs several times throughout the novel, when he threatens to kill himself or his companions. In this fashion, the denunciation of the rubber trade is undermined by these repeated references to nature as the real corrupting force in the jungle.[27] Even more significant in this respect is the intriguing affirmation that the extraction of rubber does not yield profits to anyone; that it is an activity where both slave and despoiler are victimized, thereby throwing into question the adequacy of those labels themselves:

Rubber men know very well that the vegetable gold does not enrich anybody. The potentates of the forest have only credits in their ledgers against peons who never pay, except with their lives; Indians who waste away, canoemen who steal what they are transporting. Slavery in these regions is lifelong for both slave and master: the two must die in the jungle.

A curse of failure and malediction pursues everybody who exploits the green mine. The jungle annihilates them, the jungle holds them, the jungle calls them to swallow them up.   (p. 305)

Why, then, is so much attention given to the rubber industry in *La vorágine*? Perhaps a brief survey of the history of the exploitation of rubber will offer some insights into its role in the narrative of first poetic principles so far identified.

During the last half of the nineteenth century some Latin American countries, Brazil in particular, enjoyed an unchallenged monopoly in all aspects of the world's rubber trade.[28] The tree that provided the valuable latex – *Hevea brasiliensis* – could only be found in the region covered by the Amazon jungle. The method of extracting the latex was the one that had been traditionally employed by the Indians, where a small axe was used to make numerous incisions in the tree's bark. This technique was inherently wasteful for two fundamental and related reasons: it quickly exhausted the tree's ability to yield latex and, therefore, ever-longer journeys to seek fresh trees were needed in order to maintain a consistent level of production. The British, intent on breaking the South American monopoly, bought or smuggled thousands of seeds from the South American continent. After a careful and patient study of the ideal climatic conditions, growth space, rate of extraction and other factors pertaining to exploitation, they proceeded to establish plantations in Southeast Asia – specifically Malaya and Ceylon – throughout the last two decades of the nineteenth century. Here, trees were planted in rows, with the precise distance between them for optimal growth; when the trees reached yielding age, they were tapped with an innovative herringbone pattern that maximized latex production and extended the productive life of the tree. The efficiency of this system soon created its own reward: by the end of the first decade of the twentieth century, the consumption of plantation rubber had surpassed that of wild rubber in the world's markets. The result was the so-called "Rubber Boom of 1910": "All England seemed to go wild in this frenzy of speculation. Nearly everyone who could find the money bought rubber plantation shares. The speculative fever penetrated to every walk of life, seizing with equal force the rich and the poor, the shrewd and the gullible. Fortunes were made by many overnight. In Malaya, government employees gave up their positions to take up rubber planting, even at the sacrifice of pensions they would have received upon retirement."[29] Eventually, the boom ran its course, but the future of wild Amazon rubber was sealed: by 1930, six years after the publication of *La vorágine*, wild rubber accounted for less than three per cent of the world's production of rubber.[30]

Hence, when Rivera visited the jungle in 1922–23, the rubber enterprise of the Amazon jungle was in the midst of a severe crisis from which it would never recover: the wastefulness and unpredictability inherent in its operation had taken their inevitable toll. The extraction of wild rubber was too dependent on the capriciousness of nature; trees were tapped wherever they could be found, a circumstance that often brought implicit with it a daily meandering of several miles through the jungle:

The native tapper, during his work season, rises very early in the morning while it is still dark. Barefooted, he starts out through the forest jungle carrying with him a small hatchet and tin bucket. In a day he makes two rounds of the rubber trees in a given area. On the first trip he cuts a long gash in each tree, and attaches a little tin cup to the lower end of the wound. The milky-white substance, called latex, flows out of the long wound in the bark and runs into the little cup, while he goes on to tap more trees. In the course of a day's work he travels many miles, pushing his way through the dense jungle, until he has tapped from seventy to one hundred trees.[31]

In contrast, plantation trees were – as we saw – planted in an orderly fashion and tapped to yield the maximum amount of latex possible without causing permanent damage to the tree. It can perhaps be stated that the exploitation of plantation rubber became as successful as it did because it allowed nature to thrive, but under the most carefully controlled conditions.

I would like to propose that in the inevitable comparison between the two means of production discussed above one can perceive another formulation of the need to achieve mastery over nature that was shown at work in *Tierra de promisión*. But as was seen before, this performance of mastery functioned as an allegorical restaging of the domination of language by the poet, so that now a homology can be established between the extraction of rubber and the poetic act. This is an analogy that is not difficult to conceive or sustain, since both activities can be construed as a sort of writing. This metaphoric link, which reduces both enterprises to a scriptural gesture, recurs throughout the text. For instance, with the same instrument with which he extracts latex from the rubber trees, Clemente Silva carves in their bark messages for his errant son throughout the jungle. In another suggestive passage that hints at this relationship between writing and the extraction of rubber, a tattered flyer that denounces the injustices of the *empresarios* is mended with hot latex: "I don't know how, but a copy of the newpaper *La Felpa* began to circulate clandestinely in the rubber groves and settlements. It was published in Iquitos by Saldaña Roca, and it clamored against the crimes committed in the Putumayo, demanding justice for us. I remember the frayed condition in which the sheet arrived, from being handled so much; near the Algodón channel we mended it with warm latex so that it could keep traveling from one encampment to the next" (pp. 206–7). This homology between the production of rubber and the poetic act is reinforced by the fact that Cova, for lack of paper, must write his narrative in a ledger used to record debits and credits of the rubber operation: "It's been six weeks since, at Ramiro Estévanez's behest, I began to occupy my spare time keeping a record of my adventures, using for that purpose the accounting book that El Cayeno had in his desk as a useless and dusty ornament" (p. 294). But significantly his experiences seem to him as useless as the ledger in which he records them: "Extravagant happenings, insignificant details and hackneyed pages weave the precarious web of my narrative; and I plod along with grief, noticing that my life has not achieved transcendence and that everything in it is insignificant and transitory" (p. 294). In this tale of unsuccessful *poiesis* that is *La vorágine*, it is not surprising therefore to find the already noted affirmation that the rubber industry ultimately does not yield any profits, even if its presence renders problematic the novel's self-justification as a document of social denunciation.

Although there are no references to the plantation system in *La vorágine*, the wastefulness and non-productive quality of the extraction of wild latex that the novel portrays only become "visible," as it were, when confronted with it. Rivera must have perceived in the languishing Amazon industry of wild rubber an operation contaminated by nature, the very object it was meant to exploit. The extraction of wild rubber perished because it was too close to nature, too caught – literally – in its tangled webs. Cova's systematic inability to detach himself from the jungle keeps him in constant peril of being absorbed and annulled by it. Nowhere is this clearer than in the passage where, stricken by disease, he believes himself to be turning into a tree: "I spoke, I spoke; I heard my voice and was heard, but I felt myself planted on the earth; and through my leg, swollen and deformed like the roots of certain trees, a warm and paralyzing sap ascended. I wanted to move, but the ground would not let go" (p. 328). If, as I proposed before, nature in its jungle wildness was used by Rivera as a metaphor for language, *La vorágine* becomes an allegory about the necessity of mediation between poet and language – a mediation that was conceived by the author in terms of carefully crafted poetic form. It is precisely this formal containment of the violence inherent in nature that the sonnets of *Tierra de promisión* enact time and again. In this *mise en scène* writing becomes, as Derrida has proposed in an uncannily similar context, "the possibility of the road and of difference . . . of the *via rupta*, of the path that is broken, beaten, *fracta*, of the space of reversibility and of the repetition traced by the opening, the divergence from, and the violent spacing, of nature, of the natural, savage, salvage, forest. The *silva* is savage, the *via rupta* is written, discerned, and inscribed violently as difference, as form imposed on the *hylè*, in the forest, in wood as matter."[32] Can we not see in the meticulous arrangement of the rubber plantation, with its trees planted in straight, uniform lines, and a carefully measured distance between them, a figure that recalls the finished product of Rivera's poetic praxis: the meticulously labored sonnets of *Tierra de promisión*? Conversely, one could attribute the indecisive, contradictory and indeterminate textual nature of *La vorágine* – a quality that does not escape any reader of the novel – to the fact that it reflects the absence of a powerful will-to-form in its poet/protagonist that is, in turn, mirrored by the novel's description of the rubber industry as a chaotic and unproductive enterprise.[33] This intractable quality of the text manifests itself clearly not only in the repeated failure of critical attempts to identify an overarching organizing scheme in the novel but also in the latter's generic instability as well: In one of the most curious polemics ever surrounding a novelistic text, soon after Rivera's work appeared a reviewer claimed that the novel's principal defect was that it was, in fact, written in verse. This accusation was repeated several times in subsequent months. Rivera initially tried to defend himself against the charge, but in the end acquiesced: before the second edition of *La vorágine* he revised the novel in an attempt to expunge from it the most conspicuous traces of poetic writing. Needless to say, from the perspective of the interpretation I have advanced, this surreptitious presence of poetry in Rivera's novelistic text is alluring.[34]

Rivera's fable about opposing principles of *poiesis* ultimately had its source in the anxiety that he and the other writers of his generation experienced as a result of their confrontation with the poetic praxis of the avant-garde. Interpreted as such, *La vorágine* constitutes the defense of a very long-standing conception of poetry, one that saw in a poem a privileged object characterized by an excess in signification, an excess that was itself the mark of its aesthetic value. As Barbara Johnson has defined this concept of poetic value, "the economy of the work of art is thus organized around a signifying surplus that transcends the mere exchange between signifiers and signifieds, between tenors and vehicles. This excess . . . engenders poetic value."[35] What Rivera did not realize was that in his poetic parable he unwittingly revealed a deeper truth about the nature of poetry, one that called into question this grounding conceptualization of the aesthetic phenomenon. For in his apology of poetic form, Rivera depicted the existence of a primordial anarchy in language, a dangerous disseminatory capacity that had to be effectively mastered and controlled through the poetic enterprise. But if that is the case, the poetic act must itself be construed as an act of violence that attempts to curtail, to restrict that surplus of signification. One could propose then, that rather than deriving its aesthetic nature and strength from its unbounded polysemic qualities – as Rivera's poetic ideology would propose – poetry seeks in fact to contain the proliferation of meaning inherent in language while simultaneously asserting that it is engaged in doing precisely the opposite. Hence, just as in *La vorágine* the irrepressible violence of nature in the end puts in check its status as a document of social denunciation, Rivera's characterization of language finally reveals a knowledge that undermines the very conception of poetry that marshalled it in its own defense. Could this be any other way, when the etymology of the word that refers to the substance whose exploitation Rivera condemned is allusive of its capacity to erase, to obliterate the trace of writing: "And so, because Englishmen had found something that would rub out pencil marks and leave the paper clean, this strange material with which they did it gradually became known by the colloquial term 'rubber.' The name comes from one of its less significant uses but, nevertheless, one of its earliest ones."[36]

6

Epilogue

This study has attempted to pursue a twofold objective. The first of these was an examination of the discourse of cultural autochthony that has become virtually synonymous with cultural production in Latin America. In the first chapter I argued that the preoccupation with an autochthonous cultural expression represents a particular resolution to the difficult relationship that Latin America has consistently entertained with modernity. I argued that in the end this never-ending search for an indigenous cultural identity should be understood and addressed as an equally inexhaustible stratagem to empower rhetorically the Latin American writer in the fact of modernity's threat to undermine the authority of his discourse, given the incommensurability of Latin America's circumstances and the requirements of the modern.

My second intention was to analyze the particularities of a novelistic discourse that took as its project the incorporation of that presumed autochthonous essence into the literary text. Eschewing the fundamental assumption of both the *novela de la tierra* and most of the criticism on it, namely, the referential status of the autochthonous, I have undertaken to establish the *discursive* nature of "the autochthonous" through a description of the mutually confirming relations that connect its constitutive elements. The rhetorical figure that determines this discursive space can be seen at work in the three novels studied, irrespective of the fact that each proposes a different vision of autochthony founded on national idiosyncratic exigencies. Hence, although the *gaucho* and the *llanero* are not interchangeable, the discourses that propose each as a representative of autochthony are, as I have attempted to show, analogous. Admittedly only three texts have been examined; yet my purpose has not been to arrive at a typology of a genre but to explore the discursive underpinnings of three works that are commonly acknowledged to be archetypes of that literary modality.

Furthermore, the analysis of these novels identified the existence of a parallel critical dimension in them that, as it was established early on, is a constitutive part of the enterprise of *producing* an autochthonous text. We saw that regardless of the uncomplicated assumptions of immediacy and referentiality that the novels uphold, there is an underlying level at which these presuppositions are radically questioned and finally overthrown. This deconstructive gesture appears under a different guise in each novel, but the result is the same: a thorough challenging of the text's unproblematic assumptions regarding its signifying practice. In *La vorágine*, it was noted that Rivera's metaphorical association of language with his terrifying vision of nature compromised the conception of language on which his poetic ideology was predicated. It was also shown how the author's avowed purpose in writing the novel – the execration of the rubber industry in the Amazon region – was undermined by the novel's own dialectics. In *Doña Bárbara*, we witnessed the subversion of the work's presentation of the struggle between the forces of Civilization and Barbarism. The proliferation of allegoresis that was put in evidence in the novel resulted in the questioning of the principle of allegorical propriety, and hence in the weakening of the original doctrinaire formulation of that struggle in the figures of doña Bárbara and Santos Luzardo. I also suggested that in the final analysis, the character of doña Bárbara is more attuned to the text's commentary on signification and can therefore be considered emblematic of the novel as a whole, in spite of the fact that such a conclusion contradicts the ideological framework that governs the work. Finally, in *Don Segundo Sombra* it was remarked how the text labors to underwrite its economy of signification by conspicuously establishing a homology between writing and work, a gesture that is synthetically represented by the economic metaphor of "taking stock" that organizes the novel. In Güiraldes' text this metaphor summarizes a series of authenticating strategies whose presence undermines the assumed organicity between writing and its referent that they purport to certify.

These new insights into the *novela de la tierra* present a significant challenge to the prevailing schemes of literary history. At a very immediate level, they are indicative of the necessity of a thorough re-reading and revalorization of the entire novelistic canon before the "Boom" in Latin American literature. I am not advocating, however, the sort of venture at a revaluation of these texts that recurs periodically in critical circles, and which has two major deficiencies. The first is that such a revalorization sometimes originates from a more or less covert resentment of what is thought to be the excessive or modish experimentation of contemporary Latin American literature. The other is that it attempts to vindicate these novels by calling attention to their structural and symbolic organization in order to render invalid the commonplace accusations regarding their lack of unity and aesthetic ingenuousness. A recent such attempt to rescue *La vorágine* from these charges by showing how the circle and the triangle are structuring figures in the novel, concludes by asserting the following: "The above analysis leaves no doubt about the impropriety of the condescension with which *La vorágine* has been treated by the critics of the *boom* . . . The apparently chaotic structure . . . reflects the author's vision of the world and becomes coherent when properly interpreted."[1] One of the presuppositions of my study is precisely that this kind of unifying reading cannot achieve a radical overturning of the received views on the *novela de la tierra* because it only manages to confirm the text's assumptions about its own coherence. My premise throughout has been that a more productive way to reactivate these novels is to read them against the grain, as it were, to show how this assumed coherence is called into question by the text's own contradictory dialectics. Only then will these works, which otherwise seem so inescapably tied to their historico-literary moment, be reinscribed in the contemporary critical scene.

It is now a customary attitude to extol the merits of modern Latin American literary works by measuring them against the works that preceded. But if our reading of these texts has established anything, it should be that the literature of the "Boom" can no longer define itself in contradistinction to the *novela de la tierra* except in a superficial and uncritical fashion. In fact, the condescension with which these novels are alluded to masks a continuity between them and the novels of the "Boom" that we are only now beginning to understand from the perspective offered us by the post-"Boom."[2] For regardless of the obvious differences, many of the novels of the "Boom" were still as immersed in the topic of the exploration of Latin American identity and its literary representation as was the case with the *novela de la tierra*. *Cien años de soledad*, for instance, offered a microcosmic view of Latin American history in the guise of a chronicle of the Buendía family; it also propounded magical realism as a privileged category for the apprehension and understanding of Latin American reality. In turn Cortázar's *Rayuela* was, among other things, a polemical meditation on Latin American cultural identity staged on both sides of the Atlantic. This continuity dictates that if the *novela de la tierra* is perceived nowadays to be out of contention for critical favor it is essentially because the terms in which it articulated a cultural ontology for Latin America are not deemed adequate at present.

The critical misfortunes of the *novela de la tierra* should alert us to the dangers of a conception of literary history that perceives progress in literary developments, thereby sanctioning the relegation of certain texts to oblivion. This is, nonetheless, but a reflection in critical circles of a belief that literature periodically upholds as a definition of its own modernity; one only has to bear in mind the original reception of the *novela de la tierra* as a revolutionary beginning to understand the repetitiveness of this gesture. What must be arrived at instead is a novel formulation of literary history, similar to the one envisioned by Paul de Man in an essay that has guided many of the questions raised in this study: "Could we conceive of a literary history that would not truncate literature by putting us misleadingly *into* or *outside* it, that would be able to maintain the literary aporia throughout, account at the same time for the truth and the falsehood of the knowledge literature conveys about itself, distinguish rigorously between metaphorical and historical language, and account for literary modernity as well as for its historicity?"[3] That we should end our reading of these purportedly archaic texts by understanding the need for such a radical undertaking is the best evidence one can offer for the existence of a complexity at their core that time has neither tamed nor diminished.

Notes

All translations throughout the book are mine unless otherwise stated.

1 Introduction: The exoticism of the autochthonous

1 *La expresión americana*, p. 290.
2 In *Discusión*, pp. 128–37.
3 Borges, p. 132.
4 Borges, pp. 132–33. Camels are, in fact, mentioned in the Koran; I have also been unable to locate in Gibbon's masterpiece the remark attributed to him by Borges. It would appear that this is yet another example of the typically Borgesian maneuver of manufacturing sources in order to advance an argument based on their authority. This practice does not undermine, however, the validity of Borges' critique.
5 As Emir Rodríguez Monegal explains (*Jorge Luis Borges: A Literary Biography*, pp. 418–25), although the essay first appeared in *Sur* in 1955, Borges had presented it previously as a lecture in 1951. On this and other aspects of Borges' relations with Perón's regime see Rodríguez Monegal, "Borges and Politics."
6 *The Scope of Anthropology*, p. 44. For a sustained examination of these issues see Lévi-Strauss' *Tristes Tropiques* and his "Introduction à l'oeuvre de Marcel Mauss," pp. ix–liii.
7 "The Cerebral Savage" in *The Interpretation of Cultures*, pp. 345–59. The result according to Geertz is "an infernal culture machine [that] annuls history, reduces sentiment to a shadow of the intellect, and replaces the particular minds of particular savages in particular jungles with the Savage Mind immanent in us all" (p. 355). My intention is not to join in the polemics that Geertz establishes, but to point out that the debate itself is possible only because anthropological discourse is exceptionally aware of the unavoidable presence of mediation in intersubjective circumstances.
8 Lévi-Strauss has some poignant reflections on the anthropologist's relationship to his own society in the chapter entitled "A Little Glass of Rum" in *Tristes Tropiques*, pp. 383–93.

9 "Criticism and Crisis" in *Blindness and Insight*, p. 8.
10 de Man, p. 8.
11 "The rhetoric of crisis states it own truth in the mode of error. It is itself radically blind to the light it emits." de Man, p. 16.
12 *Fact and Symbol*, p. 186.
13 Graña, pp. 186–87.
14 *The Sense of an Ending*, p. 46.
15 Preface to the *Phenomenology of Mind*, p. 83.
16 *The Savage Mind*, p. 32.
17 José Martí, "Nuestra América" in *Prosa y poesía*, pp. 363–64.
18 Martí, p. 369.
19 Martí, p. 371.
20 *Alejo Carpentier*, p. 19.
21 "The Nature of Pronouns" in *Problems in General Linguistics*, pp. 219–20. The entire fifth section of the book, entitled "Man and Language," is apposite to our discussion. The term "shifter" is derived from R. Jakobson's essay "Shifters, Verbal Categories and the Russian Verb" in *Selected Writings*, II, pp. 130–47.
22 "Modernity exists in the form of a desire to wipe out whatever came earlier, in the hope of reaching at last a point that could be called a true present, a point or origin that marks a new departure. This combined interplay of deliberate forgetting with an action that is also a new origin reaches the full power of the idea of modernity." "Literary History and Literary Modernity" in *Blindness and Insight*, p. 148.
23 *Blindness and Insight*, p. 151.
24 "México y Estados Unidos: posiciones y contraposiciones," p. 6.
25 *Children of the Mire*, p. 85.
26 Paz, *Children of the Mire*. All further references to this work will be included parenthetically in the text. Two other suggestive accounts of Latin American modernity that take as their point of departure Paz's views are the following: "Modernidad, modernismo y nueva narrativa" by Roberto González Echevarría, and Aníbal González's *La crónica modernista hispanoamericana*, pp. 5–12. See also José Joaquín Brunner, "Entonces, ¿existe o no la modernidad en América Latina?," pp. 2–5. A number of critics who have written on *modernismo* have also produced some useful insights on modernity in Latin America: Angel Rama, *Rubén Darío y el modernismo*, pp. 35–79; Noé Jitrik, *Las contradicciones del modernismo*, pp. 103–28; Françoise Pérus, *Literatura y sociedad en America Latina*, pp. 27–61.
27 Earlier, and referring to the newly independent Latin American republics, Paz had also asserted that "the new countries went on being the old colonies; social conditions remained unchanged, but now reality was hidden under layers of liberal and democratic rhetoric . . . The

groups which challenged Spanish power used the revolutionary ideas of the time but were neither able nor willing to change our society" (pp. 85–86). See also Paz's chapter on "From Independence to Revolution" in *The Labyrinth of Solitude*, pp. 117–49. The survival of colonial structures and conditions in Post-Independence Latin America is examined by Stanley and Barbara Stein in *The Colonial Heritage of Latin America*, and by Sakari Sariola in *Power and Resistance*.

28 I use the adjective "constative" in its speech-act acceptation proposed by J. L. Austin in *How to Do Things With Words, passim*.

29 Given the contradictory relation with modernity that I propose exists at the heart of cultural discourse in Latin America, characterizing that relationship becomes an equally difficult endeavor. In the most general sense, one could label this posture postmodern, if we subscribe to Richard Palmer's use of the term to describe any effort whose main thrust is "to call modernity into question – that is, to think radically about modernity" ("Toward a Postmodern Hermeneutics of Performance," p. 21). But one could also invoke Jean-François Lyotard's description of the postmodern as the breakdown of the great legitimizing myths of the West and the enactment in their place of specifically delimited and local narratives. Latin America's obsessive and solipsistic meditation on its cultural specificity could conceivably be understood as an instance of such a narrative. See *The Postmodern Condition*.

30 This relationship is studied in detail in Frances A. Yates, *The Art of Memory*. See also Jonathan Spence's marvelous book *The Memory Palace of Mateo Ricci*, where the author discusses the nature and history of spatial mnemonics.

31 Following Paz, Roberto González Echevarría has advanced that the lack of material basis for modernity in Latin America has manifested itself in a number of literary texts: "If we wanted to, we could read Esteban Echevarría's 'El matadero' as a sort of allegory of modernity, which raises its head only to be immediately destroyed by a context that is hostile to it. There is, by the way, a whole thematics of the modern hero defeated by the archaic in all of Spanish American narrative, from the Romantic novel and the anti-slavery novel up until *Los pasos perdidos*, including *Doña Bárbara* as well . . . In this context both the idea of Spanish America and of its literature are formed, so that it is precisely in Spanish American literature that the legitimacy of the modern is put in check," ("Modernidad, modernismo . . . " p. 158, my translation). The texts González mentions do indeed deal with the issue of modernity, but their explicit intent is not to question the legitimacy of the modern, but rather to denounce the factors that retard the advent of modernity in Latin America. This is an agenda that literary texts have shared with the discourses of other disciplines – history, sociology,

philosophy – throughout Latin America's intellectual and cultural history. But to say that modernity is not possible in Latin America is not tantamount to renouncing or abjuring it. Therefore, I agree with González when he proposes that "modernity in Spanish America is characterized by a fragility of which it is aware" (p. 157). But the implication that this fragility entails a de-legitimization of the modern does not necessarily follow, and is not borne out by the textual evidence adduced. As Marshall Berman's quotation below makes evident, such a fragile experience of modernity produces a desperate desire to reaffirm the modern, rather than a questioning of it. By way of contrast, my intention is to establish that while there is an embracing of the modern in Latin American discourse, there is also a dimension of it that wishes to underscore Latin America's incommensurability with modernity, a displacement away from itself that has its final resolution in Latin America's continuous affirmation of its avowed cultural difference and specificity.

32 Domingo Faustino Sarmiento, *Facundo*, pp. 9–10. Subsequent references to this work will appear parenthetically in the text.

33 For a more thorough analysis of the discursive fissures in Sarmiento's text, see my "Facundo y la sabiduría del poder."

34 *Seis ensayos en busca de nuestra expresión*, p. 26.

35 Marshall Berman, *All That is Solid Melts Into Air: The Experience of Modernity*, pp. 231–32.

36 "Historical Notes on Ideological Aspects of the Concept of Culture in Germany and Russia," pp. 207–8. See also the entry on "Culture" in Raymond Williams' *Keywords*, pp. 76–82.

37 In a recent monograph (*Questing Fictions: Latin America's Family Romance*) Djelal Kadir has advanced a compelling thesis regarding the Latin American search for cultural identity. In his view, this search is the result of a peculiar internalization by Latin America of the European dreams of utopia that were "fulfilled" by the discovery of the New World. But in order to remain as an open-ended project, the latter must resort to a series of strategies that inevitably postpone the desired epiphany. Kadir's scheme provides an interesting turn to an argument presented by Leopoldo Zea in *En torno a una filosofía americana*: "America always lives in the future, in utopia. It is only the projection of European ideals without being able to fulfill them. *As soon as it fulfilled them it would have a history and would cease being an always renewed promise.* Since America always represents the future of Europe it is always new. In this being the future of Europe, that which has not been or is, lies the continual novelty of America, its being always new territory, a land of projects" (p. 50, my emphasis). Kadir's formulation of a self-thwarting "quest romance" for Latin America could be interpreted as a mytho/poetic rendering of the rhetorical problematic that I have endeavored

to outline above. That is, what he portrays as a romance of "recurrent homelessness" could be read as a narrative version, an allegory of the primordial rhetorical disjunction, the displacement of the text away from itself that in my view characterizes the Latin American discursive situation.

38 Jean Franco has summarized the essential aspects of this position in "Criticism and Literature Within the Context of a Dependent Culture." See also Hernán Vidal's *Literatura hispanoamericana e ideología liberal*. The bibliography on dependency theory in a Latin American context is quite extensive. I have profitably consulted the following sources: André Gunder Frank, *Capitalism and Underdevelopment in Latin America*; Fernando Henrique Cardoso and Enzo Faleto, *Dependencia y desarrollo en América Latina*; Ronald H. Chilcote, "Dependency: A Critical Synthesis of the Literature" (this entire issue is dedicated to a debate on dependency theory); Helio Jaguaribe *et al.*, *La dependencia político-económica de América Latina*; and Tulio Halperín Donghi, "'Dependency Theory' and Latin American Historiography."

39 This objection is expressed clearly by the following critique of dependency theory as a comprehensive paradigm of economic and political understanding: "[Dependency theory] implied a 'zero-sum' process whereby the advances of one nation were, and could only be, made at the expense of another . . . This part of the argument has been attacked from several directions. For instance, it was implicit in this notion that dependent social formations were, to a certain extent, 'passive victims' of their place in the world capitalist economy which was the single main determinant of their internal economic and class structure. This failure to recognise the significance of autonomous Third World histories . . . represents a venture into a Euro-centrism that utterly fails to understand the two-way nature of the relationships between social formations." D. K. Forbes, *The Geography of Underdevelopment*, p. 71.

40 My argument here reflects issues that are currently debated by anthropological theory. See, for instance, Marshall Sahlins' *Historical Metaphors and Mythical Realities*, pp. 1–8, and "The Stranger King"; Johannes Fabian, *Time and the Other: How Anthropology Makes its Object*; Clifford Geertz, *The Interpretation of Cultures*, pp. 201–7; and Pierre Bourdieu's illuminating work *Outline of a Theory of Practice*.

41 Jennifer Wicke has cogently discussed some of these issues in "Postmodernism: The Perfume of Information." Or as Djelal Kadir has said: "Emergent cultures are emerging from a Eurocentered colonial past into a Eurocentered paradigm of cultural advancement . . . We appropriated [the other] as a colony, expropriated it as a former colony, to reappropriate it as cultural complement and reflective object." In "Cultural Deliberations: States of Emergency," p. 13.

42 There appears to be a consensus on the validity of this thesis in the critical literature on nationalism. Of the immense bibliography on the subject the following works have been especially useful: Ernest Gellner, *Thought and Change,* and *Nations and Nationalism*; Elie Kedourie, *Nationalism*; Aira Kemiläinen, *Nationalism: Problems Concerning the Word, the Concept and Classification*; Clifford Geertz, "After the Revolution: The Fate of Nationalism in the New States" in *The Interpretation of Cultures*, pp. 234–54; Benedict Anderson, *Imagined Communities*; and Karl E. Scheibe, "The Psychology of National Identity."

43 Gellner, *Nations and Nationalism*, p. 56. In an earlier book Gellner had proposed that "nationalism is not the awakening of nations to self-consciousness: it invents nations where they do not exist." *Thought and Change*, p. 169.

44 Kedourie, *Nationalism*, p. 68.

45 The relationship between philology and literature is not without its difficulties, which can be traced back to their simultaneous appearance as competing discourses in the nineteenth century. Michel Foucault has addressed these specifically in *The Order of Things*, pp. 294–300.

46 "Americanismo y cubanismo literarios," p. 97. Or as Pedro Henríquez Ureña said: "We have not renounced Spanish, and the problem of our very own and original expression begins there." In *Seis ensayos*, p. 21.

47 Geertz, "After the Revolution," p. 240.

48 César Graña has made the following suggestive remark: "The might and the plenty of the United States has, on the whole, excused the American intellectual, certainly since the Civil War, from the necessity of being a cultural nationalist." *Fact and Symbol*, p. 197.

49 That the search for cultural autochthony in Latin America is directly related to modernity can be ascertained precisely by the fact that this critique has obtained concurrently with the general delegitimization of the modern that has characterized Western discourse during the last twenty-five years. An account of the ongoing reconsideration of the concept of cultural identity in Latin America can be found in Roberto González Echevarría's *The Voice of the Masters*, pp. 33–44.

2 The *novela de la tierra*

1 "El sur" in *Ficciones*, pp. 170–71.

2 "Subdesarrollo y letras de osadía" in *El escritor latinoamericano y la revolución posible*, p. 50.

3 "Primitives and Creators," p. 1287.

4 *El boom de la novela latinoamericana: ensayo*, p. 77.

5 For instance, in his *Historia de la literatura hispanoamericana*, Julio A. Leguizamón entitles the section where he studies the autochthonous

novel "La novela criolla o de la tierra: Güiraldes, Rivera, Gallegos" (p. 500).

6 See Frye's now classic "Polemical Introduction" in his *Anatomy of Criticism*, pp. 3–29.

7 I am referring to *La nueva novela hispanoamericana* by Carlos Fuentes, and to the following two works by Arturo Torres Rioseco: *La novela en la América Hispana* and *Novelistas contemporáneos de América*.

8 *Beginnings: Intention and Method*, pp. 72–73. Said's book is the most comprehensive and thorough examination of the strategic importance of points of departure, origins, etc. See especially pp. 29–78 and pp. 191–275.

9 Said, p. 76.

10 Said, pp. 76–77.

11 Fuentes, *La nueva novela*, p. 9.

12 Said, p. 77.

13 *La novela en la América Hispana*, p. 244.

14 *Novelistas contemporáneos*, p. vii.

15 This is the premise informing, for instance, Hayden White's important exploration of the rhetoric of historiographic discourse. See his *Metahistory*, as well as *Tropics of Discourse* and *The Content of the Form*. For White's perceptive comments on literary history, consult his "Literary History: The Point of it All." In this regard, see also Roland Barthes's "Historical Discourse."

16 For example in his book *The Political Unconscious*, Fredric Jameson argues that genre criticism finds itself at present "thoroughly discredited by modern literary theory and practice" (p. 105). From a different perspective, Jacques Derrida convincingly dismantles the concept of genre in "La Loi du genre/The Law of Genre." See also J. Hillis Miller, "The Search for Grounds in Literary Study." Ralph Cohen attempts to revive genre studies through a radical historicization of the idea of genre (an enterprise favored by Jameson, pp. 103–50) in his "History and Genre." Adena Rosmarin's *The Power of Genre* argues that genre criticism can survive only if it becomes conscious of its suasive nature, that is, of the existence of genre only as a projection of the critic's own discourse.

17 "Epístola a la señora de Lugones" in *Poesías de Rubén Darío*, p. 223.

18 More precise information about these developments can be found in Pedro Henríquez Ureña's encyclopedic *Historia de la cultura en la América Hispánica*, pp. 81–94. The awareness of the significance of linguistic idiosyncrasy was also responsible for the interest in spoken language that one can detect, albeit sporadically and unsystematically, in such dissimilar nineteenth-century writers as Esteban Echeverría, Jorge Isaacs and Eugenio Cambaceres.

19 "El cuadro de costumbres, el cuento y la posibilidad de un deslinde."
   Although in its most "folklorizing moments" the *novela de la tierra*
   appears to recall the *cuadro de costumbres*, I believe that the following
   fundamental differences remain: (1) In thematic terms, the *cuadro* paid
   some attention to manifestations of rural culture, but was not restricted
   to it. As opposed to the exclusively non-urban thematics of the *novela de
   la tierra*, by the time the *cuadro* was introduced into Spain (and later in
   Latin America) following its English and French models, it had evolved
   into an almost exclusively urban phenomenon; (2) The *cuadro* inhabited
   a static dimension that is the antithesis of the chronological framework
   of the novel; (3) In the *novela de la tierra* the here-and-now mimetic
   representational ideology of the *cuadro* is explicitly and self-consciously
   mediated by novelistic form. This faithfulness to its deictic purpose
   explains why the *artículo de costumbres* did not develop into more complex
   literary forms, but rather into the journalistic *crónica* of the nineteenth
   century. In this last regard see Aníbal González, *La crónica modernista*,
   pp. 61–73. For a more detailed consideration of the *cuadro de costumbres*
   see Margarita Ucelay Da Cal's exemplary study *Los españoles pintados por
   sí mismos (1843–1844)*; Frank M. Duffey, *The Early Cuadro de Costumbres in
   Colombia*; and José Montesinos, *Costumbrismo y novela*.
20 *Seis ensayos en busca de nuestra expresión*, p. 39.
21 Martin S. Stabb, *In Quest of Identity*, p. 58.
22 Stabb himself admits that "in 1914, when Caso's essay 'La filosofía de
   la intuición' appeared, Spanish American intellectuals knew relatively
   little about Henri Bergson. Caso was the first Mexican to discuss the
   French philosopher at length; and he may well have been one of the first
   Spanish Americans to do so" (p. 51).
23 The text is from a speech given in 1917 entitled "La evolución de
   nuestra diplomacia" in *Mi campaña hispanoamericana*, p. 203.
24 *La raza cósmica*, p. 31.
25 Octavio Paz has devoted some illuminating pages specifically to the
   relationship between Latin America and the United States in *Cuadrivio*,
   pp. 47–55; *Postdata*, pp. 58–67; "México y Estados Unidos: posiciones
   y contraposiciones," and of course, *The Labyrinth of Solitude*, pp. 9–46.
   See also Carlos Rangel, *Del buen salvaje al buen revolucionario*.
26 The following is only a representative list of works on Latin America
   and the United States published during the period in question that
   cannot reflect the real depth of the bibliography on the subject: Justo
   Sierra, *En tierra Yankee* (1898); several articles by Manuel Ugarte,
   among them "El peligro yanqui" (1901); José Enrique Rodó, *Ariel*
   (1900); Aníbal Maurtúa, *La idea pan-americana y la cuestión del arbitraje*
   (1901); José Francisco López, *Filosofía de la historia y de las razas latina y
   sajona* (1900); Salvador R. Merlos, *América Latina ante el peligro* (1914);

Luis Araquistaín, *El peligro yanqui* (1919); Alfonso Reyes, "México y los Estados Unidos" (1920); and Arturo Capdevila, *América: nuestras naciones ante los Estados Unidos* (1926). A full appreciation of the extent and complexity of the relationship can be obtained from the definitive *A Bibliography of United States–Latin America Relations Since 1810*.

27 During the years 1911–13, Ugarte traveled throughout Latin America and Spain lecturing in most major cities on the danger that the United States implied for the southern continent. Later, in 1922, José Vasconcelos would undertake a tour with similar purposes throughout the principal Latin American capitals.

28 Stabb, p. 40.

29 Stabb later concludes that "although anti-Yankeeism coincides with the diffusion of Rodó's ideas and although there is a current of fear, suspicion, and even hostility toward the United States among some of his followers, the inclusion of *yanquifobia* in the definition of Arielism clouds the issue" (p. 40).

30 In his book *Balance y liquidación del novecientos*, Luis Alberto Sánchez argues that with very few exceptions, the anti-American rhetoric of the time did not arise from a confrontation with the political and social realities of imperialism. Of Ugarte, for instance, he says that he "limited his anti-imperialist politics to a campaign of denunciation, without unmasking also the important complicity of the native oligarchies" (p. 119). See especially pp. 71–126.

31 After the first Pan-American Conference in Washington, there were meetings of the member nations in the following years and cities during the period 1900–30:
    1901 Mexico
    1906 Rio de Janeiro
    1910 Buenos Aires
    1923 Santiago
    1928 Havana

32 For a history of the doctrine of Pan-Americanism from the perspective of the United States see Elihu Root, *Latin America and the United States*; Joseph B. Lockey, *Pan Americanism: Its Beginnings*; and Samuel Guy Inman, *Problems in Pan Americanism*.

33 Arguments on Pan-Americanism can be found in the following: J. Vargas Vila, *Ante los bárbaros* (1902?); Arthur Orlando, *Pan-americanismo* (1906); *La personalidad política y la América del porvenir* by Jenaro Abasolo Navarrete (1907); Eliseo Giberga, *El pan-americanismo y el pan-hispanismo* (1916); José Gaxiola, *La frontera de la raza* (1917), especially ch. 9, "La alianza latino-americana," and ch. 10 "El Panamericanismo"; Fernando Berenguer, *El Hispano-americanismo* (1918); Ernesto Quesada, *La evolución del panamericanismo* (1919); and Manuel Ugarte, *El destino de un*

continente (1923), especially ch. 10, "Ante la victoria anglosajona." The debate over Pan-Americanism continued unabated well into the 1930s. See, for instance, José Vasconcelos, *Bolivarismo y Monroísmo* (1935) and Víctor Raúl Haya de la Torre, *A dónde va Indoamérica* (1936), especially the essays entitled "Mutabilidad del panamericanismo" and "Equivocada defensa latina del panamericanismo."

34 pp. 310–11.

35 Manuel Ugarte, *Las nuevas tendencias literarias*, pp. 143–44. In an article written in 1911, Ugarte expressed similar thoughts on the matter: "Pan-american meetings are built on a fiction . . . Origin, language, religion: they are all different between us. How are we to discuss in common the needs and interests of two different races, of two distinct civilizations? In America today there is only one possibility of unification, and it is the one dictated by both History and origin to the peoples of the Southern part of the New World." In *La Patria Grande*, p. 29.

36 F. García Godoy, *La literatura americana de nuestros días*, pp. 20–21.

37 *Las nuevas tendencias literarias*, pp. 27–28.

38 The Panama Congress in 1826 saw delegates from Colombia, Peru, Central America and Mexico, by far the best attended; In 1847 only five countries accepted invitations to a meeting; in 1856, only three; in 1864, seven; in 1877, five. The reawakened interest in a continental union of all Latin American nations at the beginning of the twentieth century produced retrospective books such as *Congreso de Panamá y Tacubaya* (1912) by P. A. Zubieta, and *El ideal latinoamericano* (n.a., 1919).

39 Manuel Ugarte "La atracción de los orígenes" in *Mi campaña hispanoamericana* (1922), pp. 230–31.

40 The *Centenario* was truly a continental affair. For the celebration of the *Centenario* in Mexico, delegations from all Latin American countries gathered there in 1910. As part of the commemoration Pedro Henríquez Ureña and others prepared a collection of texts on the occasion entitled *Antología del Centenario*. Rubén Darío represented Nicaragua in the festivities. In Argentina, the newspaper *La Nación* published an 800-page supplement that included Darío's *Canto a la Argentina*. For the equivalent celebration in Peru the Argentine poet Leopoldo Lugones accompanied his country's delegation to Lima. See "Les écrivains du Centenaire" by Francisco Contreras, in his *Les Ecrivains contemporains de l'Amérique espagnole*, pp. 17–36.

41 Since the idea of *hispanoamericanismo* brought implicit with it an acknowledgement and appreciation of the Spanish culture that was the common heritage of all Spanish American nations, the *Centenario* did not have the anti-Spanish connotations that it could easily have had; in fact, quite

the opposite occurred. A then very popular revisionist interpretation saw the independence movement not as a separatist endeavor but as an extension of the anti-monarchical movement that had obtained in Spain at the time as well. See Manuel Ugarte, "Causas y consecuencias de la revolución americana" (1910) in his *Mi campaña hispanoamericana* (1922), pp. 23–47, and José León Suárez, *Carácter de la revolución americana* (1917). There were also a number of works that expounded on the intimate nature of the cultural bond between Spain and Latin America, such as Rafael Altamira, *España y América* (1908); Alejandro Romero García, "Genio de raza" (1908); José Roguerio Sánchez, *Autores españoles e hispanoamericanos* (1911); Manuel Gálvez, *El solar de la raza* (1913); Alfonso Reyes, "España y América" (1920); and Antonio Caso, "En América dirá su última palabra la civilización latina" (1922). In "Tres metáforas sobre España e Hispanoamérica," José Juan Arrom examines critically some of the figures that arose to express the nature of this relationship.

42 *La creación de un continente* (1912), pp. vii–ix. García Calderón's dedication of his book reads as follows: "To the memory of don Lorenzo García Calderón, representative for Arequipa to the Cortes de Cádiz in 1812, this book is dedicated by his great grandson in respectful homage."

43 Bernardo González Arrili, *El futuro de América*, p. 19.

44 Blanco Fombona's edition of Bolívar's letters had an incisive prologue by José Enrique Rodó, who had himself written a book on Bolívar (*Bolívar* [1914]) and had also dedicated a number of pages to him in his *El mirador de Próspero* (1913). A sample of the first titles published by Editorial América substantiates its focus on the historical moment of Independence: J. D. Monsalve, *El ideal político del Libertador Simón Bolívar* (1916); Carlos Pereyra, *Humboldt en América* (1917), *El general Sucre* (1917) and *El mito de Monroe* (1914); and Ricardo Becerra, *Vida de don Francisco de Miranda* (1918).

45 The memoirs published include those of Generals O'Leary, Páez, García Camba, Urdaneta, Paz and those of Fray Servando Teresa de Mier. Other books and articles of the time dealing with the Independence period are Daniel O'Leary's three works entitled *Bolívar y la emancipación de Sur América* (1915), *Bolívar y las repúblicas del sur* (1919) and *El Congreso Internacional de Panamá en 1826* (1920); Pedro Henríquez Ureña, *Traducciones y paráfrasis en la literatura mexicana de la época de la independencia* (1913); *Bolívar*, by Cornelio Hispano (pseudonym for Ismael López) (1917); Jules Mancini, *Bolívar y la emancipación de las colonias españolas* (1912); Antonio Caso, "El pensamiento de Bolívar" (1923); José Santos Chocano, "Plan de la Epopeya del Libertador" (1923); Manuel Díaz Rodríguez, "Del primer centenario de Aya-

cucho" (1924) and *Los cantores de Bolívar en el primer centenario de su muerte* by Ismael López (1930).

46 Arturo Capdevila, *América: nuestras naciones ante los Estados Unidos* (1926), pp. 61–62. See also Ricardo Rojas, *La argentinidad* (1916).

47 See his *Le Mondonovisme* and "Poètes mondovistes" in *Les Ecrivains contemporains*, pp. 114–28. Contreras expounded on the idea of *mundonovismo* in several of the reviews he wrote for the *Mercure de France*. See for instance "La nouvelle littérature" (February 16, 1911), and "Le roman mondonoviste" (June 15, 1922). For a review of Contreras' critical *oeuvre* and his concept of *mundonovismo* consult Sylvia Molloy, *La diffusion de la littérature hispano-américaine en France au XXe siècle*, pp. 77–85. See also Liliana Samurovic-Pavlovic, *Les lettres hispano-américaines au "Mercure de France"*, pp. 45–63.

48 The profound imprint that the First World War made in Latin American intellectual circles can be gauged from the extraordinary number of essays and chronicles devoted to it. See, for instance, Enrique Gómez Carrillo, *Campos de batalla y campos de ruinas* (1915), and *Crónica de la guerra* (1915); Francisco Contreras, *Les Ecrivains hispano-américains et la guerre européenne* (1917); also *L'Amérique en face de la conflagration européenne* (1916), by Sá Vianna. Daringly – although consistent with his general views – Manuel Ugarte proposed that Latin America should "avail itself of the happy circumstance to disentangle ourselves from the deceitful pan-americanism that has turned [our countries] into a hapless succession of zeros." From "Sobre la neutralidad" (1917) in *La nación latinoamericana*, p. 149.

49 *The Order of Things*, p. 251.

50 Some of these are examined in the anthology *Organic Form: The Life of an Idea*, ed. G. S. Rousseau. See also Robert Nisbet's "Genealogy, Growth and Other Metaphors," and his book *Social Change and History*, where he investigates the implications of these ideas for historiographic thought. M. H. Abrams has studied the concept of aesthetic organicism in *The Mirror and the Lamp*, especially pp. 218–25, and in his *Natural Supernaturalism*, pp. 172–79 and pp. 431–37.

51 I am referring to books such as *Von der Sprache und Weisheit der Indier* (1808) by Schlegel, *Über das Konjugationssystem der Sanskritsprache* (1816) by Bopp, Grimm's *Deutsche Grammatik* (1819) and *Geschichte der deutschen Sprache* (1848), and *Ueber das Entstehen der grammatischen Formen* (1822) by Wilhelm von Humboldt.

52 "[Language] is no longer a system of representations which has the power to pattern and recompose other representations; it designates in its roots the most constant of actions, states and wishes . . . Language is 'rooted' not in the things perceived, but in the active subject. And perhaps, in that case, it is a product of will and energy, rather than a

memory that duplicates representation. We speak because we act, and
not because recognition is a means of cognition. Like action, language
expresses a profound will to something ... At the moment when
philology is constituted there arises the tendency to attribute to
language profound powers of expression" (Foucault, p. 290).

53 Foucault, p. 290.

54 Foucault, p. 286.

55 For this overview I have also consulted the following works on
nineteenth-century theories of language: Holger Pedersen, *The Discovery
of Language*; R. H. Robins, *A Short History of Linguistics*; Tzvetan
Todorov, *Théories du symbole*; and *Linguistics and Literary Theory*, by Karl
Uitti.

56 These dicta are quoted by William A. Wilson in his *Folklore and
Nationalism in Modern Finland*, p. 30.

57 Ernest Renan, *Oeuvres complètes*, vol. III, p. 883.

58 J. G. Herder, *Reflections on the Philosophy of the History of Mankind*, p. 4.
The entire first chapter, entitled "National Genius and the Environment," is a detailed examination of this bond. For a more detailed
discussion of Herder's ideas see *Herder and After*, by G. A. Wells, and
F. M. Barnard, *Herder's Social and Political Thought*.

59 Herder, p. 20.

60 Herder, p. 8. In another section Herder claims that besides temperature, the environment includes "the elevation and depression of a
region, its nature and products, the food and drink men enjoy in it, the
mode of life they pursue, the labors in which they are employed"
(p. 16).

61 The unanimous organicity of the forces of life proposed by the
plant/culture analogy can be found in the most dissimilar writers.
Herder calls man "the most perfect animal plant" (p. 23); in *L'Avenir de
la science*, Renan refers to "the divine force that vegetates in all the
creations of the human mind" (p. 889); Taine avers that "so it is with a
people as with a plant; the same sap, under the same temperature, and
in the same soil, produces, at different steps of its progressive development, different formations, buds, flowers, fruits, seed vessels, in such a
manner that the one which follows has always the first for its condition,
and grows from its death." (From the "Introduction" to the *History of
English Literature* in *Critical Theory Since Plato*, p. 609.)

62 Renan's quotation appears in *Oeuvres complètes*, p. 847. Regardless of his
emphasis on linguistic structures, one of Vossler's aims was the
determination of a "national style" (as expressed, for instance in the
title of his *Frankreichs Kultur und Sprache*). In Spitzer the philological
interpretive apparatus was not deployed to uncover a genetic and
coherent collective essence but to reveal in the text the presence of a

similarly conceived individual subject. This internal transformation within the discipline of philology accounts to some degree for the famous polemics regarding the origins of the Spanish epic that had as its most significant antagonists Ramón Menéndez Pidal and Joseph Bédier: the Spaniard emphasized the collective, anonymous contributions to the construction of the great epic poems, whereas Bédier stressed those aspects of the text that evinced the subjectivity of the individual responsible for its composition and redaction.

63 As is well known, the transmission of Romantic philological concepts from their essential German sources (Herder, Hegel, Savigny) to Latin American intellectuals in the early nineteenth century occurred through French conduits. Writers such as Lerminier, Leroux, Bonald, Lamennais and De Maistre were widely read by, among others, Echeverría, Sarmiento and Alberdi. This connection has been thoroughly established and documented by Víctor Frankl in *Espíritu y camino de Hispanoamérica*, esp. pp. 440–519.

64 *Las nuevas tendencias literarias*, pp. 11–12. See also "El poeta y su pueblo" in *La nación latinoamericana*, p. 257.

65 *El payador* (1919), p. 14. A similar conception underlies Ricardo Rojas' *El canto popular* (1923).

66 *Obras completas*, vol. II, p. 34. This essay was written in 1915. Four years earlier Reyes had published *El paisaje en la poesía mexicana del siglo XIX* (1911), where he had advanced essentially the same thesis. Two other works that elaborate on this connection are *La creación de la pedagogía nacional* (1910), by Franz Tamayo and *Eurindia* (1924) by Ricardo Rojas. See also José María Soto, *La influencia del ambiente* (1919).

67 The specificity of the relationship between the *novela de la tierra* and philology also enables us to contrast it with two coeval literary manifestations that at times have been mentioned in the same breath as the former: Afro-Hispanic literature and *indigenista* literary production. The fundamental difference between them and the *novela de la tierra* stems from the fact that in these other instances the mediating discipline for the creation of literary texts is not philology, but rather anthropology and related ethnological research. Although the investigative activity of the philologist – the collection of popular ballads and legends, familiarization with the geographic milieu, etc. – shows a superficial similarity with the anthropologist's field work, the two should not be confused, since strikingly different assumptions inform the two disciplines.

68 Rómulo Gallegos, *Obras completas*, vol. II, pp. 642–43.

69 In *L'Avenir de la science* – a text that is a treatise on the philological method, Renan expresses this ultimate goal with recourse to a botanical metaphor: "Both the layman and the learned man can equally admire a

beautiful flower; but they do not admire quite the same things. The layman sees only vivid colors and elegant shapes. The sage hardly notices such superficial beauties, mesmerized as he is by the profound marvel of life and its mysteries. It is not precisely the flower that he admires; it is life, the universal force that manifests itself in it under one of its guises." *Oeuvres complètes*, vol. III, p. 888.

70 I have profited here from Derrida's discussion of iterability as a necessary foundation of signification in "Signature événement contexte" in *Marges de la philosophie*, pp. 365–93. See also his rejoinder to John Searle on this very issue, "Limited Inc a b c."

71 "The Critical Difference" in *The Critical Difference*, p. 5.

72 The relationship of supplementarity that I identify here is reminiscent of the logic of the supplement that Jacques Derrida has described in a number of his essays. See especially the second part of his *Of Grammatology*, and "Plato's Pharmacy" in *Dissemination*, pp. 61–171.

73 Gallegos, pp. 675–76.

74 J. E. Rivera, *La vorágine*, p. 247.

75 Letter to Héctor I. Eandi (1926) in his *Obras completas*, p. 793.

76 *On Deconstruction*, p. 199. Culler's point of departure is a pertinent essay by Jacques Derrida entitled "Living On." On the issue of frames, margins, borders, etc. see also Derrida's "Parergon" in *La vérité en peinture*, pp. 19–167. J. Hillis Miller has explored the mutually "parasitical" relationship between critic and text in "The Critic as Host." More recently, Gustavo Pérez Firmat has examined the issue of marginality in Hispanic letters in his *Literature and Liminality*.

77 *Introduction to Poetics*, p. 4.

78 *Novelistas contemporáneos*, p. viii.

79 Torres, *La novela*, pp. 166–67.

80 Torres, *La novela*, p. 170.

81 Torres, *La novela*, p. 169.

82 Gallegos, *Obras completas*, vol. I, pp. 702–3.

83 The precedent for dealing with these texts as a representative triad is well established. For example: Juan Marinello, "Tres novelas ejemplares"; Concha Meléndez, "Tres novelas de la naturaleza americana, *Don Segundo Sombra*, *La vorágine*, *Doña Bárbara*"; Trinidad Pérez, ed., *Recopilación de textos sobre tres novelas ejemplares*. A more recent example is furnished by D. L. Shaw in his *Gallegos: Doña Bárbara*: "*Don Segundo Sombra* by Ricardo Güiraldes (Argentina), *La vorágine* by José Eustasio Rivera (Colombia) and *Doña Bárbara* itself, are the classic examples of the Latin American *novela de la tierra*. Their successful incorporation into fiction of the striking natural background, the *pampa*, the *selva* and the *llano* of the subcontinent, represented an important break with the imitation of European models and a great stride forward towards

authenticity in Latin American Literature" (p. 7). Likewise, in "La novela latinoamericana," Alejo Carpentier advances the following: "We all know how three novels whose names we do not need to repeat – *Don Segundo Sombra*, *La vorágine* and *Doña Bárbara* – which appeared within a year of one another, transformed the entire panorama of the Latin American novel" (p. 24). Carpentier's comment regarding the chronology of the novels' publication dates is, as we know, incorrect.

3 Don Segundo Sombra

1 *Obras completas*, p. 735.

2 Leopoldo Lugones, "*Don Segundo Sombra*, de Ricardo Güiraldes."

3 Ernesto M. Barreda, "Conversaciones del momento. Paul Groussac." The *chiripá* is an item of gaucho attire that has no direct equivalent in English. I have therefore opted for a translation that simply conveys the spirit of Groussac's remark.

4 Most of these can be found in the highly informative *Genio y figura de Ricardo Güiraldes* by Yvonne Bordelois.

5 Ramón Doll, "*Don Segundo Sombra* y el gaucho que ve el hijo del patrón."

6 "*Don Segundo Sombra*," reminiscencia infantil de Ricardo Güiraldes, pp. 99–100. A concise exposition of anti-Güiraldes criticism can be found in Leopoldo Marechal's "*Don Segundo Sombra* y el ejercicio ilegal de la crítica," and Hugo Rodríguez Alcalá, "Sobre Ricardo Güiraldes y la crítica detractora de *Don Segundo Sombra*."

7 Bordelois, p. 154.

8 Already in 1935 – nine years after the publication of *Don Segundo Sombra* – Leopoldo Marechal was able to summarize fully the essential elements of the debate in "*Don Segundo Sombra* y el ejercicio ilegal de la crítica." One could also conjecture that the critical division was accentuated by the acerbic cultural debate that came to be associated with the groups "Florida" and "Boedo" and which dominated the literary life of the 1920s in Buenos Aires. The terms of the polemics between these two factions – intrinsic literary value vs. political commitment – are reminiscent of the two critical schools on *Don Segundo Sombra*. For an excellent study of the dynamics of these two groups see Christopher Towne Leland, *The Last Happy Men*. See also Francine Masiello's *Lenguaje e ideología: las escuelas argentinas de vanguardia*.

9 Luis Soler Cañas, *Don Segundo Sombra y Areco*, p. 55.

10 The *Bildungsroman* qualities of *Don Segundo Sombra* have been discussed by a number of critics. See, for instance, Arnold Chapman, "Pampas and Big Woods"; Bernardo Gicovate, "Notes on *Don Segundo Sombra*: The Education of Fabio Cáceres"; Elías Rivers, "*Don Segundo Sombra* y la desanalfabetización del héroe"; and "Structured Education in *Don*

Segundo Sombra," by Stephen A. Sadow. I have profited from the following general studies on the *Bildungsroman*: Jerome H. Buckley, *Season of Youth: The Bildungsroman from Dickens to Golding*; Susan R. Suleiman, "La structure d'apprentissage"; and Marianne Hirsch, "The Novel of Formation as Genre."

11 The following are systematic attempts to engage the novel in an ideological framework: *Análisis de "Don Segundo Sombra"* by Eduardo Romano; "*Don Segundo Sombra*: una novela monológica," by Jorge Schwartz; Françoise Pérus, "La constitución de la ficción: mito y realidad en *Don Segundo Sombra*"; and Christopher Leland, "The Failure of Myth: Ricardo Güiraldes and *Don Segundo Sombra*," in *The Last Happy Men*, pp. 119–47. Of these, Leland's psychohistorical interpretation is, in my view, the most imaginative and suggestive.

12 Leland, pp. 119–20.

13 In a reading of *Don Segundo Sombra* that wishes to establish that Güiraldes' novel is a product of class mystification, Jorge Schwartz attributes to irony what is in fact the text's way of preempting the sort of "corrective," demystifying reading that he envisions: "The idealized vision of the gaucho, represented by the figure of Don Segundo, is projected over Fabio Cáceres, whose ambition is to become another Don Segundo. This is an ironic paradox, since the adult Fabio Cáceres is completely distanced from the initial mythical image of Don Segundo, the one he had endeavored to imitate." Schwartz, p. 445.

14 Culler, *On Deconstruction*, pp. 214–15.

15 In an article entitled "La ruta de Don Segundo," Alberto Blasi reports on his attempt to duplicate the protagonist's journey. See also Eduardo Hugo Castagnino, *En busca de "Don Segundo Sombra"*. For a detailed account of "mistakes" of all sorts in *Don Segundo Sombra* see Juan Francisco Cáldiz's *Lo que no se ha dicho de "Don Segundo Sombra"*.

16 Emir Rodríguez Monegal, "El *Martín Fierro* en Borges y Martínez Estrada," p. 289.

17 In a provocative article entitled "La lengua como arma: fundamentos del género gauchesco," Josefina Ludmer has observed that "the popular culture of the gaucho encompasses not only the folklore that he received (and transformed) from the Spaniards, but also his customs, beliefs, rituals, rules and common law. *The great dilemma of the gaucho popular culture is that it has reached us almost exclusively through its manipulation by the literate poets, who selected certain traits and transformed others according to their purposes*" (p. 471, my emphasis). My object is not – of course – to argue that the gaucho never existed, but rather to advance that, as Ludmer implies, his historical concreteness may be essentially unrecoverable. One *can* envision, however, the reconstruction of the fundamental aspects of that culture as a structural opposite to the hegemonic

culture, a project described in more general terms by Fredric Jameson: "Since by definition the cultural monuments and masterworks that have survived tend necessarily to perpetuate only a single voice in this class dialogue, the voice of a hegemonic class, they cannot be properly assigned their relational place in a dialogical system without the restoration or artificial reconstruction of the voice to which they were initially opposed, a voice for the most part stifled and reduced to silence, marginalized, its own utterances scattered to the wind, or reappropriated in their turn by the hegemonic culture." *The Political Unconscious*, p. 85.

18 Güiraldes' reply was published in *Martín Fierro*, May 15, 1924. Quoted from *Obras completas*, pp. 647–48.

19 Ricardo Güiraldes, *Don Segundo Sombra* in *Obras completas*, p. 497. All subsequent references to *Don Segundo Sombra* are from this edition and the appropriate page numbers will be included parenthetically in the text. I have consulted *Don Segundo Sombra: Shadows on the Pampas*, Harriet de Onís' translation of the novel.

20 Horacio Jorge Becco has produced a book-length study on the novel's lexicon entitled *"Don Segundo Sombra" y su vocabulario*. See also G. A. Stanford's "A Study of the Vocabulary of Ricardo Güiraldes' *Don Segundo Sombra*." It is of interest to note that there are many editions of *Don Segundo Sombra* that append a glossary or include lexicographic footnotes, even in printings meant specifically for Argentine distribution.

21 Francine Masiello has observed in this regard that "it would seem that in the pampas the rules of the marketplace are suspended and that the gaucho's toils are a labor of love. In reality there is a paradoxical lack of productivity in the gaucho's experience as depicted by Güiraldes, so that, for instance, food and drink show up apparently as if by magic . . . Instead of representing life on the plains as taking place under the rules of mercantile exchange, the gaucho experience in the novel proposes that only nature is the context for any valorization" (p. 189).

22 Letter to "Cuti" Pereira, September 2, 1926, *Obras completas*, p. 790. The description that is the source of the disagreement appears in chapter x of *Don Segundo Sombra*, p. 390.

23 The first position would be represented by Amado Alonso, "Un problema estilístico de *Don Segundo Sombra*," in *Materia y forma en poesía*, pp. 418–28. Alonso asserts that through this stylistic duality Güiraldes avoided a simplistic folklorization of literary language. P. R. Beardsell suggests that the break is a reflection of Güiraldes' indecision between his regionalism and his admiration for a more stylistically conscious idea of art derived from European models ("The Dichotomy in Güiraldes' Aesthetic Principles"). On the other side, for example, Jorge Schwartz explains that the dichotomy reflects social reality and

consequently the ideology of the novel (p. 439). In more general terms, Antonio Candido has referred to the phenomenon as a "schizophrenic style," and observes the following: "In regional texts the man from a higher social class never has an accent, never shows any peculiarities in his pronunciation, never mangles words, which in his speech present the ideal state they have in a dictionary. On the other hand, when rural man speaks the writer gives his speech an almost teratological aspect that contaminates his every word and which singles out the speaker as different, as a picturesque show just like the trees and the animals, created for the amusement of the cultured man who thereby finds his superiority confirmed" ("A literatura e a formação do homem," p. 808). This view is echoed by Angel Rama in *Transculturación narrativa en América Latina*, p. 41.

24 Güiraldes, *Obras completas*, pp. 636–37.

25 Most critics who have noticed the predominance of the simile in the narrative ascribe it to the avowed conflict in Güiraldes' aesthetic allegiances that was summarized in the previous note. See, for example, 'El símil en *Don Segundo Sombra*, expresión de la actitud conflictiva de Güiraldes," by Pedro R. León. In another article, Hugo Rodríguez Alcalá asserts that the simile is a most effective figure for making the world of the gaucho come to life. "Sentido y alcance de las comparaciones en *Don Segundo Sombra*" in *Korn, Romero, Güiraldes* . . ., pp. 78–93.

26 In my consideration of the homology between writing and work established by *Don Segundo Sombra*, I have found useful Marc Shell's book *The Economy of Literature*, particularly the following assertion: "Poetics is about production (*poiesis*). There can be no analysis of the form or content of production without a theory of labor. Labor, like language, is symbolically mediated interaction, reconciling man and 'Nature'" (p. 9). I am proposing that in *Don Segundo Sombra* this "theory of labor" is explicitly introjected in the text itself. See also Shell's *Money, Language, and Thought*. I have also found useful Barbara Johnson's discussion of related issues in Baudelaire's conception of poetry: "Poetry and Its Double: Two *Invitations au voyage*" in *The Critical Difference*, pp. 23–51; Richard Sieburth's reading of Ezra Pound, "In Pound We Trust"; and the section on "Style as Craftsmanship" in *Writing Degree Zero* by Roland Barthes, pp. 62–66.

27 Quoted by Bordelois, p. 140.

4 *Doña Bárbara*

1 *Obras completas*, I, p. 792. All subsequent references will be to this edition and will be included parenthetically in the text. I have also consulted Robert Malloy's translation of the novel.

2 This anecdote appears in Emir Rodríguez Monegal's *Narradores de esta América*, 1, p. 113. Another account of the incident can be found in Juan Liscano's *Rómulo Gallegos y su tiempo*, p. 119. Gallegos abandoned the country temporarily to avoid assuming his new senatorial "responsibilities."

3 Rómulo Gallegos, "Cómo conocí a doña Bárbara" in *Una posición en la vida*, p. 525.

4 Gallegos, "Cómo conocí a doña Bárbara," pp. 530–31.

5 Rómulo Gallegos, "La pura mujer sobre la tierra" in *Una posición en la vida*, pp. 404–5.

6 Quoted by Emir Rodríguez Monegal in "Carlos Fuentes" in *Homenaje a Carlos Fuentes*, ed. H. F. Giacoman, p. 53.

7 Reported by A. Durán in "Conversaciones con Gabriel García Márquez" in *Sobre García Márquez*, ed. Pedro Simón Martínez , p. 36.

8 Alejo Carpentier, "Problemática de la actual novela latinoamericana" in *Tientos y diferencias*, p. 33.

9 Alejo Carpentier, "La novela hispanoamericana en vísperas de un nuevo siglo," p. 26.

10 Orlando Araujo, *Lengua y creación en la obra de Rómulo Gallegos*, 1, p. 159. In all fairness to Araujo, it must be mentioned that in the third edition of his two-volume work on Gallegos he included an appendix where he challenged his own earlier view on *Doña Bárbara*. Speaking now from a more ideologically minded stance, he decries the "rigid bipolar structure" that characterizes Gallegos' world-view.

11 Emilio Carilla discusses the long-standing dichotomy as it manifests itself in the intervening years between Sarmiento's *Facundo* and Gallegos' text in "La polaridad en *Doña Bárbara*." An earlier study of the opposition can be found in Ernest A. Johnson Jr.'s, "The Meaning of *Civilización* and *Barbarie* in *Doña Bárbara*." See also José Antonio Galaos, "Rómulo Gallegos o el duelo entre civilización y barbarie"; Mariano Morínigo, "Civilización y barbarie en *Facundo* y *Doña Bárbara*"; and Nelson Osorio, "*Doña Bárbara* y el fantasma de Sarmiento."

12 *Authoritative Fictions*, p. 54.

13 Suleiman adds: "In linguistics and information theory, redundancy is defined as a 'surplus of communication' . . . The redundancies of a communicative system reduce the quantity of information that is transmitted, but augment the probability of a correct reception of the message" (p. 55).

14 Roland Barthes, *S/Z*, p. 85.

15 S. T. Coleridge, *The Statesman Manual*, quoted in Angus Fletcher's *Allegory: The Theory of a Symbolic Mode*, p. 16.

16 The literature on allegory is both extensive and substantive. I have found useful these studies, some of them bibliographical classics: C. S.

Lewis, *The Allegory of Love*; Edward Honig, *Dark Conceit: The Making of Allegory*; Angus Fletcher, *Allegory: The Theory of a Symbolic Mode*; Morton Bloomfield, "Allegory as Interpretation"; Maureen Quilligan, *The Language of Allegory*; *The Fiction of Truth*, by Carolynn Van Dyke; and Robert Scholes and Robert Kellog, "The Problem of Control: Allegory and Satire" in *The Nature of Narrative*, pp. 105–59. My reading of the function of allegory in *Doña Bárbara* has profited particularly from the following critical meditations on that rhetorical figure: Craig Owens, "The Allegorical Impulse," parts 1 and 2; Walter Benjamin, *The Origin of German Tragic Drama*; Joel Fineman, "The Structure of Allegorical Desire"; Gerald Bruns, "Allegory and Satire: A Rhetorical Meditation"; Three works by Paul de Man: "The Rhetoric of Temporality," "Pascal's Allegory of Persuasion," and *Allegories of Reading*; and also the essays by J. Hillis Miller "The Two Allegories" and Murray Krieger "'A Waking Dream': The Symbolic Alternative to Allegory."

17 J. L. Borges, "De las alegorías a las novelas" in *Otras inquisiciones*, p. 212.

18 William W. Stowe, *Balzac, James and the Realistic Novel*, pp. 111–12. This is also the interpretive premise that underlies Fredric Jameson's excellent article on "La Cousine Bette and Allegorical Realism." Jameson employs the Freudian concept of *overdetermination* to refer to the obsessive restatement of meaning that becomes a sign of the existence of a repressed content.

19 An interesting version of this argument is advanced by Nelson Osorio. He argues that the automatic filiation between *Doña Bárbara* and *Facundo* established by critics has tended to harden the more dialectical Galleguian conceptions of Civilization and Barbarism. He claims that Gallegos envisioned the possible sublation of the two antinomies into a synthesis that was a hopeful promise for the future. See also V. González Reboredo, *Nueva visión de la novela "Doña Bárbara"*.

20 Naomi Schor has discussed insightfully the presence of interpretive moments in fiction (performed by what she calls "interpretants") in her essay "Fiction as Interpretation/Interpretation as Fiction." See also Philippe Hamon, "Texte littéraire et métalangage."

21 In general terms the presence of glossaries in many regionalist novels has been the object of harsh criticism. Angel Rama, for instance, alleges that glossaries implied that the works in question were being addressed to a Spanish audience instead of an American one, since success with that audience was regarded by the colonized mentality as "real" success (*La ciudad letrada*, p. 51). See also Rama's "La tecnificación narrativa," and his *Transculturación narrativa en América Latina*, pp. 40–43. Similarly, Alejo Carpentier has interpreted the disappearance of glossaries from modern Latin American texts as a sign of

literary maturity ("La novela latinoamericana en vísperas de un nuevo siglo," p. 34). Although the first edition of *Doña Bárbara* did not include a glossary, the second – published only a short time later – and every subsequent one have appended a glossary, presumably composed by Gallegos himself.

22 For the compilation of this brief history of the glossary I have consulted the *Encyclopedia Britannica* (1972), and the *Enciclopedia Universal Ilustrada Espasa-Calpe* (1933).

23 "The Rhetoric of Temporality," p. 190.

24 "The Structure of Allegorical Desire," p. 45.

25 "Allegory is conceived as a *supplement*, 'an expression externally added to another expression.' . . . Allegory *is* extravagant, an expenditure of surplus value; it is always *in excess*." Craig Owens, "The Allegorical Impulse," part 1, p. 84.

26 This is the conception of allegory that provides the foundation for Walter Benjamin's *The Origin of German Tragic Drama*. See Lukács' perceptive comments on Benjamin and allegory in relation to modern literature in "The Ideology of Modernism," and Fredric Jameson, *Marxism and Form*, pp. 60–83.

27 The importance of desire in *Doña Bárbara* may help us understand Gallegos' abandonment of his initial conception of the novel. In 1928, the Litografía y Tipografía Vargas in Caracas had already printed the first six chapters (64 pages) of what was to be a new novel by Gallegos entitled *La Coronela*. I have managed to examine a copy of these printed pages; the story covers roughly the account of Santos Luzardo's return to Altamira up to his encounter with the overseer Balbino Paiba, as well as the chapter that details the rape of doña Bárbara in her youth. But Santos returns to Altamira already married to a woman by the name of Luisana, who rides with him in the canoe that brings Luzardo back to his property. This development would have severely limited the eroticization of the relationship between Luzardo and Doña Bárbara that is such a key ingredient in the novel. One can also see in the transition from the earlier text to *Doña Bárbara* the radical allegorizing of what was originally conceived as an essentially Realist novel. For Santos' marriage would have prevented the mirroring of his civilizing project in his rescue and education of Marisela, which is, as we saw, further reflected in the taming of the mare La Catira by one of Luzardo's men. Furthermore, in the earlier version the encounter with the villainous Paiba is not allegorically reflected in the subduing of a horse as is the case in *Doña Bárbara*. Finally, doña Bárbara's original name of Guadalupe, an individualizing feature, is erased in the final version and transformed into Barbarita, as befits allegorical abstraction. For a reading of *Doña Bárbara* as a

confrontation between male and female principles see Sharon Magnarelli, *The Lost Rib*, pp. 38–58.

28 "*Doña Bárbara* Writes the Plain" in *The Voice of the Masters*, pp. 33–63.

29 *Ibid.*, 48.

30 *Ibid.*, 56.

31 González's dependence on allegory is explicitly acknowledged: "Contrary to the way it may appear on the primary doctrinal plane of allegorical reading in which civilization and barbarity confront each other, the radically *allegorical* reading that I am outlining here defies the possibility of such propriety in the text's signifying task" (p. 50, my emphasis).

32 *The Anatomy of Criticism*, p. 89. The relationship between allegory and criticism is also discussed by J. Fineman, "The Structure of Allegorical Desire," pp. 27–28 *et passim*.

33 *The Political Unconscious*, p. 60. See also Frank Kermode's brilliant study *The Genesis of Secrecy*, where these hermeneutical issues are the subject of a long meditation in the rich context provided by the Gospels.

34 There are signs that the ground for such a revalorization is being prepared. In "La resurrección de Rómulo Gallegos" Carlos Fuentes has recently argued for a thorough re-reading of the Venezuelan writer. See also Maya Schärer-Nussberger, *Rómulo Gallegos: el mundo inconcluso*.

5 *La vorágine*

1 Quoted by Eduardo Neale-Silva in *Horizonte humano*, p. 363.

2 José Eustasio Rivera, *La vorágine*, p. 239. All subsequent references to *La vorágine* are from this edition, and the page numbers will be included parenthetically in the text. I have had access to *The Vortex*, Earl K. James' translation of the text.

3 Eduardo Neale-Silva, *Horizonte humano: vida de José Eustasio Rivera*, p. 305. Neale-Silva's literary biography of José Eustasio Rivera is a paramount example of the genre. It is an indispensable work for anyone attempting to come to terms with Rivera's figure, an assertion that is amply confirmed by the repeated references to it throughout my discussion of his *oeuvre*.

4 Neale-Silva, *Horizonte humano*, p. 306.

5 In an interview in 1926, Rivera revealed that "in Brazil this book caused quite a stir, and the Brazilian Congress is currently considering a bill for the protection of Indians in the rubber-producing region of the Caquetá." "*La vorágine* y sus críticos," *El Tiempo*, November 25, 1926. Quoted by Neale-Silva in *Horizonte humano*, p. 306.

6 E. K. James, "José Eustasio Rivera," p. 397. Quoted by Juan Loveluck in "Notas sobre la vida y la obra de Rivera," p. 333.

7 Quoted by Neale-Silva in *Horizonte humano*, p. 298.

8 "The Factual Bases of *La vorágine*."

9 Internationally, the South American rubber industry had received some years before a devastating indictment by the British explorer W. E. Hardenburg in his book *The Putumayo: The Devil's Paradise* (1912). In the same year Pope Pius X wrote an encyclical (*Lacrimabili Statu*) to Latin America's bishops demanding that they appeal to their respective governments to bring an end to the injustices and crimes of the trade. For a more detailed account of such denunciations consult Neale-Silva, "The Factual Bases . . . "

10 Neale-Silva, *Horizonte humano*, p. 281.

11 The reporter was Benjamín Saldaña Rocca, who published in 1907 what had earlier been a sworn deposition on the crimes he had either witnessed or heard of. Quoted by Neale-Silva, *Horizonte humano*, pp. 281–82.

12 A number of critics have paid some attention to the journey motif of the novel, some of them discussing it in the context of Cova's status as a poet. See, for instance, Otto Olivera, "El romanticismo de José Eustasio Rivera"; Jean Franco, "Image and Experience in *La vorágine*"; Leonidas Morales, "*La vorágine*: un viaje al país de los muertos"; Seymour Menton, "*La vorágine*: Circling the Triangle"; Randolph D. Pope, "*La vorágine*: autobiografía de un intelectual"; and Vicky Unruh, "Arturo Cova y *La vorágine*: la crisis de un escritor."

13 Lydia de León Hazera, *La novela de la selva hispanoamericana*, p. 123.

14 Neale-Silva, *Horizonte humano*, p. 244.

15 José Eustasio Rivera, *Tierra de promisión*, pp. 19–20. All subsequent references are to this edition and will be included parenthetically in the text.

16 For an exposition of the syntactic organization of the sonnet as a literary form see Elías Rivers, "Hacia la sintaxis del soneto."

17 The passage in question from *La vorágine* reads as follows: "Where is the poetry of contemplation here, where are the butterflies that seem translucent flowers, the enchanted birds, the singing brooks" (p. 239).

18 For instance: "*La vorágine* is a clearly autobiographical novel. Rivera himself made sure it was known as such when at the beginning of the book he placed a supposed photograph of his protagonist that turned out to be a picture of himself. But even if he had not done so it would have been possible to detect it in the delight with which he both depicts his hero and narrates his adventures." Eduardo Castillo, "*La vorágine*," *Cromos*, December 13, 1924, quoted by Neale-Silva, *Horizonte humano*, p. 302.

19 *The Spanish American Novel*, p. 43.

20 *Horizonte humano*, p. 167.

21 For a detailed consideration of this moment in Colombian literary history see the following two essays: Armando Romero, "Ausencia y presencia de las vanguardias en Colombia;" and Fernando Charry Lara, "Los poetas de 'Los Nuevos'."

The bibliography on the avant-garde as a general phenomenon in Latin America is daunting. I have found particularly illuminating these critical works: David Barry, *Movimientos literarios de vanguardia en Iberoamérica*; Guillermo de Torre, *Historia de las literaturas de vanguardia*; Oscar Collazos, ed., *Los vanguardismos en América Latina*; Edward J. Mullen, "Spanish American 'vanguardismo': The Aesthetics of Revolt"; Julio Ortega, "La escritura de la vanguardia"; Nelson Osorio, *El futurismo y la vanguardia literaria en América Latina*. The *Revista de Crítica Literaria Latinoamericana*, vol. 8, no. 15 (1982) is a special issue on the Latin American "vanguardias"; Saúl Yurkiévich, *A través de la trama: sobre vanguardismos literarios y otras concomitancias*; and *Las vanguardias literarias en Hispanoamérica: manifiestos, proclamas y otros escritos*, ed. Hugo J. Verani.

22 *Horizonte humano*, p. 383.

23 Neale-Silva, *Horizonte humano*, p. 382.

24 *Poetic Closure: A Study of How Poems End*, pp. 50–51.

25 *José Eustasio Rivera en la intimidad*, p. 68.

26 *Estudios sobre José Eustasio Rivera: el arte poético ("Tierra de Promisión")*. See also Rafael Maya, "Los sonetos de Rivera," prologue to *Tierra de promisión*, pp. 5–11.

27 In a later Colombian novel (1933) that also intended to denounce the rubber trade one finds a passage that in contradistinction to *La vorágine* makes explicit the difficulties that stem from the overwhelming characterization of the jungle in Rivera's text: "The jungle? . . . The jungle was nothing. The catastrophe was not due to Nature. It was due to the men that brought illness, slavery and death to the inhabitants of the woods where the rubber trees grew." César Uribe Piedrahita, *Toá*, p. 19.

28 For this overview of the history of the rubber trade I have consulted the following books: P. T. Bauer, *The Rubber Industry: A Study in Competition and Monopoly*; J. H. Drabble, *Rubber in Malaya 1876–1922*; Harvey S. Firestone Jr., *The Romance and Drama of the Rubber Industry*; and D. M. Phelps, *Rubber Developments in Latin America*.

29 Firestone, p. 46.

30 Firestone, p. 38.

31 Firestone, p. 36.

32 *Of Grammatology*, pp. 107–8.

33 The indeterminate nature of Rivera's text has been, in my view, definitively established by Sylvia Molloy in a recent article, "Contagio narrativo y gesticulación retórica en *La vorágine*."

34 See Neale-Silva, *Horizonte humano*, pp. 362–88, for an account of this controversy.
35 "Poetry and Its Double: Two *Invitations au voyage*" in *The Critical Difference*, p. 36.
36 Firestone, p. 23.

6 Epilogue

1 Seymour Menton, "*La vorágine*: Circling the Triangle," *Hispania*, 59 (1976), 418–32.
2 For a lucid commentary on post-"Boom" novelistic production, see Roberto González Echevarría's "The Dictatorship of Rhetoric/The Rhetoric of Dictatorship" in *The Voice of the Masters*, pp. 83–85. See also his apposite reading of Sarduy and the literature after the "Boom" in *La ruta de Severo Sarduy*, pp. 243–53.
3 "Literary History and Literary Modernity" in his *Blindness and Insight*, p. 164.

Bibliography

Abasolo Navarrete, Jenaro. *La personalidad política y la América del porvenir.* Santiago: Imprenta y Encuadernación Universitaria, 1907.

Abrams, M. H. *The Mirror and the Lamp: Romantic Theory and the Critical Tradition.* New York: Oxford University Press, 1971.

Natural Supernaturalism. New York: Norton, 1973.

Ainsa, Fernando de. *Identidad cultural de Iberoamérica en su narrativa.* Madrid: Gredos, 1986.

Alonso, Amado. *Materia y forma en poesía.* Madrid: Gredos, 1955.

Alonso, Carlos J. *"Facundo* y la sabiduría del poder." *Cuadernos Americanos,* 226 (September–October 1979), 116–30.

Altamira, Rafael. *España en América.* Valencia: F. Sempere y Cía., 1908.

Anderson, Benedict. *Imagined Communities: Reflections on the Origin and Spread of Nationalism.* London: Verso Editions and NLB, 1983.

Araquistaín, Luis. *El peligro yanqui.* Madrid: Publicaciones España, 1919.

Araujo, Orlando. *Lengua y creación en la obra de Rómulo Gallegos.* 2 vols. Caracas: Ediciones En La Raya, 1977.

Arrom, José Juan. "Tres metáforas de España e Hispanoamérica" in *Certidumbre de América.* Madrid: Gredos, 1971, pp. 167–71.

Austin, J. L. *How to Do Things with Words.* London: Oxford University Press, 1963.

Barnard, F. M. *Herder's Social and Political Thought: From Enlightenment to Nationalism.* Oxford: Clarendon Press, 1965.

Barreda, Ernesto. "Observaciones del momento. Paul Groussac." *La Nación,* September 19, 1926.

Barry, David. *Movimientos literarios de vanguardia en Iberoamérica.* Mexico: University of Texas Press, 1965.

Barthes, Roland. "Historical Discourse" in *Introduction to Structuralism,* ed. Michael Lane. New York: Basic Books, 1970, pp. 145–55.

S/Z. Paris: Seuil, 1970.

Writing Degree Zero. Trans. Annette Lavers and Colin Smith. Introduction by Susan Sontag. Boston: Beacon Press, 1970.

Bauer, P. T. *The Rubber Industry: A Study in Competition and Monopoly.* Cambridge, MA: Harvard University Press, 1948.

Bayo, Ciro. *Vocabulario criollo español sud-americano.* Madrid: Sucesores de Hernando, 1911.

Beardsell, P. R. "The Dichotomy in Güiraldes' Aesthetic Principles." *Modern Language Review,* 66 (1971), 322–27.

Becco, Horacio Jorge. *Don Segundo Sombra y su vocabulario.* Buenos Aires: Ollantay, 1952.

Becerra, Ricardo. *Vida de don Francisco de Miranda.* Madrid: Editorial América, 1918.

Benedetti, Mario. *El escritor latinoamericano y la revolución posible.* Buenos Aires: Editorial Alfa, 1974.

Benjamin, Walter. *The Origin of German Tragic Drama.* Trans. John Osborne. London: NLB, 1977.

Benveniste, Emile. *Problems in General Linguistics.* 2 vols. Trans. Mary E. Meek. Coral Gables: University of Miami Press, 1971.

Berenguer, Fernando. *El Hispano-americanismo.* Havana: Imprenta El Siglo XX de la Sociedad Editorial Cuba Contemporánea, 1919.

Berman, Marshall. *All That is Solid Melts Into Air: The Experience of Modernity.* New York: Simon and Schuster, 1982.

Blanco Fombona, R. *La evolución política y social de Hispanoamérica.* Madrid: Bernardo Rodríguez, 1911.

Blasi, Alberto. "La ruta de Don Segundo." *Chasqui,* 6, no. 2 (1977), 7–14.

Bloomfield, Morton. "Allegory as Interpretation." *New Literary History,* 3 (1972), 301–17.

Bordelois, Yvonne. *Genio y figura de Ricardo Güiraldes.* Buenos Aires: Editorial Universitaria de Buenos Aires, 1966.

Borges, Jorge Luis. *Discusión.* Buenos Aires: Emecé, 1966.
  Otras inquisiciones. Buenos Aires: Emecé, 1970.
  Ficciones. Madrid: Alianza Editorial, 1985.

Bourdieu, Pierre. *Outline of a Theory of Practice.* Trans. Richard Nice. Cambridge University Press, 1977.

Brunner, José Joaquín. "Entonces, ¿existe o no la modernidad en América Latina?" *Punto de Vista,* 10, no. 5 (November–December 1987), 2–5.

Bruns, Gerald. "Allegory and Satire: A Rhetorical Meditation." *New Literary History,* 11 (1979), 121–32.

Brushwood, John S. *The Spanish American Novel: A Twentieth-Century Survey.* Austin: University of Texas Press, 1975.

Buckley, Jerome H. *Season of Youth: The Bildungsroman from Dickens to Golding.* Cambridge, MA: Harvard University Press, 1974.

Cáldiz, Juan Francisco. *Lo que no se ha dicho de "Don Segundo Sombra".* La Plata: A. Domínguez, 1952.

Calinescu, Matei. *Faces of Modernity*. Bloomington: Indiana University Press, 1977.

Candido, Antonio. "A literatura e a formação do homem." *Ciencia e cultura*, 24 (1977), 803–9.

Capdevila, Arturo. *América: nuestras naciones ante los Estados Unidos*. Buenos Aires: M. Gleizer, 1926.

Carbonell, Nestor. *Las conferencias internacionales americanas*. Havana: Montalvo y Cárdenas, 1928.

Cárdenas, Raúl de. *La política de los Estados Unidos en el continente americano*. Havana: Sociedad Editorial Cuba Contemporánea, 1921.

Cardoso, Fernando, and Faleto, Enzo. *Dependencia y desarrollo en América Latina*. Mexico: Siglo XXI, 1974.

Carilla, Emilio. "La polaridad en *Doña Bárbara*" in *Nine Essays on Rómulo Gallegos*. Riverside: Latin American Studies Program of the University of California, 1979, pp. 3–58.

Carpentier, Alejo. *Tientos y diferencias*. Montevideo: Arca, 1967.

"La novela hispanoamericana en vísperas de un nuevo siglo" in *Historia y ficción en la narrativa hispanoamericana*, ed. R. González Echevarría. Caracas: Monte Avila, pp. 19–48.

Caso, Antonio. "En América dirá su última palabra la civilización latina." *Repertorio Americano*, 4 (1922), 113–14.

"El pensamiento de Bolívar." *Repertorio Americano*, 7 (1923), 225–26.

Castagnino, Eduardo Hugo. *En busca de "Don Segundo Sombra"*. Buenos Aires: F. A. Colombo, 1967.

Chapman, Arnold. "Pampas and Big Woods: Heroic Initiation in Güiraldes and Faulkner." *Comparative Literature*, 11 (1951), 61–77.

Charria Tobar, Ricardo. *José Eustasio Rivera en la intimidad*. Bogotá: Ediciones Tercer Mundo, 1963.

Charry Lara, Fernando. "Los poetas de 'Los Nuevos'." *Revista Iberoamericana*, nos. 128–29 (1984), 633–81.

Chatelain, Fourcy. *Le Pan-Américanisme et l'équilibre américain*. Saint Amand: Bussière Frères, 1897.

Chilcote, Ronald H. "Dependency: A Critical Synthesis of the Literature." *Latin American Perspectives*, 1 (1974), 4–29.

Cohen, Ralph. "History and Genre." *New Literary History*, 17, no. 2 (1986), 204–18.

Collazos, Oscar (ed.) *Los vanguardismos en América Latina*. Havana: Casa de las Américas, 1970.

Contreras, Francisco. *Le Mondonovisme*. Paris: Mercure de France, 1917.

Les Ecrivains contemporains de l'Amérique espagnole. Paris: La Renaissance du Livre, 1920.

Les Ecrivains hispano-américains et la guerre européenne. Paris: Editions Bossard, 1917.

Cornelio Hispano (pseudonym of Ismael López). *Bolívar*. Bogotá: Juan Casis, 1917.

Culler, Jonathan. *On Deconstruction: Theory and Criticism After Structuralism*. Ithaca: Cornell University Press, 1982.

Darío, Rubén. *Poesías de Rubén Darío*. Buenos Aires. Editorial Universitaria de Buenos Aires, 1969.

de Man, Paul. "The Rhetoric of Temporality" in *Interpretation: Theory and Practice*, ed. Charles S. Singleton. Baltimore: The Johns Hopkins University Press, 1969, pp. 173–209.

Blindness and Insight. New York: Oxford University Press, 1971.

Allegories of Reading. New Haven: Yale University Press, 1979.

"Pascal's Allegory of Persuasion" in *Allegory and Representation*. Selected Papers from the English Institute, 1979–80, ed. Stephen Greenblatt. Baltimore: The Johns Hopkins University Press, 1981, pp. 1–25.

Derrida, Jacques. *Marges de la philosophie*. Paris: Minuit, 1972.

Of Grammatology. Trans. Gayatry Chakravorti Spivak. Baltimore: The Johns Hopkins University Press, 1976.

"Limited Inc a b c" in *Glyph 2*. Baltimore: The Johns Hopkins University Press, 1977, pp. 162–254.

La Vérité en peinture. Paris: Flammarion, 1978.

"Living on" in *Deconstruction and Criticism*, ed. Harold Bloom *et al*. New York: The Seabury Press, 1979, pp. 75–176.

"La Loi du genre/The Law of Genre" in *Glyph 7*. Baltimore: The Johns Hopkins University Press, 1980, pp. 176–232.

Dissemination. Trans. Barbara Johnson. University of Chicago Press, 1983.

Díaz Rodríguez, Manuel. "Del primer centenario de Ayacucho." *Repertorio Americano*, 9 (1924), 289–92.

Doll, Ramón. "*Don Segundo Sombra* y el gaucho que ve el hijo del patrón." *Nosotros*, 58 (1927), 270–81.

Domínguez, Manuel. *El alma de la raza*. Asunción: C. Zamphirópolos, 1918.

Drabble, J. H. *Rubber in Malaya 1876–1922: The Genesis of the Industry*. Oxford University Press, 1973.

Duffey, Frank M. *The Early Cuadro de Costumbres in Colombia*. Chapel Hill, NC: North Carolina Studies in the Romance Languages and Literatures, 1956.

Echegaray, Aristóbulo. "*Don Segundo Sombra*," *reminiscencia infantil de Ricardo Güiraldes*. Buenos Aires: Ediciones Doble P, 1955.

Edwards Bello, Joaquín. *El nacionalismo continental*. Madrid: G. Hernández, 1925.

El ideal latinoamericano: colección de documentos raros, protocolos de diversos congresos, memorias de eminentes pensadores, etc., que se refieren a la proyectada unión y confederación de los países centro y sudamericanos. Mexico: Imprenta de la Secretaría de Gobernación, 1919.

Fabian, Johannes. *Time and the Other: How Anthropology Makes its Object*. New York: Columbia University Press, 1983.

Fineman, Joel. "The Structure of Allegorical Desire" in *Allegory and Representation*. Selected papers from the English Institute, 1979–80, ed. Stephen J. Greenblatt. Baltimore: The Johns Hopkins University Press, 1981, pp. 26–60.

Firestone, Harvey S. *The Romance and Drama of the Rubber Industry*. Radio talks delivered by the author in "The Voice of Firestone" programs over the nationwide network of National Broadcasting Company, September 1931 through September 1932. U.S.A.: The Firestone Tire and Rubber Company, 1936.

Fletcher, Angus. *Allegory: The Theory of a Symbolic Mode*. Ithaca: Cornell University Press, 1982.

Forbes, D. K. *The Geography of Underdevelopment: A Critical Survey*. Baltimore: The Johns Hopkins University Press, 1984.

Foucault, Michel. *The Order of Things: An Archeology of the Human Sciences*. New York: Vintage, 1973.

Franco, Jean. "Image and Experience in *La vorágine*." *Bulletin of Hispanic Studies*, 41 (1964), 101–10.

"Criticism and Literature Within the Context of a Dependent Culture" in *The Uses of Criticism*, ed. A. P. Foulkes. Frankfurt: Peter Lang, 1976, pp. 269–87.

Frank, André G. *Capitalism and Underdevelopment in Latin America: Historical Studies of Chile and Brazil*. New York: The Monthly Review Press, 1967.

Frankl, Víctor. *Espíritu y camino de Hispanoamérica: la cultura hispanoamericana y la filosofía europea*. Bogotá: Biblioteca de Autores Colombianos, 1953.

Frye, Northrop. *Anatomy of Criticism*. Princeton University Press, 1973.

Fuentes, Carlos. *La nueva novela hispanoamericana*. Mexico: Joaquín Mortiz, 1969.

Galaos, José Antonio. "Rómulo Gallegos o el duelo entre civilización y barbarie." *Cuadernos Hispanoamericanos*, no. 165 (1969), 299–309.

Gallegos, Rómulo, *Obras completas*. 2 vols. Madrid: Aguilar, 1958.
Doña Bárbara. Trans. Robert Malloy. New York: Peter Smith, 1948.
Una posición en la vida. Mexico: Ediciones Humanismo, 1954.

Gálvez, Manuel. *El solar de la raza*. Buenos Aires: *Revista Nosotros*, 1913.

García Calderón, Francisco. *La creación de un continente*. Paris: P. Ollendorf, 1912.
Les Démocraties latines de l'Amérique. Paris: Flammarion, 1914.

García Calderón, Ventura. *Semblanzas de América*. Madrid: Biblioteca Ariel, 1922.

García Godoy, F. *La literatura americana de nuestros días*. Madrid: Sociedad Española de Librería, 1915.

Gaxiola, José. *La frontera de la raza*. Madrid: Tipografía Artística, 1917.

Geertz, Clifford. "The Cerebral Savage: On the Work of Claude Lévi-Strauss" in *The Interpretation of Cultures*. New York: Basic Books, 1973, pp. 345–59.

"After the Revolution: The Fate of Nationalism in the New States" in *The Interpretation of Cultures*. New York: Basic Books, 1981, pp. 234–54.

Gellner, Ernest. *Thought and Change*. London: Weidenfeld and Nicolson, 1964.

Nations and Nationalism. Oxford: Basil Blackwell, 1983.

Giacoman, H. F. (ed.) *Homenaje a Carlos Fuentes*. New York: Las Américas, 1971.

Giberga, Eliseo. *El pan-americanismo y el pan-hispanismo*. Havana: Rambla, Bouza y Cía., 1916.

Gicovate, Bernardo. "Notes on *Don Segundo Sombra*: The Education of Fabio Cáceres." *Hispania*, 34 (1951), 366–68.

Gil, Enríquez. *Evolución del panamericanismo*. Buenos Aires: Jesús Menéndez, 1933.

Giner de los Ríos, Gloria. *El paisaje de Hispanoamérica a través de su literatura*. México: Imprenta Universitaria, 1958.

Gómez Carrillo, Enrique. *Campos de batalla y campos de ruinas*. Madrid: Sucesores de Hernando, 1915.

Crónicas de la guerra. Madrid: Sucesores de Hernando, 1915.

González, Aníbal. *La crónica modernista hispanoamericana*. Madrid: Porrúa Turanzas, 1983.

González Arrili, Bernardo. *El futuro de América*. Barcelona: Araluce, 1928.

González Echevarría, Roberto. *Alejo Carpentier: The Pilgrim at Home*. Ithaca: Cornell University Press, 1977.

"Modernidad, modernismo y nueva narrativa: *El recurso del método*." *Revista Interamericana de Bibliografía*, 30, no. 2 (1980), 157–63.

The Voice of the Masters: Writing and Authority in Modern Latin American Literature. Austin: University of Texas Press, 1985.

La ruta de Severo Sarduy. Hanover: Ediciones del Norte, 1987.

González Reboredo, V. *Nueva visión de la novela "Doña Bárbara"*. Bogotá: Tercer Mundo, 1979.

Graña, César. *Fact and Symbol*. New York: Oxford University Press, 1971.

Güiraldes, Ricardo. *Obras completas*. Buenos Aires: Emecé 1961.

Don Segundo Sombra: Shadows in the Pampas. Trans. Harriet de Onís. New York: Farrar and Rinehart, 1935.

Halperín Donghi, Tulio. "'Dependency Theory' and Latin American Historiography." *Latin American Research Review*, 17, no. 2 (1982), 115–30.

Hamon, Philippe. "Texte littéraire et métalangage." *Poétique*, no. 31 (1977), 261–84.

Hardenburg, W. E. *The Putumayo: The Devil's Paradise*. London: T. Fisher Unwin, 1912.

Haya de la Torre, Víctor Raúl. *A dónde va Indoamérica*. Santiago: Editorial Ercilla, 1936.

Hegel, G. W. F. *Phenomenology of Mind*. Trans. J. B. Baillie. New York: Harper and Row, 1967.

Henríquez Ureña, Pedro. *Traducciones y paráfrasis en la literatura mexicana de la época de la independencia*. Mexico: Anales del Museo Nacional de Arqueología, 1913.

Seis ensayos en busca de nuestra expresión. Madrid: Editorial Babel, 1927.

Para la historia de los indigenismos. Buenos Aires: Facultad de Filosofía y Letras, Universidad de Buenos Aires, 1938.

Historia de la cultura en la América Hispánica. Mexico: Fondo de Cultura Económica, 1973.

Herder, J. G. *Reflections on the Philosophy of the History of Mankind*. Trans. T. O. Churchill. University of Chicago Press, 1968.

Hernández de Norman, Isabel. *La novela criolla en las Antillas*. New York: Plus Ultra, 1977.

Hirsch, Marianne. "The Novel of Formation as Genre: Between Great Expectations and Lost Illusions." *Genre*, 12 (1979), 293–311.

Honig, Edward. *Dark Conceit: The Making of Allegory*. Providence: Brown University Press, 1972.

Inman, Samuel Guy. *Problems in Pan Americanism*. New York: George Doran, 1921.

Jaguaribe, Helio *et al*. *La dependencia político-económica de América Latina*. Mexico: Siglo XXI, 1975.

Jakobson, Roman. *Selected Writings*, 2 vols. The Hague: Mouton, 1971.

Jameson, Fredric. "*La Cousine Bette* and Allegorical Realism." *PMLA*, 86 (1971), pp. 241–54.

Marxism and Form: Twentieth-Century Dialectical Theories of Literature. Princeton University Press, 1974.

The Political Unconscious: Narrative as a Socially Symbolic Act. Ithaca: Cornell University Press, 1981.

Jitrik, Noé. *Las contradicciones del modernismo: productividad poética y situación sociológica*. Mexico: El Colegio de México, 1978.

Johnson, Barbara. *The Critical Difference: Essays in the Contemporary Rhetoric of Reading*. Baltimore: The Johns Hopkins University Press, 1980.

Johnson, Ernest A. Jr. "The Meaning of *Civilización* and *Barbarie* in *Doña Bárbara*." *Hispania* 39 (1956), 456–61.

Kadir, Djelal. *Questing Fictions: Latin America's Family Romance*. Minneapolis: University of Minnesota Press, 1986.

'Cultural Deliberations: States of Emergency." *University of Minnesota Center for Humanistic Studies Occasional Papers*, no. 23 (1987).

Kedourie, Elie. *Nationalism*. New York: Praeger, 1961.

Kemiläinen, Aira. *Nationalism: Problems Concerning the Word, the Concept and Classification*. Jyväskylä (Finland): Kustantajat, 1964.

Kermode, Frank. *The Sense of an Ending: Studies in the Theory of Fiction*. Oxford University Press, 1967.

The Genesis of Secrecy. Cambridge University Press, 1979.

Krieger, Murray. "'A Waking Dream': The Symbolic Alternative to Allegory" in *Allegory, Myth and Symbol*, ed. Morton W. Bloomfield. Cambridge, MA: Harvard University Press, 1981, pp. 1–22.

Latcham, Ricardo. *El criollismo*. Santiago: Editorial Universitaria, 1956.

Leguizamón, Julio A. *Historia de la literatura hispanoamericana*. Buenos Aires: Editoriales Reunidas, 1945.

Leland, Christopher Towne. *The Last Happy Men: The Generation of 1922, Fiction and the Argentine Reality*. Syracuse University Press, 1986.

León, Pedro R. "El símil en *Don Segundo Sombra*, expresión de la actitud conflictiva de Güiraldes." *Explicación de Textos Literarios*, 4 (1975–76), 189–97.

León Hazera, Lydia de. *La novela de la selva hispanoamericana: nacimiento, desarrollo y transformación*. Bogotá: Instituto Caro y Cuervo, 1971.

León Suárez, José. *Carácter de la revolución americana*. Buenos Aires: J. Roldán, 1917.

Lévi-Strauss, Claude. "Introduction à l'oeuvre de Marcel Mauss" in M. Mauss, *Sociologie et anthropologie*. Paris: P.U.F., 1968, pp. ix–liii.

The Scope of Anthropology. Trans. Sherry Ortner Paul and Robert A. Paul. London: Jonathan Cape, 1974.

Tristes Tropiques. Trans. John and Doreen Weightman. New York: Atheneum, 1975.

The Savage Mind. University of Chicago Press, 1979.

Lewis, C. S. *The Allegory of Love*. Oxford: Clarendon Press, 1936.

Lezama Lima, José. *La expresión americana. Obras completas*, II. Mexico: Aguilar, 1977, pp. 279–380.

Liscano, Juan. *Rómulo Gallegos y su tiempo*. Caracas: Monte Avila, 1969.

Lockey, Joseph B. *Pan Americanism: Its Beginnings*. New York: Macmillan, 1920.

López, Ismael. *Los cantores de Bolívar en el primer centenario de su muerte*. Bogotá: Editorial Minerva, 1930.

López, José Francisco. *Filosofía de la historia y de las razas latina y sajona*. Buenos Aires: J. Peuser, 1900.

Loveluck, Juan. "Notas sobre la vida y la obra de Rivera." Postscript to *La vorágine* by José Eustasio Rivera. Mexico: Editorial Nacional, 1967, pp. 329–64.

Ludmer, Josefina. "La lengua como arma: fundamentos del género gauchesco" in *Homenaje a Ana María Barrenechea*, ed. L. S. and I. Lerner. Madrid: Castalia, 1984, pp. 471–79.

Lugones, Leopoldo. "*Don Segundo Sombra*, de Ricardo Güiraldes." *La Nación*, Buenos Aires, September 12, 1926.

El payador. Caracas: Biblioteca Ayacucho, 1979.

Lukács, Georg. *The Meaning of Contemporary Realism*. London: Merlin Press, 1979.

"The Ideology of Modernism" in *The Meaning of Contemporary Realism*. London: Merlin Press, 1979, pp. 17–46.

Lyotard, J.-François. *The Postmodern Condition: A Report on Knowledge*. Minneapolis: The University of Minnesota Press, 1984.

Magnarelli, Sharon. *The Lost Rib: Female Characters in the Spanish American Novel*. Lewisburg: Bucknell University Press, 1985.

Mancini, Jules. *Bolívar y la emancipación de las colonias españolas, desde sus orígenes hasta 1815*. Paris: Perrin et Cie. 1918.

Marechal, Leopoldo. "*Don Segundo Sombra* y el ejercicio ilegal de la crítica." *Sur*, Año 5, no. 12 (1935), 76–80.

Marinello, Juan. *Literatura hispanoamericana: hombres-meditaciones*. Mexico: Universidad Nacional de México, 1937.

"Tres novelas ejemplares" in *La novela hispanoamericana*, ed. Juan Loveluck. Santiago: Editorial Universitaria, 1969, pp. 421–33.

Martí, José. *Prosa y poesía*. Barcelona: Editorial Argos Vergara, 1979.

Martínez, Pedro Simón (ed.) *Sobre García Márquez*. Montevideo: Biblioteca de Marcha, 1971.

Masiello, Francine. *Lenguaje e ideología: Las escuelas argentinas de vanguardia*. Buenos Aires: Librería Hachette, 1986.

Maurtúa, Aníbal. *La idea pan-americana y la cuestión del arbitraje*. Lima: Imprenta La Industria, 1901.

Maya, Rafael. "Los sonetos de Rivera." Prologue to *Tierra de promisión* by José Eustasio Rivera. Bogotá: Imprenta Nacional de Colombia, 1955, pp. 5–11.

Mayer, Alfred. "Historical Notes on Ideological Aspects of the Concept of Culture in Germany and Russia." Appendix A to A. L. Kroeber and Clyde Kluckhohn, *Culture: A Critical Review of Concepts and Definitions*. Papers of the Peabody Museum of American Archaeology and Ethnology, Harvard University, vol. 47, no. 1 (1952), 403–13.

Meléndez, Concha. "Tres novelas de la naturaleza americana: *Don Segundo Sombra, La vorágine, Doña Bárbara*." *Revista Bimestre Cubana*, 28 (1931), 82–93.

Menton, Seymour. "*La vorágine*: Circling the Triangle." *Hispania*, 59 (1976), 418–34.

Merlos, Salvador R. *América Latina ante el peligro*. San José, Costa Rica: G. Matamoros, 1914.

Miller, J. Hillis. "The Critic as Host." *Critical Inquiry*, 3, no. 3 (1977), 439–47.

"The Two Allegories" in *Allegory, Myth and Symbol*, ed. Morton W. Bloomfield. Cambridge, MA: Harvard University Press, 1981, pp. 355–70.

"The Search for Grounds in Literary Study" in *Rhetoric and Form: Deconstruction at Yale*, ed. Robert Con Davis and Ronald Schleifer. Norman: University of Oklahoma Press, 1985, pp. 19–36.

Molloy, Sylvia. *La Diffusion de la littérature hispano-américaine en France au XXe. siècle*. Paris: P.U.F., 1972.

"Contagio narrativo y gesticulación retórica en *La vorágine*." *Revista Iberoamericana*, no. 141 (1987), 745–66.

Monsalve, J. D. *El ideal político del Libertador Simón Bolívar*. Madrid: Editorial América, 1916.

Montesinos, José. *Costumbrismo y novela: ensayo sobre el redescubrimiento de la realidad española*. Madrid: Castalia, 1960.

Morales, Leonidas. "*La vorágine*: un viaje al país de los muertos." *Anales de la Universidad de Chile*, 123, no. 134 (1965), 148–70.

Morínigo, Mariano. "Civilización y barbarie en *Facundo* y *Doña Bárbara*." *Revista Nacional de Cultura*, 26 (1963), 91–117.

Mullen, Edward J. "Spanish American 'vanguardismo': The Aesthetics of Revolt." *Language Quarterly*, 9, nos. 3–4 (1971), 11–16.

Neale-Silva, Eduardo. "The Factual Bases of *La vorágine*." *PMLA*, 54 (1939), 316–31.

Estudios sobre José Eustasio Rivera: el arte poético ("Tierra de promisión"). Bogotá: Imprenta Nacional de Colombia, 1955.

Horizonte humano: vida de José Eustasio Rivera. Madison: University of Wisconsin Press, 1960.

Nisbet, Robert. *Social Change in History*. New York: Oxford University Press, 1969.

"Genealogy, Growth and Other Metaphors." *New Literary History*, 1, no. 3 (1970), 351–63.

O'Leary, Daniel. *Bolívar y la emancipación de Sur América*. Madrid: Sociedad Española de Librería, 1915.

Bolívar y las repúblicas del sur. Madrid: Editorial América, 1919.

El Congreso Internacional de Panamá en 1826. Madrid: Editorial América, 1920.

Olivera, Otto. "El romanticismo de José Eustasio Rivera." *Revista Iberoamericana*, 18, nos. 35–36 (1952), 41–61.

Orlando, Arthur. *Pan-americanismo*. Rio de Janeiro: Rodrigues & C., 1906.

Ortega, Julio. "La escritura de la vanguardia." *Revista Iberoamericana*, nos. 106–7 (1979), 187–98.

Osorio, Luis E. *Los destinos del trópico*. Quito: Editorial Bolívar, 1932.

Osorio, Nelson. *El futurismo y la vanguardia literaria en América Latina*. Caracas: Centro de Estudios Latinoamericanos Rómulo Gallegos, 1982.

"Doña Bárbara y el fantasma de Sarmiento." *Escritura*, 8, no. 15 (1983), 19–35.

Owens, Craig. "The Allegorical Impulse," 2 parts. *October* 12 (1980), 67–86 and *October* 13 (1980), 59–80.

Palma, Ricardo. *Neologismos y americanismos*. Lima: Carlos Prince, 1890.

Palmer, Richard. "Toward a Postmodern Hermeneutics of Performance" in *Performance in Postmodern Culture*, ed. M. Benamou and C. Caramello. Madison: Coda Press, 1977, pp, 19–32.

Paz, Octavio. *Cuadrivio*. México: Joaquín Mortiz, 1965.

Postdata. México: Siglo XXI, 1971.

El laberinto de la soledad. Mexico: Fondo de Cultura, 1973.

Children of the Mire: Modern Poetry from Romanticism to the Avant-Garde. Trans. Rachel Phillips. Cambridge, MA: Harvard University Press, 1974.

"México y Estados Unidos: posiciones y contraposiciones." *Vuelta*, no. 27 (1979), 5–12.

Pedersen, Holger. *The Discovery of Language: Linguistic Science in the Nineteenth Century*. Trans. J. W. Spargo. Bloomington: Indiana University Press, 1962.

Pereyra, Carlos. *El mito de Monroe*. Madrid: Editorial América, 1914.

El general Sucre. Madrid: Editorial América, 1917.

Humboldt en América. Madrid: Editorial América, 1917.

Pérez, Trinidad (ed.) *Recopilación de textos sobre tres novelas ejemplares*. Havana: Casa de las Américas, 1971.

Pérez Firmat, Gustavo. *Literature and Liminality: Festive Readings in the Hispanic Tradition*. Durham: Duke University Press, 1986.

Pérus, Françoise. *Literatura y sociedad en América Latina*. Mexico: Siglo XXI, 1976.

"La constitución de la ficción: mito y realidad en *Don Segundo Sombra*" in *Historia y crítica literaria: el realismo social y la crisis de la dominación oligárquica*. Havana: Casa de las Américas, 1982, pp. 177–265.

Phelps, D. M. *Rubber Developments in Latin America*. Ann Arbor: University of Michigan Bureau of Business Research, 1957.

Pope, Randolph D. "*La vorágine*: autobiografía de un intelectual" in *The Analysis of Literary Texts: Current Trends in Methodology*, ed. Randolph D. Pope. Ypsilanti, Michigan: The Bilingual Press, 1980, pp. 256–67.

Pupo Walker, Enrique. "El cuadro de costumbres, el cuento y la posibilidad de un deslinde." *Revista Iberoamericana*, 44 (1978), 1–15.

Quesada, Ernesto. *Nuestra raza. Discurso pronunciado en el teatro Odeón el 12 de octubre de 1900*. Buenos Aires: Librería Bradhal, 1900.

El día de la raza y su significado en Hispano América. Buenos Aires: Araujo Hnos., 1918.

La evolución del panamericanismo. Buenos Aires: Ministerio de Agricultura de la Nación, 1919.

Quilligan, Maureen. *The Language of Allegory: Defining the Genre*. Ithaca: Cornell University Press, 1979.

Radcliff, Dillwyn F. *Venezuelan Prose Fiction*. New York: Instituto de las Españas, 1933.

Rama, Angel. "La tecnificación narrativa." *Hispamérica*, no. 30 (1981), 29–82.

Transculturación narrativa en América Latina. Mexico: Siglo XXI, 1982.

La ciudad letrada. Hanover: Ediciones del Norte, 1984.

Rubén Darío y el modernismo. Caracas: Alfadil Ediciones, 1985.

Rangel, Carlos. *Del buen salvaje al buen revolucionario*. Caracas: Monte Avila, 1976.

Renan, Ernest. *Oeuvres complètes*. 10 vols. Paris: Calman Lévy, 1937.

Reyes, Alfonso. *El paisaje en la poesía mexicana del siglo XIX*. Mexico: Tipografía Vda. de Díaz de León, 1911.

"España y América." *Repertorio Americano*, 1 (1920), 363–64.

"México y los Estados Unidos." *Repertorio Americano*, 1 (1920), 297–98.

Obras completas. 12 vols. Mexico: Fondo de Cultura Económica, 1960.

Rivera, José Eustasio. *Tierra de promisión*. Bogotá: Arboleda y Valencia, 1921.

La vorágine. Bogotá: Editorial de Cromos, 1924.

The Vortex. Trans. Earle K. James. New York: Putnam's Sons, 1935.

Rivers, Elías. "Hacia la sintaxis del soneto" in *Homenaje a Dámaso Alonso de sus amigos y discípulos con ocasión de su 60o aniversario*, vol. 3. Madrid: Gredos, 1962, pp. 225–33.

"*Don Segundo Sombra* y la desanalfabetización del héroe." *Revista Iberoamericana*, 44 (1978), 119–23.

Robins, R. H. *A Short History of Linguistics*. Bloomington: Indiana University Press, 1967.

Rodó, José Enrique. *Ariel*. Montevideo: Imprenta Dornaleche y Reyes, 1900.

El mirador de Próspero. Montevideo: J. M. Serrano, 1913.

Bolívar. Caracas: Tipografía Vargas, 1914.

Rodríguez Alcalá, Hugo. *Korn, Romero, Güiraldes, Unamuno, Ortega*. Mexico: De Andrea, 1958.

"Sobre Ricardo Güiraldes y la crítica detractora de *Don Segundo Sombra*." *Cuadernos Americanos*, 218 (1978), 217–27.

Rodríguez Monegal, Emir. *Narradores de esta América*. 2 vols. Montevideo: Editorial Alfa, 1969.

El boom de la novela latinoamericana: ensayo. Caracas: Tiempo Nuevo, 1972.

"El *Martín Fierro* en Borges y Martínez Estrada." *Revista Iberoamericana*, 40 (1974), 287–302.

Jorge Luis Borges: A Literary Biography. New York: Dutton, 1978.

"Borges and Politics." *Diacritics*, 8, no. 4 (1978), 55–69.

Rojas, Ricardo. *La argentinidad: ensayo histórico sobre nuestra consciencia nacional en la gesta de la emancipación 1810–1816.* Buenos Aires: Librería La Facultad, 1916.

El canto popular. Buenos Aires: Editorial Coni, 1923.

Eurindia. Buenos Aires: Librería La Facultad, 1924.

Romano, Eduardo. *Análisis de "Don Segundo Sombra".* Buenos Aires: Centro Editor de América Latina, 1967.

Romero, Armando. "Ausencia y presencia de las vanguardias en Colombia." *Revista Iberoamericana*, nos. 118–19 (1982), 275–87.

Romero García, Alejandro. "Genio de Raza." *El Cojo Ilustrado*, 17 (1908), 625–26.

Root, Elihu. *Latin America and the United States: Addresses*, ed. R. Bacon and J. B. Scott. Cambridge, MA: Harvard University Press, 1917.

Rosmarin, Adena. *The Power of Genre.* Minneapolis: University of Minnesota Press, 1985.

Rousseau, G. S. (ed.) *Organic Form: The Life of an Idea.* London: Routledge and Kegan Paul, 1972.

Sadow, Stephen A. "Structured Education in *Don Segundo Sombra*" in *Essays in Honor of Jorge Guillén on the Occasion of his 85th year.* Cambridge, MA: Abedul Press, 1977, pp. 97–106.

Sahlins, Marshall. *Historical Metaphors and Mythical Realities.* Ann Arbor: Michigan University Press, 1981.

"The Stranger King." *The Journal of Pacific History*, 16, no. 3 (1981), 107–32.

Said, Edward. *Beginnings: Intention and Method.* New York: Basic Books, 1975.

Samurovic-Pavlovic, Liliana. *Les Lettres hispano-américaines au "Mercure de France" (1897–1915).* Belgrade: University of Belgrade, 1969.

Sánchez, José Roguerio. *Autores Españoles e hispanoamericanos.* Madrid: Perlado Páez y Cía, 1911.

Sánchez, Luis Alberto. *Balance y liquidación del novecientos.* Santiago: Ercilla, 1941.

"El año diez" in *El pueblo en la revolución americana*, pp. 181–99. Buenos Aires: Editorial Americalee, 1942.

Santos Chocano, José. "Plan de la epopeya del Libertador." *Repertorio Americano*, 6 (1923), 239–41.

Sariola, Sakari. *Power and Resistance: The Colonial Heritage in Latin America.* Ithaca: Cornell University Press, 1972.

Sarmiento, Domingo F. *Facundo*. Introduction by Noé Jitrik. Caracas: Ayacucho, 1977.

Schärer-Nussberger, Maya. *Gallegos: el mundo inconcluso*. Caracas: Monte Avila, 1979.

Scheibe, Karl E. "The Psychology of National Identity" in *Studies in Social Identity*, ed. T. R. Sarbin and K. E. Scheibe. New York: Praeger, 1983.

Scholes, Robert and Kellog, R. *The Nature of Narrative*. Oxford University Press, 1976.

Schor, Naomi. "Fiction as Interpretation/Interpretation as Fiction" in *The Reader in the Text*, ed. S. Suleiman and I. Crosman. Princeton University Press, 1980, pp. 165–82.

Schwartz, Jorge. "*Don Segundo Sombra*: una novela monológica." *Revista Iberoamericana*, 42 (1976), 427–46.

Semillosa, Juan. *Panamericanismo cultural*. Buenos Aires: A. Pedemonte, 1924.

Shaw, D. L. *Gallegos: Doña Bárbara*. London: Grant and Cutler, 1972.

Shell, Marc. *The Economy of Literature*. Baltimore: The Johns Hopkins University Press, 1978.

  Money, Language, and Thought. Berkeley: University of California Press, 1982.

Sieburth, Richard. "In Pound We Trust." *Critical Inquiry*, 14, no. 1 (1987), 142–72.

Sierra, Justo. *En tierra Yankee*. Mexico: Tipografía de la Oficina Impresora del Timbre, 1898.

Smith, Barbara Herrnstein. *Poetic Closure: A Study of How Poems End*. University of Chicago Press, 1980.

Soler Cañas, Luis. *Don Segundo Sombra y Areco*. La Plata: Cuadernos del Instituto de Literatura, 1971.

Soto, José María. *La influencia del ambiente*. Paris: P. Rosier, 1919.

Spence, Jonathan. *The Memory Palace of Mateo Ricci*. New York: Viking, 1984.

Stabb, Martin S. *In Quest of Identity: Patterns in the Spanish American Essay of Ideas, 1890–1960*. Chapel Hill: University of North Carolina Press, 1967.

Stanford, G. A. "A Study of the Vocabulary of Güiraldes' *Don Segundo Sombra*." *Hispania*, 25 (1942), 181–88.

Stein, Stanley and Barbara. *The Colonial Heritage of Latin America: Essays on Economic Dependence in Perspective*. New York: Oxford University Press, 1970.

Stowe, William W. *Balzac, James and the Realistic Novel*. Princeton University Press, 1983.

Stuart, Graham H. *Latin America and the United States*. New York: Century Co., 1922.

Suleiman, Susan R. "La Structure d'apprentissage: Bildungsroman et roman à thèse." *Poétique*, 37 (1979), 24–42.

Authoritative Fictions: The Ideological Novel as a Literary Genre. New York: Columbia University Press, 1983.

Sux, Alejandro. *La juventud intelectual de la América Hispánica*. Prologue by Rubén Darío. Barcelona: Presa Hnos., 1911.

Taine, Hippolyte. "'Introduction' to the *History of English Literature*" in *Critical Theory Since Plato*, ed. Hazard Adams. New York: Harcourt, Brace, Jovanovich, 1971, pp. 602–14.

Tamayo, Franz. *La creación de la pedagogía nacional*. La Paz: El Diario, 1910.

Terán, Juan B. *La salud de la América española*. Paris: Casa Editorial Franco-Ibero-Americana, 1926.

Todorov, Tzvetan. *Théories du symbole*. Paris: Seuil, 1977.

Torre, Guillermo de. *Historia de las literaturas de vanguardia*. Madrid: Guadarrama, 1965.

Torres Rioseco, Arturo. *La novela en la América Hispana*. *University of California Publications in Modern Philology*, 21, no. 2 (1939), 159–256.

Novelistas contemporáneos de América. Santiago: Editorial Nascimiento, 1939.

Trask, David F. *et al*. *A Bibliography of United States–Latin America Relations Since 1810*. Lincoln: University of Nebraska Press, 1968.

Ucelay Da Cal, Margarita. *Los españoles pintados por sí mismos (1843–1844): estudio de un género costumbrista*. Mexico: Fondo de Cultura Económica, 1951.

Ugarte, Manuel. *Las nuevas tendencias literarias*. Valencia: Sempere y Cía., 1908.

La Patria Grande. Madrid: Editora Internacional, 1922.

Mi campaña hispanoamericana. Barcelona: Editorial Cervantes, 1922.

El destino de un continente. Madrid: Mundo Latino, 1923.

La nación latinoamericana, ed. Norberto Galasso. Caracas: Ayacucho, 1978.

"El peligro yanqui." *El país*, October 19, 1901. Reprinted in *La nación latinoamericana*, pp. 65–70.

Uitti, Karl. *Linguistics and Literary Theory*. Englewood Cliffs: Prentice Hall, 1969.

Unruh, Vicky. "Arturo Cova y *La vorágine*: la crisis de un escritor." *Revista de Estudios Hispánicos* (Vassar), 21, no. 1 (1987), 49–60.

Uribe Piedrahita, César. *Toá*. Buenos Aires: Espasa Calpe, 1942.

Van Dyke, Carolynn. *The Fiction of Truth: Structures of Meaning in Narrative and Dramatic Allegory*. Ithaca: Cornell University Press, 1985.

Vargas Llosa, Mario. "Primitives and Creators." *Times Literary Supplement*, November 14, 1968.

Vargas Vila, J. *Ante los bárbaros*. Barcelona: Casa Editorial Maucci, 1902?

Vasconcelos, José. *Bolivarismo y Monroísmo: temas iberoamericanos*. Santiago: Editorial Ercilla, 1935.

Verani, Hugo J. *et al.* (eds.) *Las vanguardias literarias en Hispanoamérica: manifiestos, proclamas y otros escritos*. Rome: Bulzoni, 1986.

Vianna, Sá. *L'Amérique en face de la conflagration européenne*. Rio de Janeiro: M. A. Vasconcellos, 1916.

Vidal, Hernán. *Literatura hispanoamericana e ideología liberal: surgimiento y crisis*. Buenos Aires: Ediciones Hispamérica, 1976.

Volek, Emil. *Cuatro claves para la modernidad*. Madrid: Gredos, 1984.

Wells, G. A. *Herder and After: A Study of the Development of Sociology*. The Hague: Mouton and Co., 1959.

White, Hayden. "Literary History: The Point of it All." *New Literary History*, 2, no. 1 (1970), 173–85.

Metahistory: The Historical Imagination in Nineteenth-Century Europe. Baltimore: The Johns Hopkins University Press, 1973.

Tropics of Discourse: Essays in Cultural Criticism. Baltimore: The Johns Hopkins University Press, 1978.

The Content of the Form: Narrative Discourse and Historical Representation. Baltimore: The Johns Hopkins University Press, 1987.

Wicke, Jennifer. "Postmodernism: The Perfume of Information." *The Yale Journal of Criticism*, 1, no. 2 (1988), 145–60.

Williams, Raymond. *Keywords: A Vocabulary of Culture and Society*. New York: Oxford University Press, 1977.

Wilson, William A. *Folklore and Nationalism in Modern Finland*. Bloomington: Indiana University Press, 1976.

Yates, Frances A. *The Art of Memory*. University of Chicago Press, 1966.

Yurkiévich, Saúl. *A través de la trama: sobre vanguardismos literarios y otras concomitancias*. Barcelona: Muchnik, 1984.

Zea, Leopoldo. *En torno a una filosofía americana*. Mexico: El Colegio de México, 1945.

Zubieta, P. A. *Congreso de Panamá y Tacubaya: breves datos para la historia diplomática de Colombia*. Bogotá: Imprenta Nacional, 1912.

Index

Alegría, Ciro, 111
Alonso, Amado, 184n23
anthropological fallacy, 8
anthropomorphic metaphor, 8
Araujo, Orlando, 186n10
Arciniegas, Germán, 13
Arguedas, Alcides, 13
Arrom, José Juan, 177n41
Austin, J. L., 169n28
autochthonous, the: as discourse, 75;
    compared to anthropological
    discourse, 4–5; and criticism, 6; and
    cultural crisis, 6–7, 11–12, 18–19; as
    cultural ritual, 12; and exoticism,
    3–4; and historical consciousness,
    9–11; as rhetorical formula, 15–16;
    and self-reflection, 3–4, 6
autochthonous in Latin America, the:
    rhetorical categories of, 72–78; as
    self-critical discourse, 66–70, 164
autochthony: etymology of word, 3;
    and literature, 1–3

Barthes, Roland, 117, 172n15, 185n26
Bédier, Joseph, 180n62
Bello, Andrés, 13, 33, 45
Benedetti, Mario, 38
Benjamin, Walter, 188n26
Beneviste, Emile, 16–17
Bergson, Henri, 46, 174n22
Berman, Marshall, 26, 27, 270n31
Bilbao, Francisco, 13
Blaine, James, G., 50, 51
Blanco Fombona, Rufino, 48, 53, 55
Blasi, Alberto, 183n15
Bolívar, Simón, 55, 62
Bopp, Franz, 57
Borges, Jorge Luis, 1–4, 32, 38, 108,

117; "The Argentine Writer and
    Tradition," 1–4, 6
Boutroux, Emile, 46
Brunner, José, 168n26
Bunge, Carlos O., 13

Calinescu, Matei, 31
Camino, Miguel, 63
Candido, Antonio, 185n23
Carpentier, Alejo, 111, 112, 182n83,
    187n21
Centenario, 53–56, 152, 176n40,
    176n41
centenaristas (in Colombia), 152–53
Chatelain, Foucy, 51
Contreras, Francisco, 55, 176n40
Cortázar, Julio, 166
Croce, Benedetto, 46, 117
cuadro de costumbres, 45, 174n19
Culler, Jonathan, 70, 71, 85
cultural discourse in Latin America:
    13–17; conventionality of, 16; and
    history, 17, 35; and literature, 37;
    and modernity, 17–18, 32, 19–37,
    163; as myth of foundations, 36;
    problems in articulating, 34–36, 56;
    as rhetorical formula, 15–17
culture: concept of, 7–9; and cultural
    crisis, 9; and environment, 60–61;
    epistemological sources of, 56–61;
    and historical awareness, 10–13; and
    language, 57–59; and organic
    metaphors, 59, 61; and philology,
    61; and teleology, 9, 12

Darío, Rubén, 44, 62, 176n40
de Man, Paul, 6–7, 17, 31, 130, 166
dependency theory, 30–31

Derrida, Jacques, 161, 173n16, 181n70, 181n72, 181n76
Don Segundo Sombra (Güiraldes), 75, 78, 111, 112, 115, 136, 138, 139, 164, 181n83; the "autochthonous" in, 91–93; as *Bildungsroman*, 83; critical polemics on, 80–84, 106–7; economics in, 96, 107–8; economy of signification in 100, 105, 107; genealogy in, 98; knowledge in, 97–98, 100, 105, 106; linguistic dichotomy in, 102–4; metaphor of "taking stock" as organizing conceit in, 96–97, 100–1, 106; *mise en abyme* in, 101–2; money in, 95; ownership of land in 98–99; pedagogy in, 95–96, 99; use of simile in, 105; work in, 93–95; 106, and writing, 106
Doña Bárbara (Gallegos), 46, 65, 68, 75, 76, 78, 136, 138, 139, 164, 165, 181n83; allegory in, 116–25, 130–34; the "autochthonous" in, 113–15; glossary in, 125–29; ideological message of, 111–12; interpretation and meaning in, 118, 125–29, 134–35; mimesis in, 109–10; its proliferation in, 123–25; as a *roman à thèse*, 116–17; symbols in, 110

Editorial América, 55, 177n44
Enlightenment, the, 19; in Spain, 20

Fineman, Joel, 130
Forbes, D. K., 171n39
Foucault, Michel, 56–58, 61, 172n45
Franco, Jean, 171n38
Frye, Northrop, 40, 134
Fuentes, Carlos, 40, 41, 111, 189n34

Gallegos, Rómulo, 68; his views on *Doña Bárbara*, 109–10; revalorization of, 135
García Calderón, Francisco, 53, 54, 177n42
Geertz, Clifford, 5, 35, 167n7
Gellner, Ernest, 33, 172n43
Gómez, Juan Vicente, 109
González Aníbal, 168n26, 174n19
González-Echevarría, Roberto, 16, 133–34, 168n26, 169n31, 172n49, 192n2
González Prada, Manuel, 62
Graña, César, 8, 9, 172n48
Grimm, Jakob, 57
Groussac, Paul, 79
Güiraldes, Ricardo, 69, 75, 79, 113; as analogous figure to Fabio Cáceres, 83–86; as autochthonous creator, 81–82; as landowner, 79–81, 83

Hegel, G. W. F., 12, 180n63
Henríquez Ureña, Pedro, 26, 33, 45, 172n46, 173n18, 176n40
Herder, J. G., 28, 59, 69, 114, 179n60, 179n61, 180n63
Hernández, José, 87
Hispano, Cornelio (pseud. for Ismael López), 63
hispanoamericanismo (pan-latinismo, pan-iberismo, pan-hispanismo), 52–3, 176n41
Humboldt, Wilhelm von, 57

Icaza, Jorge, 111

Jakobson, Roman, 168n21
Jameson Fredric, 134, 173n16, 183n17, 187n18
Jitrik, Noé, 168n26
Johnson, Barbara, 67, 162, 185n26

Kadir, Djelal, 170n37, 171n41
Kant, Immanuel, 28
Kedourie, Elie, 33
Kermode, Frank, 189n33

Leguizamón, Julio, 172n5
Lévi-Strauss, Claude, 4–5, 167n6, 167n8
Lezama, José, 1, 32
Ludmer, Josefina, 183n17
Lugones, Leopoldo, 62, 63, 79, 86, 176n40
Lynch, Benito, 75
Lyotard, Jean-François, 169n29

Marechal, Leopoldo, 182n6, 182n8
Marinello, Juan, 34
Martí, José, 13–14, 29, 45, 48

Martínez Estrada, Ezequiel, 13
Masiello, Francine, 184n21
Mayer, Alfred, 28, 29
Mendéndez Pidal, Ramón, 180n62
Miller, J. Hillis, 181n76
modernismo: as equivalent to European
    Romanticism, 20–21, 23
modernity, 17; as discourse, 32; and
    underdevelopment, 26–30, 32
modernity in Latin America, 18,
    46–47; and autochthonous
    discourse, 24–34; Paz's view of,
    18–22; as rhetorical phenomenon,
    22–24; and the United States, 46–53
Molloy, Sylvia, 191n323
mundonovismo, 55

nationalism: as arbitrary construct, 33;
    and language, 33–34; and philology,
    33–34
Neale-Silva, Eduardo, 143, 144, 152,
    155
Nietzsche, Friedrich, 46
novela de la tierra: compared to
    indigenista and Afro-Hispanic literary
    production, 180n67; as concept, 39;
    and criticism, 39–40, 44, 70–72, 78;
    historical context for, 45–56; and
    Neo-Kantianism, 46; as nostalgia for
    agrarian order, 46; and philology,
    64–66; its place in literary history,
    38–40, 166, as point of departure in,
    41–43, 166; rhetorical categories of,
    72–78; as self-critical discourse,
    66–70

Osorio, Nelson, 187n19

Palmer, Richard, 169n29
Pan-Americanism, 50–51, 52, 53
Paz, Octavio, 18–22, 30, 31, 168n27
Pérez Firmat, Gustavo, 181n76
Pérus, Françoise, 168n26
philology: as discursive model for the
    novela de la tierra, 64–66 as
    hermeneutical enterprise, 61; and
    literary discourse in Latin America,
    61–64
Picón Salas, Mariano, 34
positivismo, 20

Pupo-Walker, Enrique, 45

Rama, Angel, 168n26, 185n23, 187n21
Raynouard, François, 58
Renan, Ernest, 59, 61, 62, 179n61,
    180n69
Reyes, Alfonso, 13, 33, 63, 180n66
Reyles, Carlos, 75
Rivera, José Eustasio, 63; and
    centenaristas, 152–53; and *los nuevos*,
    153–54; *Tierra de promisión*, 144–48,
    154–57, violence in, 148, 154–55;
    voyage to the jungle, 141–42
Rodó, José Enrique, 48, 49, 53, 177n44
Rodríguez Alcalá, Hugo, 185n25
Rodríguez Monegal, Emir, 39, 86,
    167n5, 186n2
Romanticism, 19, 20, 23
Rosmarin, Adena, 173n16

Said, Edward, 40, 41, 42
Sánchez, Luis A., 13, 175n30
Santos Chocano, José, 62
Sarmiento, Domingo F., 13, 25, 26, 41,
    45, 75, 87, 180n63
Schlegel, Friedrich von, 57
Schor, Naomi, 187n20
Schwartz, Jorge, 183n13, 184n23
Shaw, D. L., 181n83
Shell, Marc, 185n26
Smith, Barbara Herrnstein, 154
Spitzer, Leo, 61
Stabb, Martin S., 174n22, 175n29
Stowe, William, 118
Suleiman, Susan, 116, 183n10

Taine, Hippolyte, 179n61
Todorov, Tzvetan, 71
Torres Rioseco, Arturo, 40, 41–43, 72;
    and his concept of *ambiente*, 73–75,
    76

Ugarte, Manuel, 13, 47, 48, 49, 51, 52,
    62, 176n35, 178n48

Vargas Llosa, Mario, 38
Vasconcelos, José, 13, 47, 55, 175n27
La vorágine (Riviera), 64, 69, 75, 78,
    164, 181n83; the "autochthonous"
    in, 136–39; as document of

denunciation; 139, 140–44, 157–58;
ironic presentation of protagonist in,
148–52; nature in, 139; negative
autochthony in, 136; rubber
industry in, 139–41, 142–44, 158–61;
as statement on *poiesis*, 152–62; and
Tierra de promisión, 144, 154–57;

Vossler, Karl, 61

White, Hayden, 173n15

Zea, Leopoldo, 170n37